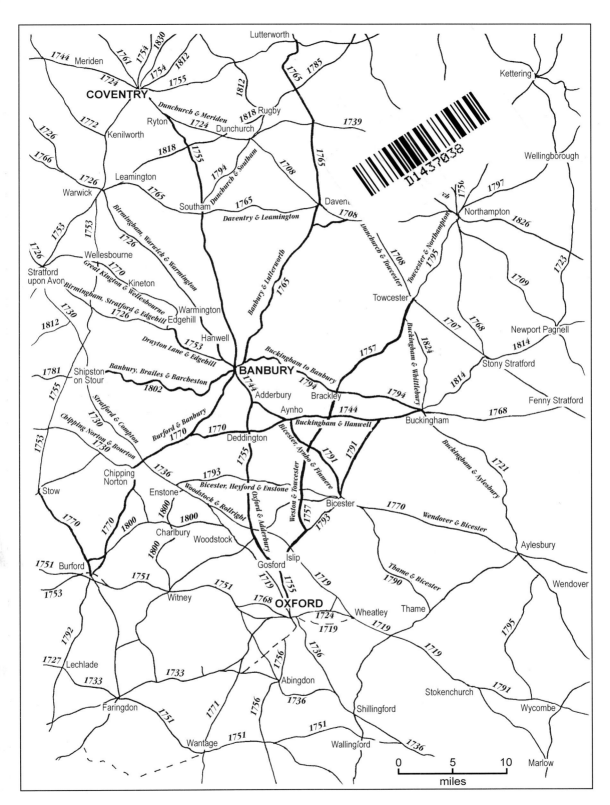

The full Turnpike network in the south Midlands
(date of first Turnpike Act shown)

Banbury: South Bar, The Monument, The Green and Horse Fair,
by Joseph Scarcebrook, 1833
(Banbury Museum: Oxfordshire Museums Collections BM 984.71.2)

A view painted in 1833 and described in 1903 by T.W. Boss (*Reminscences*, reprinted in *Cake & Cockhorse* vol. 13(3), p.74). It shows the main south-to-north highway through Banbury (see page 29). This was part of the Buckingham to Warmington or Hanwell Trust, turnpiked in 1744, rather than the later Oxford to Coventry turnpikes north and south of the town, turnpiked in 1755.

The Horse Fair is in the distance. One of the large houses on its left would originally have been the *Three Tuns*, Banbury's leading inn for a century from the 1680s, though it ceased trading around 1786. Its landlords were also much involved in the coaching and carrying business.

Boss recollected that "the cart going down the centre of the road was John Dipper's, one of the oldest Bloxham carriers. I find his name in *Rusher's List of Carriers* more than seventy years ago." In fact it first appears in 1828.

The "Monument" on the left was erected to commemorate the site of South Bar, demolished in the late eighteenth century. Boss tells us that "on three sides were given the towns and their distances [from] Banbury." The facing side points to Bath, Bristol, Cheltenham and Chipping Norton (*ie*, to start, the Banbury to Burford road, turnpiked in 1770). The Monument was in its turn demolished in 1845.

TURNPIKE ROADS TO BANBURY

Originally published as
No 14 in the series on *Roads across the Upper Thames Valley*
by Alan Rosevear,
but subsequently much revised and enlarged

The Banbury Historical Society

General Editor: J.S.W. Gibson

TURNPIKE ROADS TO BANBURY

Alan Rosevear

with additional text and indexes by
Jeremy Gibson

Volume 31

2010

Published 2010 by
The Banbury Historical Society,
c/o Banbury Museum, Spiceball Park Road, Banbury OX16 2PQ,
in association with Robert Boyd Publications,
260 Colwell Drive, Witney, Oxfordshire OX28 5LW

ISBN 978 0 900129 29 2 (B.H.S.)
ISBN 978 1 899536 48 1 (Robert Boyd Publications)

This volume has been produced with the aid of a substantial grant from
the Greening Lamborn Trust
which is acknowledged with gratitude.

Printed by
Information Press, Southfield Road, Eynsham, Oxford OX29 4JB
from computer-generated text prepared by
Alan Rosevear
with additions and layout by Jeremy Gibson

Jacket and Frontispiece illustration:
South Bar and Horse Fair, Banbury, 1833,
Joseph Scarcebrook
(by kind permission, *Oxfordshire Museums Collection*, BM 984.71.2)

Contents

Maps

Graphs

Income from leasing individual gates

Tables

Roads across the Upper Thames Valley
produced by Alan Rosevear

PREFACE

Turnpike trusts were set up by Acts of Parliament to improve the through-routes that had been neglected by Parish administration. A dozen independent turnpike trusts maintained the road network in the Banbury and Buckingham area. The main Buckingham to Birmingham road and the Oxford to Coventry road were managed by relatively large trusts, set up in the middle of the eighteenth century. Smaller trusts, set up later in the century, were responsible for subsidiary routes into the market towns. Carrier and coach services using these turnpikes paid tolls that financed maintenance and road improvements. The turnpike trusts were wound-up in the late nineteenth century, leaving as their legacy an occasional milestone or toll-house and the framework of our modern road network.

My thanks are due to the late Christine Kelly for her encouragement to extend this series to cover Banbury and the assistance of staff at Record Offices and Libraries for their assistance and patience.

Alan Rosevear

All enquiries to
<Rosevear1@aol.com>, or http: //www.turnpikes.org.uk

Names of Places and Turnpike Trusts

At the time of the Turnpike Trusts spelling of place names had not been standardised. Little attempt has been made here to rectify this, so readers will often find the same places in varied versions. This is also the case with the Trusts themselves. Every road would have been between one place and another. The order of their names is frequently reversed, quite apart from the occasions when one or both ends were extended to other places. They may bear alternative names. In particular, the Trust operating north-west from Banbury towards Coventry ran to Ryton – also known as Finford – Bridge (see page 50). Both names were used throughout. The Adderbury to Kidlington Trust (formed from the Finford Bridge to Oxford Trust) was referred to as the Kidlington to Deddington Trust but locally as the Oxford to Adderbury Road (page 58). The same could be the case with the names of Toll-gates.

Place names may be duplicated. There is a Drayton close to Banbury; and also one close to Daventry. 'Bourton' can mean Bourton-on-the-Hill (termination of one Trust), Bourton-on-the-Water (both in Gloucestershire) or Great or Little Bourton, near to Banbury. Middleton Stoney (Oxon.) on the Weston-on-the Green to Towcester Turnpike should not be confused with Middleton Cheney (Northants.) on the Buckingham to Banbury Turnpike.

An attempt has been made to identify (by county) or cross-reference these variations in the Index of Places (page 205) and the separate Index of Turnpike Roads (page 213).

A Note from the General Editor

A version of this book was published by the author a good many years ago, in his series listed on a previous page. I asked if he would allow an amended edition to be published by the Banbury Historical Society, to which he agreed. He promptly supplied the text on disc and illustrations in hard copy; the long delay in its appearance for our Society is no fault of his.

Much of this has been because all the preparation work has been carried out, as usual, on my computer, and it is only relatively recently that appropriate programs have been acquired allowing merging of text and illustrations. A certain additional amount of both have been added (including the valuable list of Turnpike Trustees). It is quite possible that this material may have introduced mistakes, despite Tony Newman's proof-reading, for which the author is in no way responsible. For these I must apologise in advance. The maps also needed re-lettering, and once again I must thank my friend Jeff Long for his patient expertise in this task. All this has resulted in the book's appearance being very different to the original publication.

Authors agreeing to allow their work to be published by a record society need to possess enormous patience, and receive, of course, no remuneration. Alan Rosevear is only the latest of our contributors who has uncomplainingly accepted these disadvantages. Our Society has been very fortunate in him and his predecessors; we must just hope that the eventual outcome has made the wait worthwhile.

J.G.

Abbreviations
to be found in footnotes

C&CH	*Cake & Cockhorse* (Banbury Historical Society)
JHC	Journal of the House of Commons
JOJ	*Jackson's Oxford Journal*
PP	Parliamentary Papers
RUTV	*Roads across the Upper Thames Valley*
VCH Oxon	*Victoria History of the County of Oxford*

1. Historic Roads in the Cherwell Valley

1.1 Highways around Banbury

Banbury lies on the northern edge of the upper Thames Valley. Routes from Berkshire, Buckinghamshire and southern Oxfordshire approach the town along the Cherwell valley from the south-east. North of Banbury there are two relatively easy routes into the Midland Plain, across the Jurassic ridge that forms this edge of the Thames Valley. Other important lines of communication follow the high limestone ridge, north-eastwards across the Redlands to Northamptonshire and south-westwards along the Cotswolds to Gloucestershire. The building of the M40 has now made Banbury a major node for trunk roads between London and the Midlands giving this area a new importance on the national road network.

Despite this apparently important position, Banbury itself was not a focus for long distance journeys before the medieval period. The main Roman roads such as Akeman Street, Watling Street and Fosse Way did not serve the site of Banbury. Several straight tracks, presumably engineered by the Romans, cross the north Cotswolds, connecting the Roman settlements at Alchester (near Bicester), Fleet Marston and Lactodurum (Towcester) with communities such as that at Thornborough (near Buckingham). The Romans would have developed lines of communication that were already used by the local population beside the Cherwell and over the hills. There is some evidence for two Romanized roads crossing the Cherwell, at Twyford and near North Aston. The former aligns with a road from Stratford upon Avon through Broughton and on, via Hinton in the Hedges, to Thornborough. The latter route runs over a natural, stone-bottomed ford to Somerton[1] and then goes on to Bicester. Minor Roman highways must have linked the rich farms in this region of the Cotswolds, but it is difficult to distinguish these from tracks created at later dates. However, the nodes in this network of Roman roads and tracks differed from that of later administrators and traders. Once the Roman Empire was displaced, many of these early roads fell into disrepair and material would have been robbed from any metalled surfaces. Only where the needs of the new residents corresponded to those of the Romans did sections of these early roads survive.

---

[1] Wickham Steed, V., *Roman roads of the Banbury District* (1967).

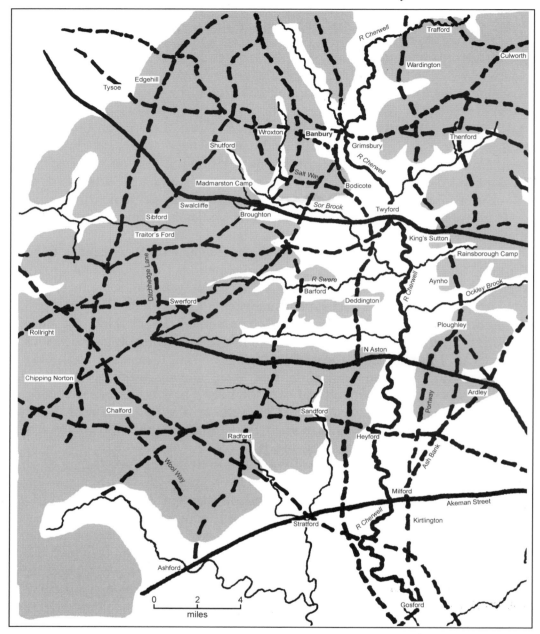

Fig. 1: Early tracks and roads entering north Oxfordshire.

Key — suggested Roman roads — — other tracks ▓ higher ground

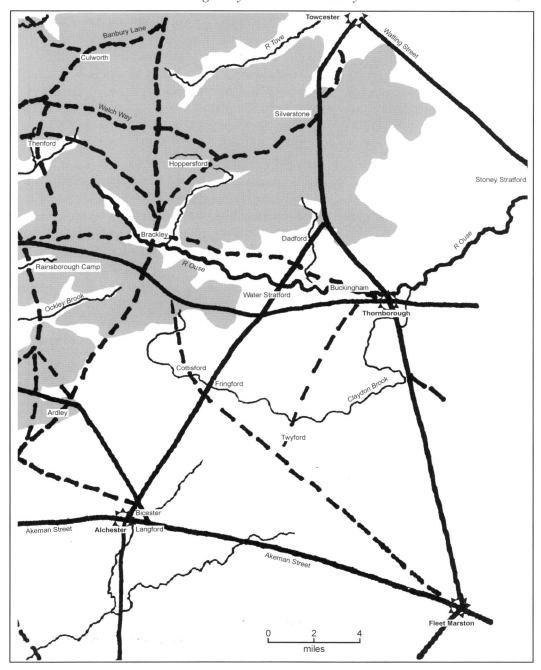

Fig. 1: Early tracks and roads entering north Oxfordshire.

Key ━━━━━ suggested Roman roads

▬ ▬ ▬ other tracks   ▓ higher ground

Economic and social factors directed the paths of long distance travellers who trod down the vegetation to create these ancient trackways. The relatively dry and open ridgeways of southern England have long been regarded as the earliest highways in the region. Close to Banbury, the Cotswold ridgeway from Gloucestershire becomes the Jurassic Way into Northamptonshire. However, the contemporary view, exemplified by the work of Christopher Taylor,[2] casts doubt on the uniqueness of the Jurassic Way and it is now thought that a large number of pathways criss-crossed these uplands and Banbury had no obvious position of importance in this network. A number of tracks that may be of ancient origin are illustrated in Fig. 1 (pages 2-3). Many of these routes stay on the high ground, following ridges between river valleys and only descending to cross streams at specific places. The Saxon villages which grew up beside these roads sometimes took the name "ford", indicating the importance of the crossing to the community. Several of these old tracks were still in use even during the turnpike era, when they became drove roads that could be used without tolls. Banbury Lane (a part of the Jurassic Way), the Welsh Way and Dornford Lane are examples. An earlier use of one track is recalled in the name, Salt Way. This is said to be the path used by pack horses carrying salt from Droitwich, through Stratford to places with salt-rights, such as Princes Risborough.[3]

There is more evidence of ancient tracks on the eastern bank of the Cherwell Valley than on its western bank. A track called the Portway is an old trade route that runs north from Akeman Street. It crosses the Ockley Brook just north of the old Hundred meeting place, beside the tumulus of Ploughley Hill. An ancient earthwork, Ash Bank, seems to mark the line of an old road north of Kiddington. The road through Ardley was referred to in the thirteenth century as the *Via Regia* and in medieval times was probably the main road south from the large wool market in Brackley. This road used to go across what is now Middleton Park, west of the present B430. It is not clear whether this could also have been the ancient highway along which Saxon traders carried goods between the Mercian commercial centre at Northampton and the Wessex port at Southampton, gateway to the Continent. A more likely path for the earliest traders would have been the old Roman road from Towcester to Bicester. Except for the section through Stowe Park this road is still followed and so would have facilitated travel southwards from Northamptonshire as far as Akeman Street. From here the ford below the Saxon town of Oxford could be used to cross the Thames and the highway south through Abingdon led on to the main towns of Wessex.

[2] Taylor, C.C., *Roads and Tracks of Britain*, Dent, London (1979).
[3] Houghton, F.T.S., "Saltways", *Trans. Birmingham Arch. Soc.*, **54** (1932), 1-17.

The ridgeway through Brackley probably did not become important until medieval times when the Cotswolds, rather than Northampton alone, were the destination of merchants from the Continent. Early English monarchs definitely preferred the road through Silverstone, Brackley and Ardley.[4] An itinerary taken from an early fifteenth century manuscript at Titchfield Abbey in Hampshire recommends travel through Middleton and Brackley on the road north from Oxford towards Yorkshire.[5] Records from a similar period[6] show that travellers from Merton College, Oxford, also followed this highway to the North East.

The old ridgeway tracks do not lead to a river crossing at Banbury. The Welsh Way at Trafford, north east of Banbury, crosses the upper reaches of the Cherwell. Below the site of the present town, the Roman road crossed the river at Twyford and further downstream there are other ancient crossing places near Somerton, Heyford, Enslow and Milford. Wickham Steed[7] concludes that the earliest crossing near Banbury was at Grimsbury, north of the town. She speculates that the name Grimsbury refers to the superstitious belief of the Saxon farmers that the old buildings beside a Roman road were the work of the Devil. It may be significant that Banbury did not take the name "ford" suggesting that, for the Saxon settlers, providing a crossing of the Cherwell was not the main function of this site.

The road running north/south through Banbury has probably been most important in development of the town. The Titchfield itineraries of about 1400 recommend the road from Oxford on the west bank of the Cherwell, through Deddington, Banbury and Southam, to reach Coventry and the North West.[8] This road was used occasionally by Henry III and Edward I in their journeys north, though the Brackley road was more frequently used by all the Plantagenet kings.[9] It suggests that in the medieval period this road up the Cherwell valley was a route of local importance rather than one of the great highways between the Thames Valley and other regions of the country.

---

[4] *Roads across the Upper Thames Valley [RUTV]* 5: The Wallingford, Wantage and Faringdon Turnpike.

[5] Dickins, B., "Premonstratension Itineraries from Titchfield Abbey", *Proceedings of Leeds Philos. & Lit. Soc*, **4** (1938), 349-361.

[6] Martin, G.H., "Road travel in the middle ages, some journeys of the warden and fellows of Merton College, Oxford, 1315-1470", *J. of Transport History*, **3** (3) (1976), 159-178.

[7] Wickham Steed, V., *Roman roads of the Banbury District* (1967).

[8] As note 5 above.

[9] *RUTV* 9.

1.2 The Borough of Banbury

The Bishop of Lincoln developed the borough in the mid-twelfth century, attracting merchants to the new market place and building a castle from which to administer his extensive estates in Oxfordshire.[10] There are few natural barriers limiting access to the town and the existing trackways were easily adapted so that trade flowed into this market on the west bank of the upper Cherwell. It was important that a bridge crossed the Cherwell but this was to serve the town, rather than travellers in transit between other major towns. A bridge existed at Banbury in 1294[11] and some thirteenth century stonework survived in the nineteenth century structure. In the eighteenth century it was described as having seven pointed arches to carry it over the Cherwell and the Mill Stream. The cutwaters were carried up to the parapet and a level causeway led to the bridge from either bank. The old bridge was modified to accommodate the canal arch, changed again when the railway was constructed and has now been replaced by a modern flyover.

The Bishop of Lincoln would probably have commissioned the original bridge, using a similar Gothic style to that of contemporary church architecture. Maintenance of the bridge would have remained the responsibility of the builder but by the sixteenth century a hermit had been installed at the foot of the bridge to collect alms for its upkeep. Later still, a Bridgemaster, appointed by the borough, became responsible for maintenance of this bridge. Despite the existence of Banbury Bridge, the main road to London passed over the Cherwell at Nell Bridge near Aynho. Hence, most long distance travellers from both London and Oxford would have entered the town through the South Bar and left through the North Bar.

Banbury was not an important stop on the itineraries of early kings of England.[12] The royal hunting lodge at Woodstock to the south was the region's principal road hub from where the highways to Brackley and Cirencester led across the Cotswolds. Despite the presence of the bishop's castle at Banbury, there were no rich monastic institutions to stimulate the local economy. As a result, the road network would have served mainly the needs of the regional markets. However, by Tudor times, royal patronage and monastic power had declined and in the new mercantile era Banbury grew into a significant market centre. Harrison's description of the principal highways of Tudor England gives Banbury the status, previously assigned to Woodstock, as the hub of the road network in the northern Cotswolds.

---

[10]   Crossley A., *VCH Oxon*, **10** (1972), 6; part reprinted as *Banbury, a history*, Oxon. County Library Service (1984).

[11]   As note 10, *VCH Oxon*, **10**, 23.

[12]   *RUTV* 9.

In the 1540s, John Leland passed through this area during his travels on behalf of Henry VIII. He approached via Burchestar (Bicester) and Brakeley (Brackley) which he entered "*by a litle stone bridge in a botom, of one arche, undar the whiche Use riveret rennithe, there being a letle streme. From this bridge the great streate of the towne goith up apon a pratie hille: at the pitch whereof there turnithe nothar streat by este to Seint Peter's, heade churche of the town. The towne of Brakeley by estimation of olde ruines hath many stretes in it, and that large.....This towne florished in the Saxon tyme ontyll the danes rasid it. It florishid syns the Conquest, and was a staple for wolle*".[13] Leland rode eastwards, apparently through Twyford, his route being "*from Brakeley to Kyngs Southtowne 4 miles of, al by champayn corne and gresse.... From Southtowne to Banbyri a 3. miles, all by champaine baren of wood. Scant a mile bynethe Southtowne I passyd by a stone bridge of one arch over Charwell ryver*"

Leland wrote that "*The moaste part of the hole towne of Banbyri standithe in a valley, and is inclosyd by northe and est with low grownde, partely medowes, partely marsches; by southe and southe-west the ground somewhat hillithe in respecte of the site of the towne. The fayrest strete of the towne lyethe by west and easte downe to the river of Charwelle. And at the west parte of this streat is a large area invironed with meatlye good buildinge, havynge a goodly crosse with many degrees about it. In this area is kept every Thursday a very celebrate market. There renithe a prile of freshe watar throwghe this area. There is another fayre strete from southe to northe; and at eche end of this strete is a stone-gate. There be also in the towne othar gates besydes thes. Yet is there nothere eny certayne token or lykelyhod, that ever the towne was dichid or waullyd. There is a castle on the northe syde of this area havynge 2. wardes, and eche warde a dyche. In the utter is a terrible prison for convict men.*" Leland rode to Warwick from Banbury and later returned through Southam and Banbury on his journey from Coventry to Bicester.

The disadvantages of Banbury's new position on a main line of communication between the Midlands and London were highlighted during the Civil War. The first battle of the conflict took place at Edgehill, north-west of Banbury. On the 23rd October 1642, Royalist troops from Northampton moved against a Parliamentary force heading from Warwick towards London. Although there was no clear victor, the Royalists moved back through Banbury, capturing the castle.

---

[13] Toulmin Smith, L., *Leland's Itinerary in England and Wales*, Centaur, London (1964); and Gibson, J., "Travellers' Tales", Part 1, *Cake & Cockhorse [C&CH]*, **5**.7 (1973), 127-29.

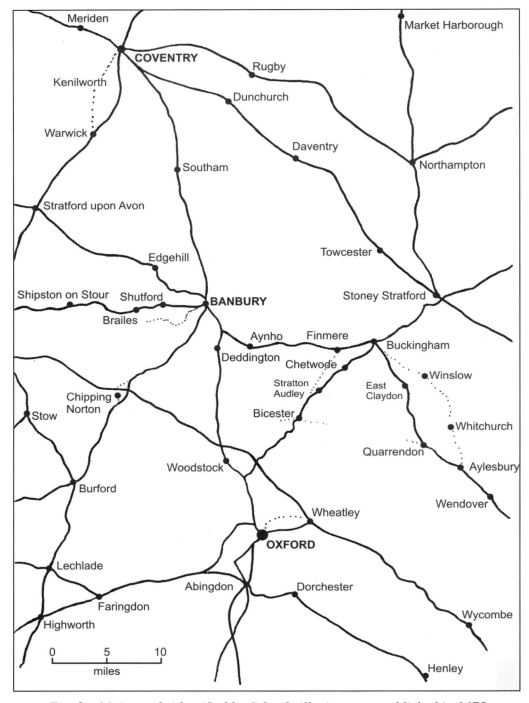

Fig. 2a. Main roads identified by John Ogilby in a map published in 1675
(present line of roads as ....)

For over three and a half years the King's men garrisoned this castle in what was avowedly a puritan area. By the time that the castle was retaken for Parliament, in 1646, many of the buildings had been severely damaged.[14] Nevertheless, the town soon revived and the market regained its prosperity and drew in more trade.

1.3 Road Maps from the Seventeenth Century

John Ogilby published the first detailed English road maps in 1675. These strip maps gave Banbury a similar status to Oxford as a principal node on the road network of southern England. The modern pattern of main roads can be discerned on Ogilby's maps (Fig. 2a). A main road ran north from Oxford, through Banbury to Coventry. The road from London to Buckingham had an extension through Banbury to Stratford with a branch from Banbury to Chipping Campden. The Buckingham to Banbury road passed through Aynho (not Brackley) using Nell Bridge rather than Twyford to cross the Cherwell. A third road connects Banbury with Bristol, the important trading port for Stuart England. These highways would eventually form the framework for the turnpikes passing through Banbury. Ogilby's highway from Oxford to Cambridge passed through both Bicester and Buckingham.

Ogilby described the highway from London through Buckingham (fig. 2b, page 10) as *"affording a very good road to Aylesbury but not so pleasant to Banbury and Bromsgrove"*. His detailed commentary mentions landmarks such as the gallows half a mile outside Aylesbury and the various church towers visible for up to several furlongs on either side of the road. The approach to Buckingham was *"an indirect* [winding] *way for the most part open, being indifferently* [generally] *arable and pasture"* and then over *"a stone bridge of six arches."* Buckingham *"contains about 300 houses, sends Burgesses to Parliament, hath a well furnished Market on Saturdays and six fairs"*. From Buckingham to Banbury Ogilby recommended *"repassing the Owse you leave the town by the Lady Smiths House and Park* [Stowe] *and Ratley Church on the right; at 63m you come to Tinewick a discontinued* [dispersed] *village, and at 64m, entering Oxon, you pass through Fenmore another scattered village"*. The strip map states that between *"Fenmore"* and the *"Cotisford"* turn there is *"a great coney warren"*. It is noted that Aynho affords *"good reception for travellers"* and that the road crosses *"the Charwell at 73.2m* [73 miles and 2 furlongs from London], *over Nell-Bridge of 6 arches stone-built"*. Banbury is described as *"a large and well-built town containing several good Inns and Accommodation"*, and *"its Market on Thursday is well stored with Provisions and hath 7 fairs yearly. It subscribes to none in the County, Oxford excepted, for Wealth and Beauty"*.

---

[14] As note 10, *VCH Oxon* **10**, 10.

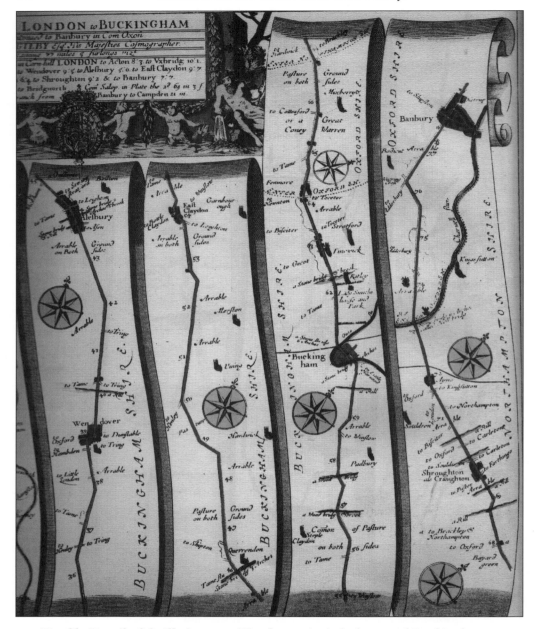

Fig. 2b. Detail of Ogilby's route, Wendover via Aylesbury and Buckingham to Banbury.

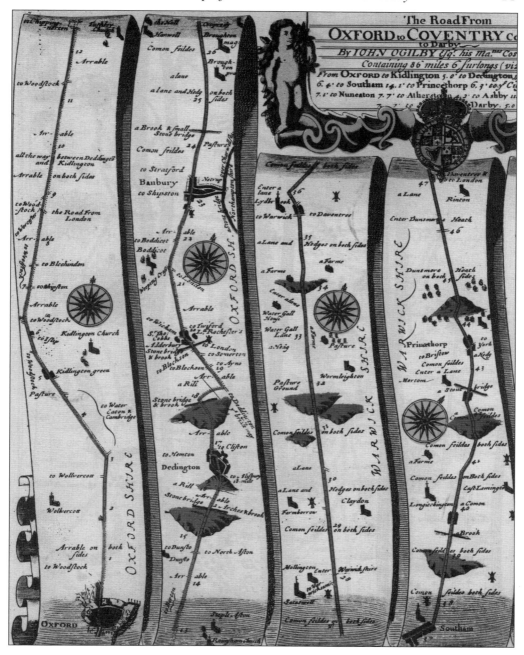

Fig. 2c. Detail of Ogilby's route from Oxford via Banbury towards Coventry.

The road to Drayton is *"an open way"* leading over *"two small waters and an indifferent straight way"* to Wroxton. A branch from this road to Campden left Banbury by the West Bar but near the edge of the Cotswold scarp Ogilby recommends a different route to that followed by the modern road. His road goes through *"Shutford, another village with an Inn in it"* and on by Sibberts [Sibford] Heath, *"entering Warwickshire you descend a large Hill of 11f, at the foot of which lies Brailes, a dis-united village extending 10f on the road, having an Inn or two in it for accommodation"*. From here it follows the modern road to Shipston *"by a direct way brings you at 13.6m to a stone bridge of six arches over the River Stour"*.

Ogilby considers the road from Bristol to Banbury as *"affording generally good way and reasonable entertainment"*. He makes no comments on the highway through Burford, by Bruern Abbey and Bloxham. No mention is made of Chipping Norton, so it would appear that the highway by-passed the town. Navigational features on the map include not only the towers of local churches but also the windmills at North Newington and Wickham. Additional notes on Banbury state that *"it has a fair large church which with the town not long since suffered much by fire; this town is of note for being the place where Kenric King of the West Saxons put the Britains to flight"*. The third road that Ogilby describes through Banbury is that from Oxford to Coventry (fig. 2c). This *"in general is no very good road, yet every where replenisht with good towns and fitting entertainment for travellers"*. He notes that south of Deddington the road passes over *"a stone-bridge of two arches over a brook"*: Deddington *"has an indifferent good Market on Saturdays"* and *"at which place was lately found a Medicinal Spring"*. Adderbury is *"a village of good accommodation in which are the seats of Lord Rochester and Sir Thomas Cobb, then at 21.3m you come to Weeping-Cross, a noted place where four ways meet"*. North of Banbury is *"a straight way crossing a brook"*. Southam is noted as *"a place of good accommodation, enjoys a considerable market on Mondays"*. The final section is across *"Dunsmore Heath by Rinton Church on the right, you are conveyed at 47.6m to Winford Bridge of stone, whence you cross the River Avon"*.

Two of Ogilby's roads to Buckingham differ significantly from the modern routes. His road from Oxford to Cambridge follows the present line to Bicester but deviates from the old Roman road south of Newton Purcell, passing through Chetwode to approach Buckingham from the south rather than the west. Ogilby's road from Aylesbury to Buckingham heads west along Akeman Street before turning north-west at Quarrendon so that it goes to the west of the modern road, passing through East Claydon rather than Winslow.

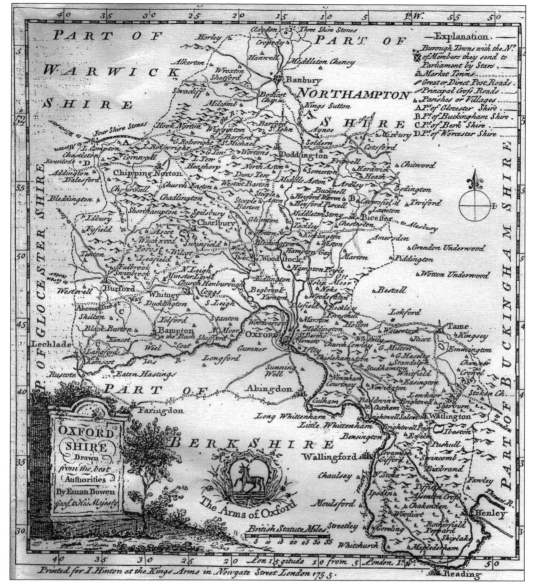

Fig. 3. Bowen's map of Oxfordshire, published 1755
(based on surveys by Ogilby and Morden in the seventeenth century)

Robert Morden's county maps of 1695 were derived from Ogilby's survey but incorporated comments from local informants. Unfortunately his description of roads close to county boundaries seem incomplete and so the relative importance of roads approaching Banbury is difficult to judge. The road eastwards from Banbury to Buckingham is shown as going through Aynho on the Oxfordshire map but on the Buckinghamshire map there is no road marked through Tingewick whereas the road to Brackley is clearly shown.

None of the roads into Warwickshire are marked on the Oxfordshire map but roads go south-westwards not only to Chipping Norton but also through Rollright to Stow. The first of these was eventually turnpiked; the second remains a minor road.

The map of Oxfordshire (Fig. 3, page 13) published by Emanuel Bowen in 1755, draws on the survey work of Ogilby and Morden, representing the road network at the end of the 17th century.

1.4 A Deteriorating Road Network

The state of the roads across England had worsened considerably in the 17th century. A statute passed in the reign of Elizabeth obliged each parish to organise labour, equipment and materials to repair their own roads. However, as heavy long distance traffic increased, an unfair burden was placed on parishes through which ran the main highways. Where main roads crossed clay vales and river valleys, the highway became deep and founderous and was frequently unusable in the winter months. Defoe wrote in 1724/6 that *"...the soil of the midland part of England, even from sea to sea, is of a deep stiff clay, or marly kind, and it carries a breadth of near 50 miles at least, in some places much more; nor is it possible to go from London to all part of Britain, north, without crossing this clayey dirty part."* Examples he gives are the *"road as it leads to Coventry, and from thence to West Chester, the deep clays reach through all the towns of Brickhill, Fenny and Stony Stratford, Towcester, Daventry, Hill Morton or Dunchurch, Coventry, Coleshill and even to Birmingham for very nearly 80 miles. If you take the road to Worcester it is the same through the Vale of Aylesbury to Buckingham, and westwards to Banbury, Keynton, and the vale of Evesham, where the clays reach, with some intermission even to the banks of the Severn"*.

It was against this background of increasing commercial traffic using unmetalled and indifferently managed roads, that the turnpike system was devised.

2. The Turnpike System

2.1 Reorganising the Maintenance of Roads

Turnpikes were created during the eighteenth century to assist local communities maintain and improve the main roads passing through their area. A group of turnpike trustees were empowered, by specific Acts of Parliament, to levy tolls on users of a particular road running through several parishes. The trust had to apply these funds to improve this same section of highway and augmented the historic contribution of statute labour that still had to be provided by the parishes.

Turnpikes were a response to local demand for improving the means of transporting goods by road. At the time, petitioners justified the cost and inconvenience of turnpiking by expecting increased markets for local goods, particularly agricultural produce. The wider markets and better prices allowed landlords to demand higher rents and brought new business to the market towns. Turnpiking was financed, administered and operated by individuals drawn from the local business and agricultural communities. There was no central Government transport plan, though Parliament provided the means by which the old, communal institutions were replaced with a cash-based system. As the great laissez-faire economist Adam Smith remarked, in 1776, the scale and grandeur of the road was *"suited to what commerce can afford to pay"*.[1] The new roads assured speed and reliability of distribution rather than lower costs. However, the local community was stimulated to consider wider business horizons and to develop new products. As a result capital was diverted away from financing large inventories of stock to investing in new manufacturing equipment. Thus, the turnpikes became part of a virtuous cycle that helped to drive industrialisation and a national economy.

Defoe explains that *"these are (Midland) counties which drive a very great trade with the city of London, and with one another, perhaps the greatest of any counties in England; and that, by consequence, the carriage is exceeding great, and also that all the land carriage of the northern counties necessarily goes through these counties, so the roads had been ploughed so deep, and materials have been in some places so difficult to be had for repair of the roads, that all the surveyors rates have been able to do nothing; nay, the very whole country has not been able to repair them; that is to say, it was a burden too great for the poor farmers; for in England it is the tenant, not the landlord, that pays the surveyors of the highways.*

---

[1] Rule, J., *The Vital Century*, Longman, Harlow (1991).

"This necessarily brought the country to bring these things before Parliament; and the consequence has been, that turnpikes or toll-bars have been set up on several great roads in England, beginning at London, and proceeding through almost all those dirty deep roads, in the midland counties....."

The earliest phase of turnpiking, until the 1720s, dealt mainly with the great roads radiating out of London. The second phase around 1750 brought the important cross-routes into the care of trusts. In the third phase after 1770 the remainder of the main roads across England were turnpiked, creating most of the trunk road network with which we are familiar. A few minor roads and exceptional routes, such as Telford's improvement of the road to the Ireland Ferry at Holyhead, were turnpiked after 1800.

2.2. Turnpike Acts

2.2.1 General features

The creation of a turnpike road required an Act of Parliament to define the conditions under which the road could be improved and the means by which the costs were to be recouped. The first Turnpike Act, in 1663, covered improvements to the Great North Road out of London. It was administered by the justices for the counties through which it passed. However, later Acts, including all those relating to the Thames Valley (Appendix 1, Page 143) involved trusts made up of local gentry (including some justices), clergy, landowners, merchants and tradesmen. Unlike the later canal and railway companies, turnpike trusts did not construct totally new facilities but widened and improved an existing transport network. Consequently, the trusts could not raise money by issuing shares and were obliged to raise loans through mortgaging the anticipated income from tolls. The trustees were to handle substantial amounts of money and so care was taken to ensure they were responsible citizens who would swear an oath to serve the purposes of the trust. They were unpaid and were forbidden to make personal profit from the turnpike, although the indirect benefits from improved trade was an obvious motive for their support.

The initiative to turnpike a road was probably taken by a small number of local gentlemen but they had to gain the support of a cross-section of the community if their Act was to succeed. A County M.P. normally presented the case to Parliament and steered it through the Committees. Evidence was taken from those familiar with the area; in several instances this is recorded in the Journal of the House of Commons (*JHC*). Opposition came from those who had an historic right to use the roads and concessions were common in early Acts (e.g. for those attending a particular Fair).

ANNO QUADRAGESIMO SEPTIMO

GEORGII III. REGIS.

Seff. 2.

****

Cap. 91.

An Act for enlarging the Term and Powers of Two
Acts of the Fifth and Twenty-fifth Years of His
present Majesty, for repairing the Road from *Banbury*, in the County of *Oxford*, through *Daventry*
and *Cottesbach* to *Lutterworth*, in the County of
Leicester.   [8th *August* 1807.]

WHEREAS an Act was paffed in the Fifth Year of the Reign of
His prefent Majefty, intituled, *An Act for repairing and widening* 5 G. 3. c. 105.
the *Road from the Turnpike Road in* Banbury, *in the County of*
Oxford *through* Daventree *and* Cottefbach, *to the South End of* Mill Field
in the Parifh of Lutterworth, *in the County of* Leicefter : And whereas
another Act was paffed in the Twenty-fifth Year of the Reign of His prefent
Majefty, intituled, *An Act to enlarge the Term, and explain and amend the* 25 G. 3. c. 128.
Powers of an Act, *paffed in the Fifth Year of the Reign of His prefent Majefty, intituled*, ' *An Act for repairing and widening the Road from the Turn-
' pike Road at* Banbury, *in the County of* Oxford, *through* Daventry *and
' Cottefbach*, *to the South End of* Mill Field, *in the Parifh of* Lutterworth,
' *in the County of* Leicefter :' And whereas the Truftees appointed to put
the faid Act into Execution have made a confiderable Progrefs in the
Repairs of the faid Road, and for that Purpofe have borrowed feveral
Sums of Money upon the Credit of the Tolls thereby granted, which
Tolls are infufficient for Payment of the Interefb of the Sums borrowed
on the Credit of fuch Tolls, and for the proper Maintenance and Repair
of the faid Road; and the faid principal Money fo due and owing cannot be
repaid,

Fig. 4a. An example of a published Turnpike Act: Banbury to Lutterworth, 1807.

2.2.2 Components of the Act

By the eighteenth century the format of Turnpike Acts had become fairly
standard (Figs. 4a-c). A preamble specified the route in very general terms and
then asserted that the road was in a poor state and could not be amended by
the present laws, i.e. by statute labour. Trustees were generally named in
descending order of status. Lords and knights who had local interests headed
the list, followed by other gentry. Clergy from parishes through which the
road passed were included, probably to signal the support of local interests but
also to secure the statute labour.

ANNO QUINQUAGESIMO PRIMO

GEORGII III. REGIS.

∗∗∗

Cap. 2.

An Act for more effectually repairing the Road from
the Sessions House in the Town of *Buckingham*,
to *Hanwell*, in the County of *Oxford*.
[22d *March* 1811.]

WHEREAS an Act was passed in the Seventeenth Year of the
Reign of His late Majesty King *George* the Second, intituled,
An Act for repairing the Road from the Town of Buckingham, 17 G.2. c. 43.
in the County of Bucks, *to* Warmington, *in the County of* Warwick: And
whereas another Act was passed in the Ninth Year of the Reign of His
present Majesty, intituled, *An Act to continue the Term and enlarge the* 9 G.3. c. 52.
*Powers of so much of an Act, made in the Seventeenth Year of the Reign of
His late Majesty, as relates to the Road from the Town of* Buckingham, *in
the County of* Bucks, *to the North Extent of the Parish of* Hanwell, *in the
County of* Oxford, *leading towards* Warmington *Gate*: And whereas
another Act was passed in the Thirty-second Year of the Reign of His
present Majesty, intituled, *An Act for continuing and amending Two Acts* 32 G.3. c.134.
of the Seventeenth Year of King George *the Second, and the Ninth Year of
His present Majesty, so far as relates to repairing the Road from the Town of*
Buckingham *to the North Extent of the Parish of* Hanwell *in the County of*
Oxford: And whereas great Progress has been made in the Repair of
the said Road, and considerable Sums of Money borrowed upon the Credit
of the Tolls, now remain due, which cannot be repaid, nor the said Road
properly amended and kept in Repair, unless the Term granted by the
said Acts be continued, and the Powers and Provisions thereof altered
and enlarged, and the present Tolls increased:

Fig. 4b. A published Turnpike Act: Buckingham to Hanwell, 1811.

The number of trustees varied: relatively short turnpikes (e.g. Drayton to
Edgehill) had under a hundred trustees whereas those passing through many
parishes (e.g. Banbury to Lutterworth) had over two hundred. More than ten
per cent of the original trustees were landed gentry but as trustees retired or
died new members could be appointed and the composition of the trust
changed. By the early nineteenth century, the number of aristocratic trustees
had fallen and up to half of the active trustees were local clergymen (Table 1,
page 20).

ANNO QUINQUAGESIMO NONO

GEORGII III. REGIS.

Cap. cxxii.

An Act to continue the Term and alter and enlarge the Powers of an Act of His prefent Majefty's Reign, for repairing the Road from the Guide Poft in the Village of *Adderbury*, in the County of *Oxford*, through *Kidlington*, to the End of the Mileway in the City of *Oxford*. [2d *July* 1819.]

WHEREAS an Act was paffed in the Thirty-feventh Year of the Reign of His prefent Majefty King *George* the Third, intituled *An Act for more effectually repairing, improving, and keeping in repair the Road leading from the Guide Poft in the Village of* Adderbury, *in the County of* Oxford, *through* Kidlington, *to the End of the Mileway in the City of* Oxford: And whereas the Truftees appointed in or by virtue of the faid Act have proceeded in the Execution thereof, and have borrowed a confiderable Sum of Money upon the Credit of the Tolls thereby authorized to be collected, a confiderable Part of which ftill remains due and owing: And whereas the Money borrowed and due as aforefaid cannot be paid off and difcharged, and the faid Road effectually amended and kept in repair, unlefs the Term of the faid Act be continued, and fome of the Powers thereof altered, amended, and enlarged: May it therefore

ANNO TERTIO

GEORGII IV. REGIS.

Cap. xcv.

An Act for more effectually repairing the Road leading from the *Cross-of-Hand* near *Finford Bridge* in the County of *Warwick*, through the Town of *Southam* in the same County, to the Borough of *Banbury* in the County of *Oxford*.
[24th *June* 1822.]

WHEREAS an Act was passed in the Twenty-eighth Year of the Reign of His late Majesty King *George* the Second, intituled *An Act for repairing and widening the Roads leading from the Cross-of-Hand near* Finford Bridge *in the County of* Warwick, *through the Town of* Southam *in the same County, to the Borough of* Bambury *in the County of* Oxford, *and from the* Guide Post *in the Village of* Adderbury *in the same County, through* Kidlington, *to the* Mile Way *leading towards the City of* Oxford; *and also the Road leading from a Place called the* Two Mile Tree *near the City of* Oxford, *over* Gosford, *otherwise* Gossard Bridge, *to a certain Gate entering upon* Weston-on-the Green *in the said County:* And whereas another Act was passed in the Twentieth Year of the Reign of His late Majesty King *George* the Third, intituled *An Act for continuing the Term, and altering and enlarging the Powers of an Act passed in the Twenty-eighth Year of the Reign of His late Majesty King* George *the Second, for repairing and widening the Roads leading from the* Cross-of-Hand *near* Finford

Fig. 4c. Published Turnpike Acts: Adderbury to Oxford, 1819;
Finford Bridge to Banbury 1822.

The Turnpike System

Table 1: Number and status of trustees named in Turnpike Acts
Entry relating to the initial Act is in italics

Year	Turnpike Trust	Trustee Total	Number in category			as percentage of Total		
			Aristo	Clerk/ Dr	Other	Aristo	Clerk/ Dr	Other
1719	*Stokenchurch to Woodstock*	*164*	*21*	*27*	*116*	*13*	*16*	*71*
1730	*Woodstock to Rollright Lane*	*72*	*15*	*18*	*41*	*21*	*25*	*54*
1731	*Chappel on the Heath to Bourton*	*150*	*20*	*32*	*99*	*13*	*21*	*65*
1739	Stokenchurch to Woodstock	210	7	69	134	3	33	64
1744	Chappel on the Heath to Bourton	27	0	9	18	0	33	67
1744	*Buckingham to Warmington*	*96*	*9*	*12*	*78*	*9*	*13*	*78*
1751	*Crickley Hill to Campsfield*	*189*	*14*	*26*	*152*	*17*	*14*	*79*
1751	Woodstock to Rollright Lane	80	11	22	49	14	27	59
1753	*Drayton Lane to Edge Hill*	*96*	*14*	*18*	*66*	*15*	*19*	*67*
1755	*Finford to Banbury*	*251*	*16*	*23*	*214*	*7*	*18*	*75*
1755	*Adderbury to Weston*	*238*	*24*	*40*	*180*	*10*	*17*	*73*
1756	*Weston to Towcester*	*125*	*21*	*22*	*84*	*17*	*18*	*66*
1765	*Banbury to Lutterworth*	*243*	*17*	*43*	*185*	*7*	*18*	*75*
1770	*Burford to Banbury*	*317*	*14*	*75*	*228*	*4*	*24*	*72*
1790	*Bicester to Aynho*	*79*	*7*	*17*	*55*	*9*	*22*	*70*
1800	Fyfield District	41	5	6	30	12	15	73
1802	*Banbury to Barcheston*	*113*	*6*	*17*	*91*	*5*	*15*	*80*
1804	Woodstock to Rollright Lane	69	6	24	40	7	35	57
1807	Banbury to Lutterworth	26	0	12	14	0	46	54
1811	Buckingham to Hanwell	86	5	19	65	6	22	72
1812	Bicester to Aynho	38	3	5	30	8	13	79
1818	Adderbury to Kidlington	20	1	6	13	5	30	65
1820	Weston to Towcester	75	9	22	44	12	29	59
1821	Crickley Hill to Campsfield	112	5	43	64	4	38	57
1821	Gosford	36	4	7	25	11	19	69
1822	Finford to Banbury	83	5	23	55	6	28	66

Year	Turnpike Trust	Trus-tee Total	Number in category			as percentage of Total		
			Aristo	Clerk/ Dr	Other	Aristo	Clerk/ Dr	Other
1822	Drayton to Edgehill	44	2	13	29	5	30	66
1825	Woodstock to Rollright Lane	48	6	16	26	13	33	54
1828	Banbury to Lutterworth	71	0	32	39	0	45	55
1832	Burford to Banbury	108	8	35	65	7	32	60
1832	Buckingham to Hanwell	75	3	23	49	4	31	65
1834	Barrington to Campsfield	94	7	22	65	7	23	69
1840	Banbury to Lutterworth	85	1	34	50	1	40	59
1846	Woodstock to Rollright Lane	29	6	8	15	21	28	51
1859	Finford to Banbury	46	2	23	21	4	50	46

Table 1 *contd.*: **Number and status of trustees named in Turnpike Acts**

The Act specified trustees' powers and the manner in which disputes were to be settled. Occasionally specific nuisances were mentioned such as preventing windmills being built close to the Crickley Hill to Campsfield Turnpike.

The trust was empowered to collect tolls at turnpike gates erected at key points. Tolls reflected both the ability (or preparedness) of travellers to pay and the degree of damage it was judged they might do to the road. Except where the road spanned two counties, only one payment was normally needed per day on the roads covered by a particular trust. The charges were specified in the Act and had to be displayed at the toll-gates. There were exemptions for pedestrians, clergy, soldiers on the march, voters at elections, traffic to and from church or funerals and some local traffic involved in agricultural activities. Later, when mail coaches used the turnpikes they had right of free passage and the gatekeeper was obliged to open the gate as soon as he heard the horn of the approaching coach. Commercial traffic carried the bulk of the charges and in the eighteenth century charges were based on the size of the vehicle (e.g. four or two wheel coaches) and the horses drawing it. Examples of charges are given in Appendix 2. The charge of 3d. per horse meant that a coach or waggon pulled by four horses would pay about a shilling to travel about twenty miles along the turnpike. By the nineteenth century, horse-power and the width of the wheels were used as the basis of tolls. The advent of horseless steam traction led to arbitrary tolls or charges per axle, giving a total toll equivalent to a two or four horse vehicle.

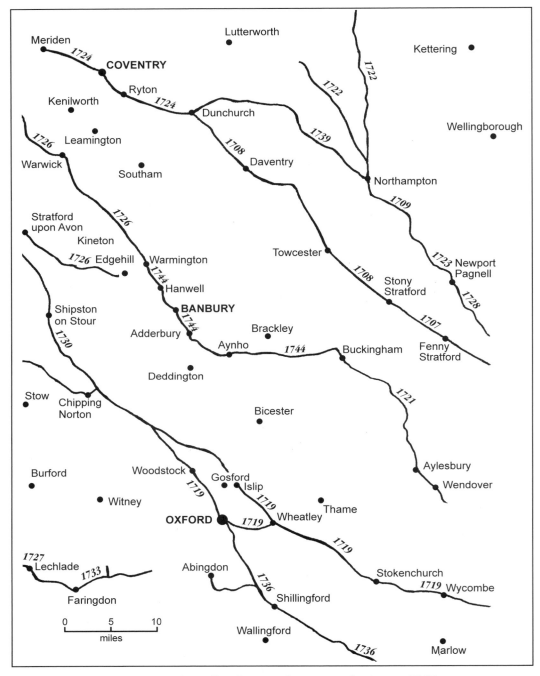

*Fig. 5. South Midlands turnpikes created prior to 1745
(date of first Turnpike Act shown).*

The income that trusts received from collecting or leasing tolls varied greatly (figures in Appendix 2). Some trusts collected less than £400/a (e.g. Gosford, Drayton to Edgehill, Upton to Wellesbourne, Buckingham to Towcester) but had low expenditure either because they administered short stretches of road (the first two examples) or looked after roads which carried relatively little traffic. The larger local trusts had incomes of over £1000/a (e.g. Burford to Banbury, Buckingham to Hanwell) whereas the main trunk roads had incomes of several thousand pounds per year (e.g. Stokenchurch to Woodstock, Hockliffe section of the Holyhead Road).

2.3 Turnpikes in North Oxfordshire

Although the turnpikes and their system of administration disappeared more than a hundred years ago, some documents have survived in county record offices and further information can be gleaned from newspapers and private papers. The main eighteenth century roads in the Banbury area are considered in two main groups below. Individual turnpike trusts are described in subsequent chapters (3 to 6).

2.3.1 Principal roads across the region

None of the roads through Banbury warranted inclusion in the first phase of turnpiking prior to 1720 (Fig. 5). Two main roads from London to Birmingham, through Coventry and Oxford, were clearly more important trunk routes and were turnpiked in the first two decades of the eighteenth century. The former, running through Northamptonshire and Warwickshire, is the most important of these; its history has been recorded by Cossons.[2] The road from London through Oxford was for much of its distance the Great road to Worcester, recorded by Ogilby. The highway from Uxbridge, through Beaconsfield and Stokenchurch to Woodstock was turnpiked under two trusts in 1719. The Worcester road from Chappel on the Heath, above Chipping Norton, to the Cotswold scarp at Bourton Hill had been turnpiked in 1731, and the remaining section of the Worcester road north of Woodstock was turnpiked in 1736. This latter trust also had responsibility for a branch northward to Rollright Lane that became increasingly important as one of the main roads to the growing industrial centre of Birmingham.

---

[2] Cossons, "Warwickshire turnpikes", *Birmingham Arch. Soc., Trans & Proc.*, LXIV, 53-100 (1946).

2.3.2 Roads centred on Banbury

Highways across the Avon at Stratford and Warwick were turnpiked during the early phase of turnpiking. It was 1744 before the London road through Buckingham to Birmingham became the first turnpike road to serve Banbury. This highway connected with the existing Warwick turnpike road at Warmington and, in 1753, a second road was turnpiked from Banbury to join the Stratford road at Edgehill. These initiatives were part of a general improvement of roads running south and east from the industrial Midlands towards London and augmented rather than replaced other routes. These turnpikes are considered in Chapter 3.

The main north/south road through Banbury was turnpiked soon afterwards in 1755; again this was a consequence of business activity in Warwickshire, particularly around Coventry. The two trusts covering this road are considered in Chapter 4.

The remaining roads to, rather than through, Banbury were turnpiked during the third phase of turnpiking. The road north-eastwards to Daventry, Watling Street and Lutterworth was turnpiked in 1765 and the road south-westwards to Chipping Norton and Burford in 1770. Final connections between the main parts of the network were completed during the closing stages of turnpike mania. An alternative road from Buckingham was improved in 1791, a branch southwards from the existing turnpike at Aynho was part of general improvements of the network around Bicester in 1791 and the road from Banbury to the Oxford to Birmingham road at Shipston was turnpiked in 1802. The trusts covering these roads running north-eastwards from Banbury are considered in Chapter 5 and those to the west are dealt with in Chapter 6.

The full turnpike network across the region is illustrated in Fig. 6.

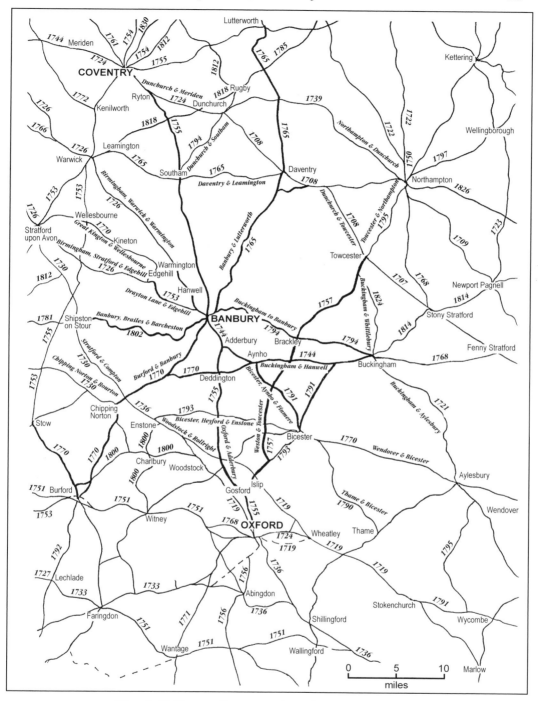

*Fig. 6. Full turnpike network in the south Midlands
(date of first Turnpike Act shown).*

2.3.3 Individual involvement in Turnpike Trusts

Four classes of people were associated with turnpikes.

- The trustees had a responsibility to ensure that the turnpike served the purposes laid down under the Act of Parliament.
- The officers of the trust had specific roles to ensure that the turnpike was administered effectively and was financially sound.
- The lessees of the tolls and their toll-collectors were generally independent of the trust and were concerned to extract sufficient toll revenue to cover their lease.
- The users of the turnpikes were concerned to ensure that the improvements in travel resulting from passage along a turnpike matched the cost they incurred in paying the toll.

The turnpike acts listed the trustees and so we know the names of many of the men who sponsored and watched over the turnpikes (see the alphabetical list of trustees, pages 163-193). Some individuals acted as trustees for a number of turnpikes, particularly where these covered adjacent sections of a main road. Aristocratic families such as Dashwood, North, Parker, Spencer were particularly active supporters of local trusts. This broad involvement was also evident among the local gentry and the enthusiasm was often carried over several generations (e.g. families such as Blencowe, Bowles, Cartwright, Cope, Holbech, Lee, Lenthall, Walford, Willes and Wyatt around Banbury and Dowdeswell, Rowney and Stickland in the Cotswolds).

Some trustees acquired considerable experience from their position on different trusts. The Revd Henry Homer, rector of Birdingbury in Warwickshire, was a Commissioner (trustee) on the Finford to Banbury Trust and the Dunchurch to Stonebridge Trust. In 1767 he published a lengthy pamphlet, analysing the method of road construction and recommending the best means of managing roads.[3] His main conclusion was the need for *"some check upon the obstinacy and temerity of waggoners"* who dragged over-weight vehicles along the turnpikes.

The conscientious William Cotton Risley, vicar of Deddington from 1835 to 1848, regularly recorded in his diary attending turnpike trustees' meetings at Aynho and at the Fox at North Aston. In January 1837 Clifton & Aynho was let for £150, Deddington £65, and Swerford Heath at £36. Meetings at North Aston concerned repairs to the Adderbury to Oxford road and appointing a surveyor (1841, 1844).[4]

---

[3] *An enquiry into the means of preserving and improving the Publick Roads of this Kingdom with observations on the probable consequences of the present plan*; Henry Homer; Bodleian Library, Oxford. Oxf 1767, 8° G Pamphlet (1865) 1. 24755 e80.
See Appendix 4, pp. 154-155.

[4] Smedley-Stevenson G., *Early Victorian Squarson*, BHS 29, 2007, see index 'Turnpike', 254.

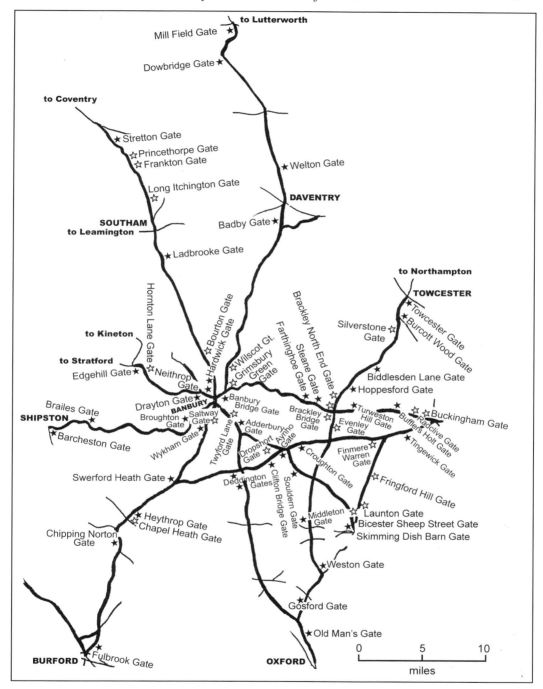

*Fig. 7. Location of toll-houses in the area around Banbury and Brackley, roughly
between Coventry, Towcester, Buckingham, Bicester, Oxford, Burford,
Chipping Norton, Shipston-upon-Stour, Stratford-upon-Avon and Warwick.
Black stars = permanent location; white stars = location used for a few years only.
See also Fig.11, pages 46-47, for more details of the Banbury, Bicester, Brackley areas.*

The clerk or clerks to the trust were paid officials appointed by the trustees. They were usually local solicitors, who dealt with the legal aspects of the trust and administrated the routine operation of the turnpike. During the eighteenth century the clerk often acted as treasurer as well, but by the nineteenth century this was specifically forbidden, presumably because it had led to corruption. Surveyors were paid officials who took responsibility for the building and maintenance of the road, toll-gates and toll-houses.

Often short sections of the road were allocated to locally recruited surveyors. They were empowered to dig out road-making materials within the parishes and take all measures necessary to remove obstructions and nuisances such as overhanging trees, poor drainage or narrow roadways. They also co-ordinated the statute labour and teams which parishioners were obliged to provide. In addition surveyors could purchase materials and services from outside the area. As techniques in road construction improved, consultant engineers such as McAdam were appointed as chief surveyor with local surveyors to deal with day to day work. Names of officers (Appendix 3) appear in the surviving papers and from the early nineteenth century, these individuals were listed in the formal returns which trusts were legally bound to submit to government agents.

The names of lessees of tolls (Tables 2 to 7[5]) can be found in the administrative papers for the trusts. These records are very patchy but are clear evidence that some individuals operated at a regional level, leasing gates on several turnpikes at the same time. The location of the individual toll-gates is shown in Fig. 7 (page 27) and typical income from these gates is illustrated in the tables of Appendix 2.

There is least information about the users of the turnpikes. Obviously everyone in the earlier categories used the road which they helped to run. However, there is only fragmentary evidence of how the traveller judged the operation of the turnpikes. Where comments have been traced they appear below, within the sections covering particular turnpikes.

---

[5] Tables 2 to 7 appear on pages 39, 41, 49, 54, 64 and 73.

3. Buckingham to Birmingham Turnpikes

Until 1725 Buckingham was a county town and so historically was connected to London by the King's highway. Banbury was on the road between Buckingham and the county town of Warwick. However, by the eighteenth century it was the industrial towns beyond Warwick which were determining the transportation needs of the region. The two roads from Birmingham to the edge of Warwickshire over the bridges at Warwick and Stratford were turnpiked, in 1726, under a single trust. In 1753, the section south-east from Edgehill to Banbury (Drayton Lane) was turnpiked separately, but by an Act of 1770, the single Birmingham to Warwick & Warmington, and to Edgehill & Stratford Turnpike Trust was broken up. The powers of the original trustees were restricted to the Birmingham to Stratford road (the Henley Road) and a new trust was created to deal with the Birmingham to Warwick & Warmington section. At the same time another trust was formed to turnpike the road from Wellesbourne & Kineton to Upton, near Edgehill. To the east of Buckingham, the London road from Wendover and Aylesbury had been turnpiked in 1721. Turnpiking the road between Warmington and Buckingham in 1744 completed the improvement of this main radial route from London to Birmingham (Fig. 5, page 23).

3.1 The Buckingham to Warmington Trust

3.1.1 The road covered by the Act

The road from Buckingham, via Aynho and Banbury to Warmington, was illustrated by Ogilby and so is judged to have been an important highway in seventeenth century England. The route ran on ground that would have remained relatively dry. An ancient route (Fig. 1, pages 2-3) crossed the Cherwell at Twyford but by the sixteenth century Nell Bridge carried the main road. It is not clear why the bridge was built downstream of the old twin ford at Twyford, though it does give better access to Adderbury which had aspirations as a market. Both Nell Bridge and Twyford bring traffic on to the western bank of the river well to the south of Banbury and so avoid the low lying ground on the eastern bank closer to Banbury Bridge. Upkeep of Nell Bridge was a county responsibility and so the turnpike trustees were not burdened directly by any costs in using it. From this crossing the turnpike went north of Adderbury, approaching Banbury through the South Bar and passing along the Horse Fair, to the west of the town centre.

The petition to Parliament in February 1743 was made by the Bailiff, Burgesses and inhabitants of Buckingham.[1] It stated that *"the road from Buckingham to Warmington in the County of Warwick, by reason of the heavy carriages frequently passing the same, is become so ruinous that in the winter season the said road is dangerous to travellers and cannot by the ordinary provisions applied by the laws and statutes of this realm be effectively repaired unless some further provisions be made for raising money to be applied for that purpose"*. In evidence to the Committee,[2] Mr Thomas Shirley said that *"it is a road of great resort, many carriages as well as passengers on horseback passing through the same"*. Mr John Parish provided evidence that the road was bad and could not be improved under present provisions. The majority of the highway was in Buckinghamshire and the involvement of Banbury was incidental. Nevertheless, the town would have benefited from the traffic generated by the improved carriageway on this alternative route for coaches travelling between Birmingham and London.

The trust controlled roads through parishes in four counties. Responsibility to four sets of justices must have complicated the administration. So it is not surprising that when the trust sought to renew its powers, in 1768, the section north of Banbury was shortened so the road ran from the Sessions House in Buckingham to the northern boundary of Hanwell in the County of Oxfordshire. In seeking an extension of the powers of the trust for a further 21-year period, Thomas Walker used the normal justification that the road had been improved but was so heavily used that it required further provisions. In addition, £475 of loan taken to make improvements was still outstanding and an additional period of toll collection was necessary to repay this.

3.1.2 Trust Administration

Judging by newspaper advertisements in the 1770s, the road was administered in two divisions. The Oxfordshire section was referred to as the Weeping Cross Turnpike (Fig. 8a), named after the ancient crossroads where the Saltway to Twyford road crosses the Oxford road south of Banbury. This division had only one gate, at the Weeping Cross, and was administered from Banbury. The gates at Finmere Warren (Oxfordshire/Buckinghamshire border) and Dropshort (Fig. 8b), were administered from Buckingham. The Finmere Gate was close to where Ogilby noted the great coney warren. The location of Dropshort Gate is a matter of conjecture, though it was probably on the hill between Aynho and Nell Bridge.

---

[1]   *JHC* **24**, 536.
[2]   *JHC* **24**, 605.

WEEPING-CROSS TURNPIKE, Nov. 9, 1775.

NOTICE is hereby given, That the next Meeting of the Trustees of this Turnpike will be held at the Three Tuns in Banbury, in the County of Oxford, on Tuesday the 21st day of this instant November, at ten o'clock in the forenoon, for the purpose of putting into further execution the powers vested in them by certain Acts of Parliament made for repairing the Turnpike Road leading from Buckingham in the County of Bucks, to the north extent of the parish of Hanwell, in the County of Oxford.   By Order of the Trustees,
RICHARD BIGNELL, Clerk.

TURNPIKE TOLLS to be LETT.

THE Trustees of the Turnpike Road leading from Buckingham, in the county of Bucks, to the North extent of the parish of Hanwell, in the county of Oxford, do intend, at their next General Meeting, which will be held at the Lord Cobham's Arms Inn, in Buckingham, on Monday the sixteenth day of October, 1775, to lett by lease, to the best bidder, all the Tolls arising from the two several Turnpike-gates on the said Road, called Dropshort-gate, and Finmere-Warren-gate; and any person inclined to take the same, and being able to give sufficient security, is desired to deliver to Mr. Miller, of Buckingham, at least ten days before such Meeting, his proposal in writing, sealed up, signifying the highest yearly sum he is willing to give for the same.

NOTICE is hereby given, That the Tolls arising at the Toll Gate upon the Turnpike Road leading from Buckingham to the North Extent of Hanwell Field, in the County of Oxford, called or known by the Name of Weeping-Cross Gate, will be lett by Auction to the best Bidder, at the Red Lion in Banbury, in the County of Oxford, on Wednesday the 25th Day of July next, between the Hours of Three and Four in the Afternoon, in the Manner directed by the Act passed in the Thirteenth Year of the Reign of his Majesty King George the Third, "for regulating the Turnpike Roads," which Tolls produced the last Year the Sum of Four Hundred and Forty Pounds above the Expences of collecting them, and will be put up at that Sum. Whoever happens to be the best Bidder must at the same Time give Security, with sufficient Sureties, to the Satisfaction of the Trustees of the said Turnpike Road, for Payment of the Rent agreed for, and at such Times as they shall direct. That at such Meeting the Trustees will borrow and take up at Interest the Sum of 100l. at Four per Cent. and any Person willing to advance the same is desired to attend.

June 10th, 1792.   R. BIGNELL, Clerk.

Fig. 8a-c. Advertisements relating to the Buckingham to Hanwell Turnpike. Weeping Cross, Finmere Warren and Dropshort.

The Weeping Cross Gate (Fig. 8c) raised more than twice as much revenue as the other two gates; in 1785 Weeping Cross tolls were let for £525, the other two for £253. The road was steadily improved by the trust but also by individual subscriptions for specific purposes. In 1770 a meeting was convened at the Three Tuns in Banbury to discuss the possibility of a subscription to finance the building of a causeway along the road between Twyford and Adderbury because it was often flooded when the Cherwell overflowed.[3]

The 1811 Act defined the trust in two divisions. The upper division ran from Buckingham to the sign of the Red Lion in Aynho, and a lower division from Aynho to Hanwell. Meetings were held at the Red Lion in Aynho. The financial records of the divisions were reported separately so that finance raised in one division was directed only to repair of that section of road. A further renewal of the Act in 1832 redefined the boundary as the eastern edge of Aynho parish: the trustees were to meet at the Cartwright Arms in Aynho (the Red Lion re-named). The upper division was administered from Buckingham by its clerk Thomas Hearn and the lower division from Oxfordshire by Richard Bignell; Mr Cave was employed as surveyor for both sections (Appendix 3).

The toll-gates were relocated in the nineteenth century (Fig. 8d). The first gate on the road west from Buckingham was at Tingewick, on the northern side of the village street. The next gate was at Croughton near Aynho, although this may have replaced an earlier gate at Astwick a little to the east. The third gate was placed north of Adderbury to levy tolls on traffic joining the turnpike from the direction of Oxford. Another toll-gate, located at Twyford Lane south of Weeping Cross, was probably a side-gate let with the Adderbury Gate to intercept traffic on the alternative crossing of the Cherwell (Fig. 8e). The final gate was at Neithrop on the road leading north-west out of Banbury. This deployment of the gates was not altered during the remaining life of the trust (Figs. 8f and 8g). The road north-westwards from Hanwell was administered by the Birmingham to Warmington Trust. Their nearest gate was at Burton Ground, north-west of Warmington.

---

[3] *Jackson's Oxford Journal [JOJ]*, Sept. 1770.

TOLLS TO BE LET.

NOTICE is hereby given, That a Meeting of the Trustees acting under and by virtue of an Act of Parliament made and passed in the 51st year of the reign of his present Majesty King George the Third, entitled " An Act for more ef- " fectually repairing the Road from the Sessions " House, in the town of Buckingham, to Hanwell, " in the county of Oxford," will be held at the Cobham Arms Inn, in Buckingham aforesaid, on Monday the 9th day of August next, between the hours of Eleven o'clock in the forenoon, and Two o'clock in the afternoon; at which time and place the Tolls to arise at the two several Turnpike Gates upon the upper Division of the said Road called or known by the names of the Tingewick and Astwick Gates, will be LET by AUCTION, to the best bidder, in the manner directed by the Act passed in the 13th year of the reign of his present Majesty, " for re- gulating the Turnpike Roads," for such term as shall be stipulated by the said Trustees; which Tolls produced during the year ending the 29th day of June instant, the sum of £458, over and above the expence of collecting the same, and will be put up at that sum.

Whoever happens to be the best bidder must at the same time pay such deposit and give such se- curity, with sufficient sureties, as the Trustees shall approve of, for payment of the rent agreed upon, at the times and in such manner as they shall direct.

And at such Meeting new Trustees will be elec- ted in lieu of those who are deceased or neglected to act; and such other business done as by the several Acts is required.

THOMAS HEARN, jun.
Clerk to the said Trustees.

Buckingham, June 30, 1819.

Turnpike Tolls to be Let.

NOTICE is hereby given, That a Meeting of the Trustees acting under and by virtue of an Act of Parliament made and passed in the 51st year of the reign of his late Majesty King George the Third, intituled " An Act for more effectually re- pairing the Road from the Sessions House, in the town of Buckingham, to Hanwell, in the county of Oxford," will be held at the Town Hall, in Banbury, on Saturday the 9th day of September next, at Eleven o'clock in the forenoon; at which time and place the Tolls to arise at the several Gates upon the said Road, called or known by the names of the Adderbury, Twyford-lane, and Neithrop Gates, will be LET by AUCTION, to the best bidder or bidders, for such term as shall be agreed on by the said Trustees, which Tolls produced the last year the sums following, viz:—

The Adderbury and Twyford-lane Gates, £575
The Neithrop Gate, ... 253
at which sums they will respectively be put up.

Whoever happens to be the best bidder must, at the same time, pay down such sums by way of de- posit as the Trustees shall agreed upon, and give security, with sufficient sureties, to the satisfaction of the Trustees, for payment of the remainder of the rent agreed for, at such time as they shall direct.

And at such Meeting the Trustees intend to do and transact such other business as by the several Acts is required.

RICHARD BIGNELL,
Clerk to the said Trustees.

Middleton Stoney, August 9, 1820.

Fig. 8d. Tingewick Gate *Fig. 8e Adderbury, Twyford, Neithrop.*

BUCKINGHAM AND HANWELL TURNPIKE ROAD.
TOLLS TO BE LET.

NOTICE is hereby given, that a Meeting of the Trustees of the Lower Division of the said Road will be held at the Town Hall, in the borough of Banbury, in the county of Oxford, on Wednesday the 19th day of June next, at Twelve o'clock at noon; at which Meeting, between the hours of Twelve o'clock at noon and Two in the afternoon, the Tolls arising from the Adderbury, Twyford Lane, and Neithrop Gates, upon the said Road, will be LET by AUCTION, to the best bidder or bidders, for such term as may be determined on, not exceeding three years from the 1st day of July next, in manner directed by the Acts of the third and fourth years of the reign of King George IV., " For regulating Turnpike Roads," which Tolls produced last year the sum of 1151l., and they will be put up again at that sum.

The taker will be required to pay in advance one month's rent, and to give security, with sufficient sureties, to the satisfaction of the Trustees, for payment of the rent monthly, so that at all times one month's rent be kept paid in advance.—Dated the 23d day of May, 1844.

RICHARD BIGNELL, } Clerks to
B. W. APLIN, } the Trustees.

Fig. 8f. Adderbury, Twyford Lane and Neithrop Gates.

BUCKINGHAM AND HANWELL
TURNPIKE ROAD.

NOTICE IS HEREBY GIVEN, that the General Annual
Meeting of the Trustees of the Lower Division of the said
Road will be held at the Town Hall, in the Borough of Banbury, on
Tuesday, the 21st day of February next, at Twelve o'clock at noon,
when a statement of the debts, revenues, and expenditure of the
said Turnpike Road, from the first day of January, 1870, to the
thirty-first day of December, 1870, will be submitted to the Trustees
then assembled, and that at such Meeting the said statement will
be audited and allowed. An estimate of the probable expenditure
of the Trust for the current year, commencing on the first day
of January, 1871, will be laid before the Trustees; and at the
said Meeting new Trustees will be elected in the place of those
who are dead or refuse to act, and such other business will be
done and transacted as the circumstances of the Trust may
require.
Dated the 26th day of January, 1871.
B. W. APLIN,
Clerk to the Trustees.

Fig.8g. Buckingham and Hanwell Turnpike Road, Lower Division.

3.2 The Drayton Lane to Edgehill Trust

3.2.1 The Road covered by the Act

This relatively short section of road connected Banbury with the existing turnpike road from Stratford upon Avon to Edgehill. The earlier Birmingham to Warwick and Stratford Turnpike, established in 1726, had gone no further than the top of Edgehill, close to the county boundary. An ancient highway from Stratford ran along the watershed between the Stour and the Dene, through Ettington and climbed the hill to the Sun Rising Inn. The first Birmingham trust may have improved this road and the Drayton to Edgehill Trust had an easier task of maintaining the road into Banbury across relatively dry, undulating ground. Historically the main axis of travel north-west of Banbury had been towards Warwick and even the road to Drayton would carry some traffic bound for Warwick along the route down to Kineton. When the Birmingham trust was re-organised in 1770 a new trust was created to turnpike the road from Wellesbourne and Kineton up the scarp face to Ratley and then along the crest of the Cotswolds to Upton, near Edgehill. The Stratford to Edgehill Turnpike was administered by a separate trust from 1779 onwards.[4] Judging from the income from leasing tolls, the two roads down the scarp face had a similar status (Appendix 2). The road from Drayton fed traffic onto both roads but still appears to be a less important road than the direct route to Warwick through Warmington

---

[4] *JHC* **38**, 37.

The petition to Parliament in March 1753 was made by the Mayor, Aldermen, Burgesses and other principal inhabitants of the Borough of Banbury.[5] It stated that *"the road leading from Banbury towards Stratford upon Avon in the County of Warwick, which passes through the village of Drayton, through Roxton Lane unto a house known by the name of the Sun Rising, upon Edge Hill in the County of Warwick, is in many parts become so deep and founderous that for several months of the year the same is very dangerous for horsemen and almost impassable for carriages, and in some places so narrow that carriages cannot pass each other without great inconvenience and danger"*. Mr Francis Edge, in evidence to a Committee,[6] said that *"there is a very considerable trade carried on in Banbury and it has been a great thoroughfare for passengers who travel from London through the townships of Uxbridge, Amersham, Wendover, Aylesbury and Buckingham to Stratford upon Avon and from thence to Birmingham, that there has been a free communication from Banbury with the several towns aforesaid, but that now the great road leading through the Borough to Edge Hill and to Stratford upon Avon is become so deep and founderous that it is dangerous."*.

The tolls levied on the Warmington road had presumably increased the traffic on this alternative, toll-free highway. The resulting Act specified that the turnpike trust was responsible for the road *"leading from the Guide Post in Drayton Lane through Drayton Town and Wroxton Lane as far as a certain Well usually known by the Name of Moulds Well, and from thence turning to the right hand and passing between the Sign of the White Horse and a Piece of Ground called Stretchwell Piece, on to the Post dividing the Chipping Norton and Stratford upon Avon Roads in the County of Oxford, and from thence along the Great Stratford upon Avon Road, through Upton Lane, to the House called Sun Rising on the Top of Edge Hill in the County of Warwick, and which is the direct Road from the Town of Banbury in the County of Oxon, unto the Town of Stratford upon Avon in the County of Warwick"*.

3.2.2 Trust Administration

The trustees held their first meeting in Banbury on the 5th June 1753, electing John Makepeace as clerk, Samuel Welchman as surveyor and Francis Edge as treasurer. Edge, who was clearly a leading figure in securing the Act, was landlord of the Three Tuns in Banbury and most of the early meetings were held on his premises.[7]

---

[5] *JHC* **26**, 650.
[6] *JHC* **26**, 675.
[7] See Gibson, J., "The Three Tuns in the Eighteenth Century", *C&CH* **8**.1 (1979), 5.

It was agreed that "*gates be, with all speed erected in Drayton Lane, near the Roebuck*" and "*at or near the Sun Rising on Edge Hill*". An initial loan of £500 was secured on the credit of the tolls from these gates. Joseph Tubb was appointed collector at Drayton Lane and Joseph Turner at Edgehill, each at a salary of 6s. per week. Until a gate was erected, the surveyor was to "*put up a bar or chain*" at which tolls could be collected and a temporary hut was to be built at Edgehill. The permanent toll-house at Edgehill was built by Thomas Calliot for just under £20. There was a staircase, presumably to cope with the slope, and post and rails were made from the gate to the corner of the house called the Sun Rising and a side gate was also installed adjacent to the toll-house. The surveyor later made "*a mound from the house called the Sun Rising to the toll-house at the end of Upton Lane to prevent carriages from avoiding payment at the gate*". Only £2 was spent to fit out the toll-house in Drayton Lane, though this was consistently busier than the Edgehill Gate (Fig. 9a).

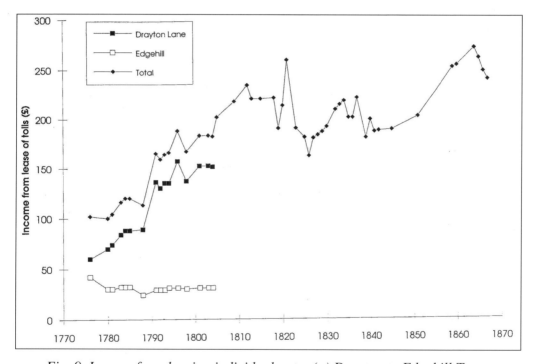

Fig. 9. Income from leasing individual gates (a) Drayton to Edgehill Trust. Compare with Fig. 12, page 52.

There may have been resistance to the imposition of charges, since by June 1753 the trustees had decided to lower the tolls to less than the maximum which they were empowered to impose by the Act. In particular the toll on a cart was cut from 8d. to 4d. and for a drove of cattle from 10d. to 5d. per score and sheep from 5d. to 3d. per score. In May 1755 a further concession was made for toll-free carriage for *"loads of bushes for fuel; one for each labourer and poor female household in the Parish of Drayton"*.

Improvements were made to *"take down the hill at the end of the road at Edgehill"* in 1796 and in 1810 costs were incurred improving the bridge at Drayton. In 1819, permission was sought from the Earl of Guilford *"to take down an old oak which stands in the road near Drayton Bridge, the tree being a great nuisance to all travellers"*. A new section of road was constructed along an existing footpath and across Shepherds Close in Wroxton, at a cost of £98; the trust had to seek permission from Trinity College, Oxford, who owned the land.

The income of the road was relatively low, even allowing for the short section of road involved. The inhabitants of the parishes of Drayton, Wroxton, Balscot, Alkerton and Ratley had to provide between two and three days statute duty, labouring on the road each year. This road was an important factor in persuading the Royal Mail to bring a service through Banbury and the local business community was concerned that it was kept in a good state. A Parliamentary Select Committee[8] noted that *"in consequence of the mail now using the road great sums of money had been expended"*, though this high expenditure would not need to continue. The leases to collect tolls at these two gates were auctioned annually, usually at the Red Lion in Banbury (Fig. 10a) but later at the Town Hall, Banbury (Fig. 10b).

NOTICE is hereby given, That the Tolls arising at the Toll Gate upon the Turnpike Road from the Guide-Post near the End of Drayton Lane, near Banbury, in the County of Oxford, to the House called the Sun Rising, at the Top of Edge Hill, in the County of Warwick, called or known by the Name of the Drayton Gate, will be lett by Auction to the best Bidder, at the House of William Pratt, the Sign of the Red Lion at Banbury, in the said County of Oxford, on Wednesday the Twenty-fifth Day of July now next coming, between the Hours of Two and Four of the Clock in the Afternoon, in the Manner directed by the Act passed in the Thirteenth Year of the Reign of his Majesty King George the Third, "For regulating the Turnpike Roads," which Tolls produced the last Year the Sum of One Hundred and Thirty-six Pounds above the Expence of collecting them, and will be put up at that Sum. Whoever happens to be the best Bidder, must at the same Time give Security, with sufficient Sureties, to the Satisfaction of the Trustees of the said Turnpike Road, for Payment of the Rent agreed for, and at such Times as they shall direct.

Adderbury,   CHRISTOPHER APLIN,
18th June, 1792.   Clerk to the said Trustees.

AUGUST 8th, 1794.

NOTICE is hereby given, That the Tolls arising at the Toll Gate upon the Turnpike Road at Edge-Hill, in the County of Warwick, called or known by the Name of the Edge-Hill Gate, will be LETT by AUCTION to the best Bidder, at the Town-Hall in Banbury, in the County of Oxford, on Tuesday the Sixteenth Day of September, 1794, between the Hours of Eleven and Twelve of the Clock in the Forenoon of the same Day, in the Manner directed by the Act passed in the Thirteenth Year of the Reign of his Majesty King George the Third, "For regulating the Turnpike Roads," which Tolls produced the last Year the Sum of Twenty-nine Pounds above the Expences of collecting them, and will be put up at that Sum. Whoever happens to be the best Bidder must at the same Time give Security, with sufficient Sureties, to the Satisfaction of the Trustees of the said Turnpike Road, for the Payment of the Rent agreed for, and at such Times as they shall direct.

CHRISTOPHER APLIN, Clerk to the said Trustees.

Figs. 10a and 10b. Advertisements relating to the Drayton to Edgehill Turnpike.

---

[8] *Parliamentary Papers [PP]* **4**, 1821.

In 1844 the trustees decided to erect a new side-gate at Hornton Lane, in the parish of Ratley, to intercept traffic entering from the Warwick road (Fig. 10c). This was let with the Drayton Lane Gate (Fig. 10d).

> ### Drayton and Edgehill Turnpike Road.
>
> NOTICE is hereby Given, that the Trustees of the Turn-pike Road under an Act passed in the Third year of the Reign of His late Majesty, King George the Fourth, "For more effectually repairing the Road from the Guide Post near the end of Drayton Lane, near Banbury, in the County of Oxford, to the House called the Sun Rising, at the Top of Edgehill, in the County of Warwick," will meet at the House of Charles White Fowler, in Banbury aforesaid, on Wednes-day, the thirteenth day of March next, at the hour of Twelve o'clock at Noon, in order to consult about erecting a Toll Gate, Bar, or Chain, across or on the side of the said Turnpike Road, in the Parish of Ratley, in the said County of Warwick, at or near a certain Highway leading out of the said Turnpike Road, to Hornton, in the said County of Oxford.—Dated the 20th day of February, 1844.
>
> W. WALFORD,
> Clerk to the Trustees.

Fig. 10c and d. Advertisements relating to the Drayton to Edgehill Turnpike..

> ### Drayton and Edgehill Turnpike Road.
>
> NOTICE IS HEREBY GIVEN, that the GENERAL ANNUAL MEETING of the Trustees of the above Turnpike Road will be held at the Red Lion Inn, in Banbury, in the County of Oxford, on Monday, the 13th day of February, 1871, at Twelve o'clock at noon, for the purpose of Auditing the Accounts for the past year, electing new Trustees, and transacting such other business as may be requisite, and at which meeting, between the hours of Twelve at noon and Two in the afternoon, the TOLLS arising at the Drayton and Edgehill Gates, and the Hornton Lane Chain, will be LET BY PUBLIC AUCTION to the best bidder or bidders, either together or in Lots, from the 1st day of March next until the 1st day of November next, in the manner directed by the General Turnpike Act, which Tolls produced at the last letting the sum of £228. The Taker will be required to pay down one month's rent in advance, and give security to the Trustees for payment of the remainder of the rent monthly in advance.
>
> Dated this 11th day of January, 1871.
>
> JOHN FORTESCUE,
> Clerk to the Trustees.

Minutes from all the trust's meetings have survived and from these a complete list of gatekeepers (and later lessees) has been compiled (Table 2).

Table 2: Drayton to Edgehill Turnpike Trust

Trustees (active)

1753: John Willes, William Cartwright, Thomas Bradford, Edward Burford, Edward Busby, William Deacter, Richard Air, Thomas Gill, Edward Hughes, Anthoney Kock [Keck], Sanderson Miller, Edw Barker, John Miller, John Newman, Samuel Seagrave, William Talbot, John Wardle, Samuel Trohnan, Benj Aplin, William Greenall, Nathanial Sansbury.

Toll gatherers or lessees

Lessees known to have leases on other Gates in this area are shown **emboldened**.

Amos, Thomas of Neithrop (Edgehill & Drayton 1825)
Avenill, William (Edgehill & Drayton 1864, 65, 66)
Belson, Henry of Neithrop, farmer (Edgehill & Drayton 1839)
Bennett, Thomas of Bloxham, victualler (Drayton 1804)
Blencome, William (Edgehill & Drayton 1813, 15)
Cantell, Charles of Ensham (Edgehill & Drayton 1832)
Carless, William of Neithrop (Edgehill & Drayton 1823, 27)
Connell, Matthew of Lathbury Gate (Edgehill & Drayton 1812)
Cummings, George of Buckingham Gate (surity 1837)
Davis, Richard (Edgehill & Drayton 1809)
Drury, John of Banbury (Drayton 1784)
Edwards, Thomas (Edgehill & Drayton 1820, 24)
Edwards, William of Banbury Bridge Gate and Red Lion (Edgehill & Drayton
    1841-51)
Foxhill, John of Boddington (Edgehill & Drayton 1822)
Galey, John of Addlestop Gate Glos (Edgehill & Drayton 1833)
Gould, Richard of Neithrop, surveyor (Edgehill & Drayton 1828, 29, 30, 31)
Grundy, John of Neithrop (Drayton 1791)
Hawkes, Edward of Hardwick Gate (Edgehill & Drayton 1837)
Hiron, Joseph (Edgehill 1780)
Holmes, Richard (Edgehill & Drayton 1805)
Ingram, Thomas of Drayton (Drayton 1788)
Ingram, William of Neithrop (Edgehill 1788, 94)
Jackman, John of Emberton Gate, Bucks (Edgehill & Drayton 1840)
Jones, John (Edgehill & Drayton 1817, 18, 19)
Jones, William of Drayton, labourer (Edgehill & Drayton 1835)
Keene, Thomas of Yarnton (Edgehill & Drayton 1821)
Lambert, John (Drayton 1780)
Millard, John of Tingewick Gate (surity 1837)
Neville, William (Edgehill 1803)

Table 2: Drayton to Edgehill Turnpike Trust: *Toll gatherers or lessees*, *continued.* Lessees known to have leases on other Gates in this area are shown **emboldened**.

Palmer, John (Edgehill 1755-74)

Parkes, Thomas of Drayton, labourer (Edgehill & Drayton 1836)

Porvell, Jos of Sun Rising (Edgehill 1794)

Pratt, William of Red Lion Banbury (Edgehill 1797; Drayton 1796)

Price, John (Drayton 1781, 3)

Robins, William of Brackley Gate (Edgehill & Drayton 1834)

Sammon, Thomas of Bicester Gate (Edgehill & Drayton 1859, 60)

Slutter, John (Edgehill 1780)

Smith, John (Edgehill 1798)

Thomson, Thomas of Banbury, Shagweaver (Edgehill 1791; Drayton 1801)

Tubb, Joseph (Drayton 1753-76)

Turner, Joseph (Edgehill 1753)

Turner, Richard (Edgehill 1775)

Washbrook, John of Hourton [Hornton?] (Edgehill 1783-5)

Watts, Edw (Edgehill 1779)

Wheeler, Mary of Adderbury Gate (Drayton 1785, 93)

Yeoman, Daniel (Edgehill & Drayton 1826)

Young, William of Witney Gate (Edgehill & Drayton 1840)

3.3 The Great Kington Trust

The road from the Edgehill down to Kineton on the road to Stratford and Warwick was turnpiked in 1770 by an "*Act for repairing and widening the road from Upton, in the Parish of Ratley, to the North End of Bridge Street in the Town of Great Kington, and from thence to the Guidepost at the town of Wellesbourne Hastings in the County of Warwick*". This trust was clearly run from Kineton (Kington) and trustees met on 18th April 1770 for their first meeting at the sign of the Red Lion in Great Kington.

In the first year they borrowed £1,300 to improve the road and construct two toll-houses. At the first meeting they ordered that "*a gate or turnpike be forthwith erected across the said road on the north side of or near to the Pound in the town or village of Wellesbourne Hastings*". A second gate was to be built "*at the boundary or fence which divides the common field of Great Kington and the Liberty of Radway*". A sidegate was ordered to be put across the road leading out of the road from the foot of Fursehill to Stratford, through the village of Walton with a second sidegate in Wellesbourne where the road crossed the Halford Bridge to Warwick road.

The trustees paid Samuel Eglington, a mason of Great Kington, the sum of £64 to construct one bridge of two arches at the east end of Bolan Lane in Kington and a second bridge of one arch over a brook at the other end of the lane. John Rogers of Banbury contracted to improve the main road from the west corner of Robert Croft's House in Great Kington to a place where Lord Warwick begins to repair. The road was to be 12 feet wide with stones 18 inches thick and two months were allowed for the job. The trust took some time to decide on the best route down Edgehill. They placed a chain across the road at the foot of Edgehill, in or near the Parish of Radway. Walter Watson of Upper Shuckborough was asked to survey and estimate the cost of improving the road "*from the top of Edgehill, at the west corner, through the village of Radway to the place in Edward Tompkins ground where the road down Edgehill called the Redway and the road from Radway to Great Kington unite and likewise view the road from the top of Edgehill at the west corner, along and down the said hill by the Redway unto the said place in Tompkins ground where the two roads unite*". In 1781 the trust resolved that they should turnpike from the castle on Edgehill to Upton by a route "*along the present road which leads from the castle towards Ratley unites the road from Ratley to Upton and proceeds along the last mentioned road along the head of the valley until it comes within 457 yards of Mr Childs' Gate, called Iron Gate, and going such last mentioned distance in as straight a line as possible.*"

The minutes book for the first 30 years of the trust has survived, giving some details of early administration (Table 3).

Table 3: Great Kington to Wellesbourne Turnpike Trust

Trustees (active)	
Toll gatherers or lessees	Barrett, Edward (Wellesbourne 1771)
	Homer, Thomas of Millway Gate (Wellesbourne & Kington 1801)
	Hopper, John of Wellesbourne, breaches maker (Wellesbourne & Kington 1808)
	Hornby, James (Kington 1771)
	Knibb, Joseph of Oakley Gate Newport Pagnell (Wellesbourne & Kington 1785, 1800)
	Parish, Thomas of Radway (Wellesbourne & Kington 1784)
	Sabin, John of Hornton, labourer (Wellesbourne 1799)
	Sharp, Thomas of Stratford, silversmith (Wellesbourne & Kington 1779)

Several regular travellers "compounded" to make a single payment for the right to pass through the gates during the year. Requests came from Revd Richard Hopkins of Wellesbourne who was "allowed to compound for the tolls which he may be liable to pay for riding thru' the said gate or chain at Wellesbourne as one shilling for the ensuing year". John Bustin, a miller of Wellesbourne paid 1s.6d. for "horses only" and John Green paid 5s. for "riding with horses" whereas Isaac Horton and his sons paid 7s.6d. The Wellesbourne Gate was consistently more valuable on those occasions when the gates were let separately. For instance at the first letting in 1771, Edward Barrett took Wellesbourne Gate for £70 and James Hornby took Great Kington for only £12 whereas in 1842 Wellesbourne was let for £214 and Great Kington for £92.

3.4 The Buckingham to Banbury Trust

The 1791 Act provided an alternative route to Banbury from Buckingham, via Brackley to the Daventry Road near the Cherwell crossing (Fig. 10e).

> New intended ROAD from BUCKINGHAM through BRACKLEY to BANBURY.
>
> NOTICE is hereby given, That an adjourned Meeting of the Subscribers to the abovementioned Road will be held at the CROWN INN, in Brackley, on Wednesday the 19th Instant, at Eleven o'Clock in the Forenoon, for the Purpose of inspecting the Plans and Estimates which will be laid before them, and for considering of a Petition to Parliament for Leave to bring in a Bill to enable them to carry the same into Execution; at which Time and Place all Persons desirous of giving their Support to such Undertaking, are particularly requested to attend. Dated at Brackley, Jan. 11, 1791.

Fig. 10e. Advertisement relating to the Brackley Road.

In the 20th century, it was this secondary turnpike road which displaced the Aynho route as the modern A-class road between Buckingham and Banbury. The Act covering the Buckingham-Banbury road passed through Parliament at the same time as the Act dealing with the Aylesbury-Bicester-Aynho Road, so there may have been active competition between Brackley and Bicester for traffic bound north-westwards through Buckinghamshire. The evidence given to the Parliamentary Committee by William Collison[9] put the case for the Brackley Road. *"The road leading from the town of Buckingham to the town of Brackley in the County of Northampton is greatly out of repair in some parts narrow and incommodious and there is not any direct convenient carriage road from the said town to Brackley and to the town of Banbury and that amending and widening the said road from Buckingham and Brackley and rendering the course thereof more direct than at present and making or providing a commodious carriage road from Brackley to communicate with the Daventry and Banbury Turnpike Road at a convenient distance from the town of Banbury and keeping such respective roads in good repair, will be of great benefit to all persons having occasion to travel between the said towns of Buckingham and Banbury."*

---

[9] *JHC* **46**, 307.

This seems to be a Brackley led initiative with the road to Banbury as a secondary feature. As was to be the case on the Bicester-Aynho Road, the traveller to Banbury still faced tolls on gates controlled by other turnpike trusts before reaching Banbury Market (Banbury Bridge Gate on this road and Adderbury Gate on the Aynho Road).

The Act was renewed in 1810, improvements made in 1812, but in 1851 this trust was amalgamated with the Towcester to Weston on the Green Turnpike Trust which it crossed at Brackley. The united trust and its toll-gates will be dealt with in Section 5.1 (page 66).

3.5 *The Bicester to Aynho Trust*

3.5.1 The New Route

This road was eventually to become part of the A41, the main trunk road in the area, but it was not turnpiked until 1791. It follows a relatively easy path along a watershed from Bicester to reach the older Buckingham road at Aynho. Traffic from Aylesbury was now able to reach Banbury without an excursion into the valley of the Ouse through the old county town of Buckingham.

The Aynho road was slightly to the north of the ancient highway from Bicester to Ardley and merged with the old Portway at Souldern. From here the road coincided with the old route down through the Aynho Hills and over the Ockley Brook to meet the existing turnpike road west of Croughton. Improvement of this route had been part of a new turnpike proposal considered a decade earlier.[10] A meeting held at the Dog (Talbot), Middleton Stoney discussed an application to Parliament to improve the road from Kidlington to Aynho, through Gosford, Bicester and Souldern. However, this plan was overtaken by the creation of the Gosford Trust in 1781, although the section from Weston to Bicester was not turnpiked until it was taken into the Bicester to Enstone trust in 1793.

The Bicester to Aynho Act passed through Parliament alongside the Bill to renew and extend the powers of the Aylesbury to Bicester Trust (created in 1770). The press notices[11] actually link the two applications and Mr Henry Churchill of Bicester, clerk to the Bicester to Aylesbury Trustees, gave evidence in support of both Acts.[12] It must be assumed that this was a concerted action by interests in Oxfordshire to bring trade through their towns. The Aylesbury & Bicester Trust had borrowed £3,300 to improve the old Akeman Street and had not raised sufficient surplus on the tolls even to pay interest on this. Mr Churchill stated that *"the roads leading from the Market*

---

[10] *JOJ*, Sept. 1780 and Oct. 1782.
[11] *JOJ*, Aug. 1790.
[12] *JHC* **46**, 127.

Place in Bicester in the County of Oxfordshire through parts of Bicester, Caversfield, Bucknell, Stoke Lyne, Fritwell and Souldern to the Turnpike Road in the Parish of Aynho are in a ruinous condition and in many places narrow and incommodious and cannot be effectively mended, widened and kept in repair by the ordinary course of Law". Mr Churchill added that "*for the greater convenience of travellers it may be necessary to make some small deviations from the present line of the road*". The published Act had provision for "*a private or field way leading along a certain lane in Bicester King's End called Bell Lane*" to be closed and shut up and for " *a public road that leads from the end of Bell Lane to and through Crockwell Brook to the Well called Crockswell*" to be discontinued except for the driftway to Dove House Close.

3.5.2 Trust Administration

The trust appears to have erected its first toll-gate in Sheep Street, Bicester. A notice in June 1792, a year after the Act, proposed that further gates be erected near the Rising Sun in Bicester and across Launton Lane in Caversfield (Fig. 10f).

BICESTER and AYNHO TURNPIKE ROADS.

NOTICE is hereby given, That a Meeting of the Trustees of the above Turnpike Road will be held at the King's Arms, in Bicester, on Friday the 13th Day of July next, at Eleven o'Clock, for the Purpose of appointing new Trustees in the Room of several dead and of others who refuse to act, and to consult about erecting the Toll House, Gate, and Side Bars following; to wit, a Toll House and Gate upon the said Road in or near the Parish of Aynho aforesaid; one Side Bar or Gate in the Lane adjoining to the Public House, called the Rising Sun, in Bicester, and one other Side Bar or Gate by the Side of the said Turnpike Road in the Village of Caversfield, across the Road leading from thence towards Launton. Also at this Meeting will be lett for one Year from the 16th Day of July next, A Messuage or Tenement now used as a Toll House, with the Garden adjoining, situate in the Sheep Street, Bicester, together with the Tolls thereto belonging or payable, which said Tolls, Turnpike House, and Garden will be lett according to the Directions of the Statute made in the Thirteenth Year of his present Majesty's Reign "For regulating Turnpike Roads;" and produced in the last Year over and above the Charges of collecting, the Sum of One Hundred and Fifty-one Pounds, and will be put up to Auction at such Sum. Whoever happens to be the Best Bidder, must immediately give Security to the Satisfaction of the Trustees for Payment of the Rents agreed upon, and at such Times as the said Trustees shall direct.

Bicester, HENRY CHURCHILL,
June 20, 1792. Clerk to the Trustees of the said Turnpike Roads.

Fig. 10f. Advertisement relating to the Bicester to Aynho Turnpike.

These were subsequently known as Skimming Dish Barn and Launton Lane Gates and were generally let with the main Bicester Gate (Fig. 10g). A gate near Souldern, just south of the junction with the old Buckingham road at Aynho, controlled the northern end of the road.

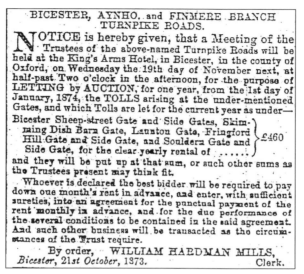

Fig. 10g Advertisement relating to the Bicester to Aynho Turnpike.

The toll-house was a simple, stone-built two storey cottage that still stands at the point where the road branches to by-pass the village.

Souldern toll house.

A side-gate was eventually placed across the old Portway, which still carried some traffic along the eastern edge of the Cherwell valley towards the London Ford crossing (Fig. 11a).

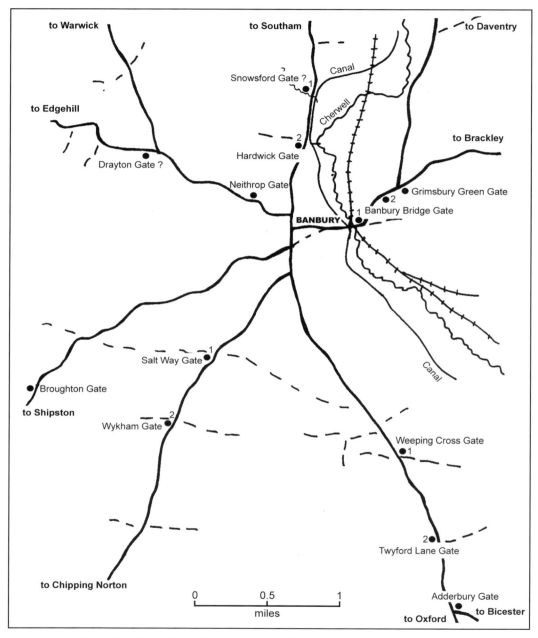

Fig. 11a. Location of toll-gates on the network around Banbury.
See also Fig. 7, page 27, for the wider scene.

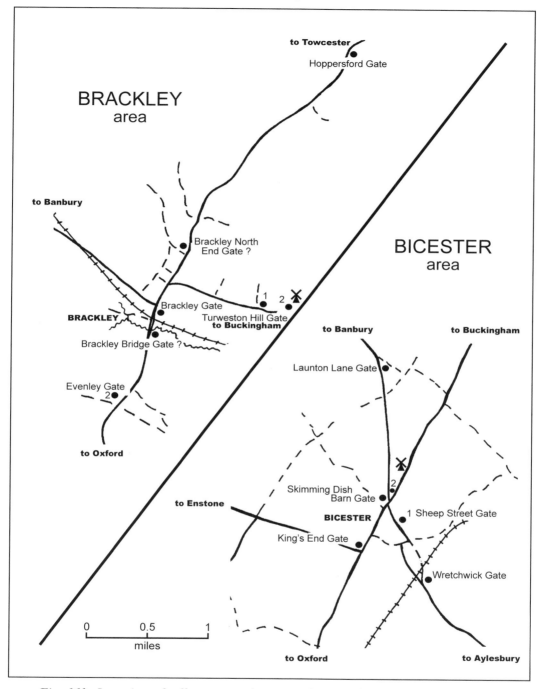

to Towcester
Hoppersford Gate

BRACKLEY
area

BICESTER
area

to Banbury

Brackley North
End Gate ?

1 2 ✕

Brackley Gate

BRACKLEY

Turweston Hill Gate
to Buckingham

Brackley Bridge Gate ?

to Banbury   to Buckingham

Launton Lane Gate

Evenley Gate
2

to Oxford

✕

Skimming Dish
Barn Gate
2

BICESTER

to Enstone

1 Sheep Street Gate

King's End Gate

Wretchwick Gate

0   0.5   1
miles

to Oxford   to Aylesbury

Fig. 11b. Location of toll-gates on the network around Brackley and Bicester.
See also Fig. 7, page 27, for the wider scene.

When the trust applied for a continuation of its powers in 1812, a second branch, north-east from Bicester was incorporated into the Act. It was part of the old Roman road from Bicester to Towcester; the trust was to repair the section from Bicester to the junction with the Buckingham, Aynho to Banbury Road at Finmere. This road had been covered by an Act of 1768 for a cross road from Newport Pagnell to Woodstock but this trust seems to have failed fairly quickly (see Section 5.3 below).

The trustees generally met at the King's Arms in Bicester. A new minutes book which commenced in 1825 has survived and this gives some background to the Administration. It indicates that the highway and the infrastructure on both branches of the road required improvement during 1825, implying that the powers of the 1812 Act were only implemented at this later date. The trustees agreed that it *"is highly proper that the hills between Souldern Gate and Aynho should be lowered and improved"* and £80 was set aside for this purpose. The bridge at the bottom of the Aynho dip was in a dilapidated state, warranting renewal, and the trust attempted to get some action from the county justices who were responsible. The posts and rails beside the road between Souldern and Aynho were whitewashed; these rails prevented travellers falling into the ditches beside the brook. Iron Mile posts were purchased for both branches and a direction post was placed at the Finmere end of the branch stating miles to Bicester and Oxford. The trust also purchased two new carts, at a total price of 16 guineas.

3.5.3 Toll-house Operation

The improvements noted in 1825 included work on existing toll-houses. John Froxley the lessee of Souldern Gate (page 43) complained that there was no privy and that the gate was out of repair. The trustees instructed the surveyor to rectify this *"at as little expense to the trust as can be"*.

In 1826 George Peak was paid £20 to build a toll-house on the Finmere Branch at Fringford Hill, midway along the road. In 1829 the trust sought to move the old toll-gate from the end of Sheep Street, Bicester, to a position outside the town nearer the junction of the roads leading to Aynho and Finmere. Their surveyor, John Edward Maynard, agreed to erect the new house with two gates for the branch roads and a sidegate at a cost of £130. He also agreed to purchase from the trust the site of the old gate and the materials for the same amount.

The other toll-houses were in regular need of maintenance, e.g. repairing the windows, installing a lamp and painting the gate at Souldern cost £17.16s. in 1833. In February 1846 the trust installed gas lighting at the Sheep Street Gate, having given the Bicester Gas, Coke & Coal Company permission to lay pipes a year earlier.

The Sheep Street Toll-house was whitewashed in 1847 and the Fringford Toll-house whitewashed and coloured a year later. A shed costing £10 was erected so that the collector from Souldern could be protected when collecting tolls at the Fritwell Lane sidegate. The three Bicester gates were generally let to a single person but the Souldern Gate was often let separately (Table 4, below). For instance in 1831 Bicester, Skimming Dish Barn Gate, Launton Gate and Fringford Gate were all let to John Hirons of Bicester, milkman, for £331 whereas Souldern Gate was let to the existing gate keeper at Souldern, Mr Smith, for £212. The lessees were not always happy with their investment. In 1833, Hirons complained of *"the loss sustained by the prevalence of the cholera at Bicester last year"*. He claimed he had lost £33.15s.9d. and was allowed a rebate of £20 by the trustees. In 1866 the lessee complained of a loss *"on account of the prevailing cattle plague taking all kinds of stock off the road"*; he was allowed £24.

Table 4: Bicester to Aynho Turnpike Trust

Trustees (active)	1825; William Ralph Cartwright, Thomas Lewis Coker, William Cartwright, Revd WF Browne, Revd Thomas Fawcett, Revd John Knipe, Revd WJ Palmer, Revd HL Bennett. 1834: Lord Viscount Chetwynd
Toll gatherers or lessees (lessees known to have leased gates on other Gates in this area are shown emboldened)	**Allen, William of Middleton Gate** (Bicester 1825, 6; Fringford 1826) Bowerman, James Jnr (Bicester 1828; Fringford 1828) **Cumming, John of Newport Pagnell** (Bicester 1849, 50-53, 7; Souldern 1849, 50-53, 7) **Foxley, John (Souldern 1825, 6, 7, 8)** Gardner, William of Launton, road surveyor (Bicester 1827; Fringford 1827) **Gardner, Thomas of High Wycombe Gate** (Bicester, Fringford & Souldern 1855) **Garrett, Thomas of Theyford Bridge Gate** (Souldern 1861) **Harris, John Jnr of Souldern Gate** (Bicester 1836, 8, 9, 40-46; Fringford 1836, 8, 9, 1840-6: Souldern 1837, 9, 40-46) Harris, James (Bicester 1866; Fringford 1866; Souldern 1866) Hirons, John of Bicester, milkman (Bicester 1831, 3, 5, 7; Fringford 1831, 5, 7) Ingram, Samuel of Bicester (Souldern 1830) Maynard, John E of Bicester, ironmonger (Bicester 1830, Fringford 1830) **Owen, Robert of St Marys Gate Wisbech** (Bicester, Fringford & Souldern 1863) **Salmons, Thomas of Bicester Kings End Gate & Gt Linford Gate** (Bicester 1859,1864; Fringford 1859, 64; Souldern 1859, 64) Smith, William of Souldern (Souldern 1831, 3) **Tidmarsh, Samuel of Adderbury Gate** (Bicester 1834; Souldern 1834) Timms, John (Bicester 1824) **White, William of Hockliffe Gate & Hartwell Gate, Aylesbury** (Bicester 1854, 6, 1858, 61, 62, 67; Fringford 1854, 6, 8, 61, 2, 7; Souldern 1854, 6, 8, 67) **Woods, John of Fringford Hill Gate** (Souldern 1838) Wyatt, William of Northampton, market gardner (Souldern 1836)

4. Coventry to Oxford Turnpikes

4.1 Divisions of the Road

The north/south road through Banbury was one of Ogilby's roads, connecting London and Oxford with the thriving mercantile and manufacturing centre of Coventry. In the eighteenth century the initiative for turnpiking this road came from the gentlemen of Coventry. The inhabitants of Oxford were slower to respond but soon saw an opportunity to benefit from a joint case for the road running the full length of the Cherwell valley. There had been a similar situation thirty years previous when Oxford had appended its case for turnpiking two additional branches into the city from the London to Worcester road.[1]

The case for the Oxford to Coventry road was laid before Parliament in January 1755. It was supported by the leading gentlemen and civic officials from the City of Coventry and Borough of Banbury.[2] This group sought to improve *"the road from the Borough of Banbury and thence to the town of Southam to the turnpike road leading from Dunchurch through the City of Coventry at a place called Finford Bridge, commonly called Ryeton Bridge"*. Furthermore, they set forth that *"three miles of the road leading from the City of Coventry towards the Borough of Banbury is upon a turnpike road leading from Dunchurch to Stonebridge and if a turnpike road should be carried from Banbury to Finford Bridge, it would considerably increase the income arising from tolls on the said turnpike and be greatly advantageous to the country in general"*.

In parallel with this, the Mayor, Corporation and principal inhabitants of the City of Oxford and the gentlemen, clergy and freeholders residing on or near the road leading from the City of Oxford to the village of Adderbury in the County of Oxford presented a second petition.[3] They stated that *"the road from the City of Oxford, from a place there called End of Mile Way, through Kidlington to Adderbury to a certain place known by the name of the Guide Post, is so deep and ruinous that it is dangerous for horsemen and almost impassable for carriages many months of the year"*. They too stated that the problems could not be remedied by present Laws; i.e. statute labour by the parishes.

---

[1] *RUTV* 8.
[2] *JHC* **27**, 70.
[3] *JHC* **27**, 76.

It was agreed that these two petitions should be considered together and evidence was taken from witnesses later that month.[4] Mr Christopher Wright and Mr Richard Parrot said that the Banbury to Coventry road, *"from the badness of the soil, had become so ruinous that it is dangerous, in many places, for carriages or passengers to pass except in very dry seasons and in many places so narrow that two carriages cannot pass each other"*. Richard Parrot added that, *"by reason of the ruinous condition of the roads, constant recourse cannot be had to and from the coal pits near Coventry which greatly increases the price of coals about Southam and in other parts of the country"*. Parrot, who was the principal financier of the Ryton to Banbury section of the road, also owned coal pits at Hawkesbury and so would be a major beneficiary of increased trade. He was later to be a supporter of the Coventry to Oxford canal.

Christopher Wright stated that *"a great number of the trustees of the turnpike road from Dunchurch to Stonebridge have signed the said petition and are willing to give any assistance in their power towards the reparation of the said road from Finford to Banbury"*. This reinforces the view that this was a road to benefit the mining and manufacturing towns in Warwickshire rather than an initiative driven by the needs of Banbury.

In support of the case for the Banbury to Oxford section, Mr Francis Edge (of the Three Tuns, Banbury)[5] said that *"the road is, from the number of heavy carriages passing along the same, and the nature of the soil, so ruinous as to be dangerous to travellers and almost impassable for carriages many months of the year"*. Before it was passed, the Oxford petitioners incorporated an additional section of road into the scope of the bill. The final recommendation describes the road as being *"from the Cross Hand near Finford Bridge to Banbury and from the Guide Post near the vill of Adderbury to the Mileway leading to the City of Oxford"* and *"to allow out of the monies arising from the tolls of the said roads an annual sum towards repairing of two miles of road through Gosford to Weston"*. The latter section connected with the road from Weston to Towcester, the other radial leading northwards from Oxford,[6] which was also in the process of being turnpiked.[7]

Although the cases for the two sections of the Coventry to Oxford road were presented to Parliament as one, the trust did not have jurisdiction over the whole road. The highway from Adderbury to the North Bar in Banbury was already in the care of the Weeping Cross Trust. The separate sections of the new turnpike were administered as two divisions; an Oxfordshire division covering the road south of Adderbury and a Warwickshire division dealing

---

[4] *JHC* **27**, 103 and 135.
[5] See Gibson, J., "The Three Tuns in the Eighteenth Century", *C&CH* **8**.1 (1979), 5.
[6] *RUTV* 8.
[7] Act of 1756 – Section 5.1.

with the road north of Banbury. Several individuals were trustees for both divisions (e.g. Benjamin Aplin,[8] Sir Theophilus Biddulph, Thomas Bradford, Edward Busby and Thomas Cartwright), but the two sections of the road were administered separately. No records survive for the southern division but the separate minutes book for the Ryton Bridge to Banbury section is in the Bodleian Library. This provides information on the first fifty years of this division (Table 5, page 54; Fig. 12).

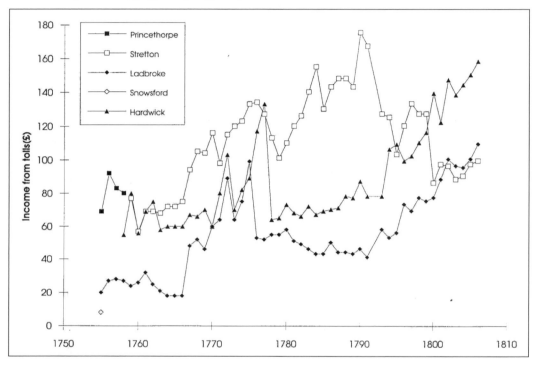

Fig. 12. Income from leasing individual gates: Ryton Bridge to Banbury Trust. Compare with Fig. 9, page 36.

Evidence to Parliament in 1777-79 was given separately by representatives from the two divisions of the trust. Thomas Walker Esq. presented the case for the Adderbury to Kidlington Division including the branch to *"Gosford, otherwise Gossard Bridge to a certain gate entering upon Weston on the Green"*.[9] John Newcombe put the case for the first division from the Cross Hands through Southam to Banbury.[10]

---

[8] See Brooks, K.R.S., "Aplins - The oldest solicitors' practice in Banbury", Pt. 1, *C&CH* **16**.6 (2002).

[9] *JHC* **36**, 240.

[10] *JHC* **37**, 496.

Soon after this, in 1781 a new Act was passed creating a separate trust to deal with improvement of the road across the Cherwell at Gosford. The petition was on behalf of those residing near and often travelling the road from the gate on the turnpike road at or near the south end of Weston on the Green to the turnpike road near Kidlington Green. In evidence[11] Mr Edward King said the road was *"often totally impassable for carriages"* and *"improvements would be of great advantage to the petitioners as well as of public utility"*. An Act of 1797 finally separated the two divisions on the main Oxford to Coventry road and created two completely separate trusts, Ryton Bridge to Banbury and Adderbury to Kidlington. The northern division normally held meetings at the Craven Arms in Southam (Fig. 13a) and the southern division at the Fox and Crown in North Aston, both midway along the respective sections of road.

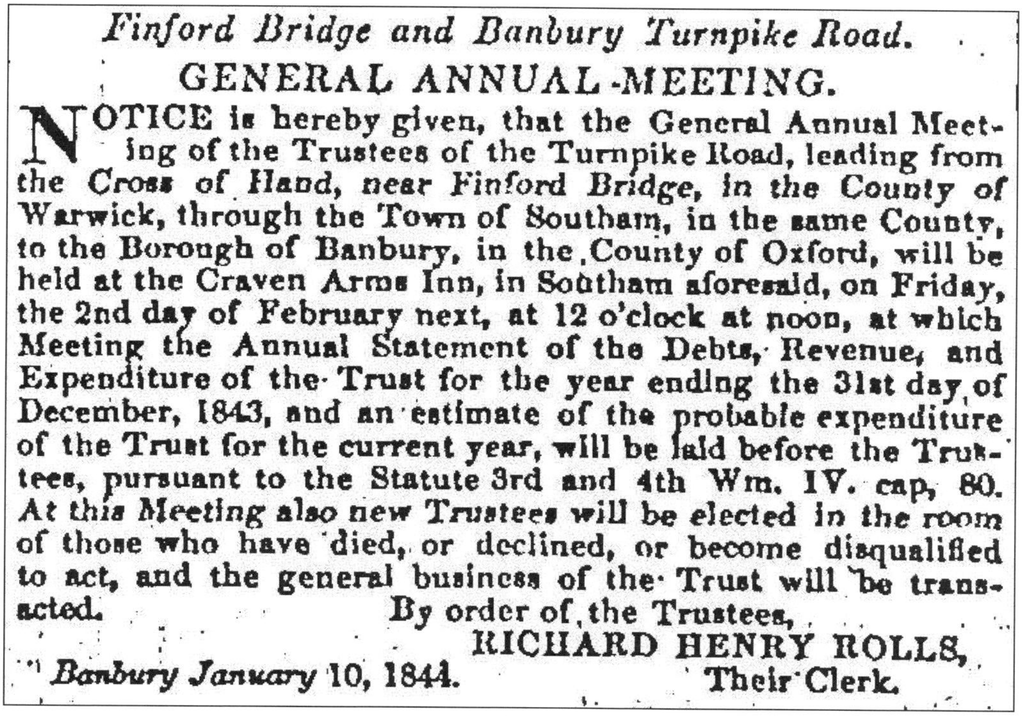

> ## Finford Bridge and Banbury Turnpike Road.
> ### GENERAL ANNUAL MEETING.
>
> NOTICE is hereby given, that the General Annual Meeting of the Trustees of the Turnpike Road, leading from the Cross of Hand, near Finford Bridge, in the County of Warwick, through the Town of Southam, in the same County, to the Borough of Banbury, in the County of Oxford, will be held at the Craven Arms Inn, in Southam aforesaid, on Friday, the 2nd day of February next, at 12 o'clock at noon, at which Meeting the Annual Statement of the Debts, Revenue, and Expenditure of the Trust for the year ending the 31st day of December, 1843, and an estimate of the probable expenditure of the Trust for the current year, will be laid before the Trustees, pursuant to the Statute 3rd and 4th Wm. IV. cap. 80. At this Meeting also new Trustees will be elected in the room of those who have died, or declined, or become disqualified to act, and the general business of the Trust will be transacted. By order of the Trustees,
> RICHARD HENRY ROLLS,
> *Banbury January* 10, 1844. Their Clerk.

Fig. 13a. Advertisement relating to Banbury to Coventry Turnpike.

---

[11] *JHC* **38**, 138.

Table 5: Ryton (or Finford) to Banbury Turnpike Trust

Trustees (active)	1755/6: Theo Biddulph, G H Thuroy, Thomas Vyner, John Biker, William Huddesford, Henry Homer, Thomas Congrove, V Palmer, Thomas Burbery, T Basley, Jonathan Michener, William Wheeler, William Daniel, Thomas Williams 1780/1: Theo Biddulph, William Daniel, Henry Homer, Thomas Knightly, George Bryant, Thomas Williams of Ladbroke, Birn George Snow, Charles Wheeler, William Bellamy 1802: Theo Biddulph, Charles Palmer, Birn George Snow, T Gill, Nathaniel Arnold, J Biddulph, Edward Tomes, J Sandys, J B Bunifield.
Toll gatherers or lessees (lessees known to have leased gate on other Gates in this area are shown enboldened)	Bailey, William (Hardwick 1804) Burgess, Jonathan (Ladbrook 1758-60) Burgess, George Snr (Stretton 1763-80; 1794; Ladbroke 1804/6) Burgess, George Jnr (Stretton 1804/6) Butler, William (Hardwick 1808) Elkington, (Stretton 1787) Field, James (Hardwick 1764) Gascoyne, Abraham (Ladbrook 1756/7) Glaze, William (Hardwick 1758-63, 1770-87; 1794) Hobley, Francis (Hardwick 1794/5, 1805/6/7/8) **Ingram, William (Stretton 1793/6/7/8; Ladbrook 1794/5)** Lane, John (Hardwick 1756/7) Loftus (Stretton 1792) Neuele, William (Hardwick 1793) Sanders (Stretton 1807) Smith, Richard (Stretton 1794/9; Hardwick 1797/8/9) Warner, William (Ladbrook 1780-87) Webb, Robert (Princethorpe 1756; Stretton 1757-61) Wright R (Hardwick 1802)

4.2 The Ryton (or Finford) Bridge to Banbury Trust

4.2.1 Toll Collection

The first entries in the minutes book are for the week of 9th June 1755 when income was received from three toll-gates at Princethorpe, Ladbrooke and Snowsford (the sums of £1.18s.3d, 12s.7½d. and 1s.3d. respectively). This is clear evidence that the trustees had acted very quickly to organise toll collection; the Parliamentary Committee had only deliberated the case in January of that year. The treasurer, John Spicer, made payments to the surveyor, Joseph Parker, presumably to finance improvements to the road, and to Richard Pratt for stone. A one-off payment was made to Mr George Salmon *"on the bill for his journey and attendance in London when the Bill was depending in the House of Commons, £5.15s.6d."*

Eleven of the trustees attended the first recorded meeting in this account, on 28th October 1755. They approved bills to Mr Pain for erecting the toll-house at Ladbrooke (cost £37.6s.6d.) and to William Sharman in part consideration money for *the piece of ground whereon the toll-house at Princethorpe is erected, £1*. Six months later they paid Robert Webb, of Princethorpe, £1.7s.0d. for posts and rails around the gate and the sum of £6; his salary of 4s. per week as collector of tolls at Princethorpe Gate. The same salary was paid to Abraham Gascoyne as collector of tolls at Ladbrooke Gate. The third gate at Snowsford only operated until Sept 15th 1755 and raised just £8.1s.7d. in tolls during three mouths of operation. This gate was probably beside one of the streams running down to the Cherwell, north of Banbury. It was replaced in June 1756 by the Hardwick Gate, located on the northern edge of Banbury (Fig. 11a, page 46), and John Lane was appointed collector of the tolls. The initial toll-house at Hardwick Gate was probably a simple one-storey building with a thatched roof. In 1767, the trust paid 17s. for straw and thatching of the toll-house at Hardwick Lane and again in 1776 William Glaze, the collector, was given £1.6s. "for thatching his house". In 1790 the toll-house, gate and sidegates at Hardwick were moved at a relatively low cost of £24; presumably it was still a simple building. New window frames and glazing in the new toll-house cost only £2.2s.4d. The surviving toll-house, on the east side of the road, is probably a later nineteenth century structure.

Hardwick Gate toll-house

Ladbrooke toll-house

The gate at the village of Ladbrooke was situated so as to levy traffic through Southam and from the turnpike road between Daventry and Leamington (Fig. 7, page 27). Erecting a new gate at Ladbrooke cost £12 in 1800. In May 1757 the original Princethorpe Gate was moved into Stretton Lane closer to Coventry and the bridge over the Avon. Robert Webb was paid £2.12s.8d. in expenses as a result of the change. After these initial modifications, the location of the three principal gates remained fixed for the remaining life of this turnpike trust. In the nineteenth century, as traffic patterns changed, the trust built additional gates to intercept traffic bound for the markets at Banbury and Coventry. A ticket gate at Frankton (Fig. 13b) augmented the Princethorpe Gate and gates at Bourton and Itchington (Fig. 13c) caught additional traffic on the southern section.

For much of the eighteenth century the gates nearest Coventry earned the greater revenue (initially Princethorpe and then Stretton: Fig. 12, page 52). The Hardwick Gate nearer Banbury was the next most profitable but in the nineteenth century its income began to overtake that of the Stretton Gate, perhaps indicating an increasing importance of road traffic into Banbury markets.

FINFORD BRIDGE AND BANBURY TURNPIKE
ROAD.
TOLLS TO BE LET.

NOTICE IS HEREBY GIVEN, that the TOLLS arising at the several Toll Gates upon the Turnpike Road leading from the Cross of Hand, near Finford Bridge, in the county of Warwick, through the town of Southam, in the same county, to the borough of Banbury, in the county of Oxford, called or known by the names of the Hardwick Gate, with the Side Bars thereto belonging, the Ladbroke Gate, and the Stretton Gate, with the Side Bars, and the Ticket Gate at Frankton, will be LET by AUCTION to the best bidders, at the Craven Arms Inn, in Southam aforesaid, on Friday, the 26th day of July next, between the hours of eleven o'clock in the forenoon and three o'clock in the afternoon, in the manner directed by the Acts passed in the third and fouth years of the reign of his Majesty King George the Fourth for regulating Turnpike Roads, which Tolls produced the last year the sum of £1,097, above the expenses of collecting them. The Tolls will be let in parcels or lots, and each parcel or lot will be put up at such sum, and subject to such conditions, as the Trustees shall think fit.

Whoever happen to be the best bidders must respectively give security, with sufficient sureties, to the satisfaction of the Trustees of the said Turnpike Road, for payment of the rent at which the Tolls may be let monthly in advance.

RICHARD HENRY ROLLS,
Clerk to the Trustees.

Banbury, June 25, 1844.

Figs. 13b and 13c. Advertisements relating to Banbury to Coventry Turnpike.

FINFORD BRIDGE AND BANBURY
TURNPIKE ROAD.
TOLLS TO LET.

NOTICE IS HEREBY GIVEN, that at a meeting of the Trustees of the Turnpike Road, leading from the Cross of Hand, near Finford Bridge, in the County of Warwick, through the town of Southam, in the same County, to the borough of Banbury, in the County of Oxford, the Tolls arising from the several Toll Gates on the same Road, called or known by the name of the Hardwick Gate and Side Bars, the Bourton Side and Ticket Gate, the Ladbrooke Gate and Side Bar, the Long Itchington Gate and Side Bar, the Stretton Gate and Side Bars, and the Ticket Gate at Frankton, will be LET BY AUCTION, to the best bidder, at the Craven Arms Inn, in Southam aforesaid, on Friday, the 25th day of August next, between the hours of Twelve o'clock at noon and Three o'clock in the afternoon, in the manner directed by the Acts passed in the 3rd and 4th years of the Reign of His Majesty King George the 4th for regulating Turnpike Roads, which Tolls produced last year the sum of £667 above the expenses of collecting the same. The Tolls will be let either in one lot or in parcels or lots and will be put up at such sums and subject to such conditions as the Trustees shall think fit. Whoever happens to be the best bidder must give security, with sufficient sureties, to the satisfaction of the Trustees of the Turnpike Road for payment of the Rent at which such Tolls may be let, monthly in advance.

And NOTICE is hereby further given that at the time and place aforesaid, the Trustees will if they think fit to do so, elect new Trustees in the room of any such as may have died or declined or become disqualified to act, and the general business of the trust will be transacted.

D. P. PELLATT,
Clerk to the said Trustees.

Banbury,
24th July, 1871.

4.2.2 Finance

In 1765 the trust expended £5 on a *"new road from Hardwick Gate to the Bridge"* and further expenditure of £7.2s.0d. was made, in 1768, on this new road and fencing of the side of the road towards the holloway. This was presumably the road along the causeway and over river towards Grimsbury

The treasurer's account, in June 1755, records the first receipt of £100 investment by Mr Parrot. A slow release of loan money to the trust by Richard Parrot continued until 1765. During the early years finances were precarious as expenditure on road improvement exceeded the income from tolls. The trust eventually borrowed £1,300 from Parrot but did not begin to pay interest on this until 1768 when £26 was paid for the half year (five percent per annum). By the end of the century the loan had climbed to £1,700 and the interest was being paid to Mr Parrot's heirs, including Mrs Wright (Mr Wright had given evidence in support of the Bill). In 1772, John Newcombe took over the task of treasurer from John Spicer and was responsible for renewal of the powers of the trust in 1780. He died in March 1792 and the accounts record the complicated transfers of money collected by the gate-keepers and held by the treasurer. One officer seems to have acted as treasurer and secretary, since the next treasurer, Henry Rolls, was responsible for obtaining the *"renewal of the Finford Turnpike Road Bill, in 1803"*, for which he submitted an account of £283.19s.6d. Other costs associated with the renewal included advertisements in the Coventry and Oxford newspapers that cost £1.11s.6d. and £1.15s. respectively.

4.3 The Adderbury to Kidlington Trust

This trust was formed from the southern division of the Finford Bridge to Oxford Trust by an Act 1797. However, the trustees had always operated independent from the northern division, with John Walker, an attorney from Oxford, acting as clerk. The name by which the trust was known varied though by the nineteenth century it was most commonly called the Kidlington to Deddington Trust (Fig. 13d) but was referred to locally as the Oxford to Adderbury Road (Fig. 13e).

The road ran from the Guide Post in the village of Adderbury, through Kidlington, to the End of the Mileway in the City of Oxford. In evidence to Parliament Samuel Churchill said *"that the trustees had borrowed heavily to improve the road"*. In addition *"the road near the termination of the turnpike at or near a place called The Diamond House in the City of Oxford is not sufficiently amended and kept in repair and it would be advantageous to the neighbourhood and the public if the same were put in the care and management of the trust"*.

KIDLINGTON and DEDDINGTON TOLLS
To be LETT.

NOTICE is hereby given, That the TOLLS arising at the Toll-Gates upon the Turnpike Road at Kidlington and Deddington, in the County of Oxford, known by the Names of the Old Man's Gate and Deddington, will be LETT by AUCTION, to the Best Bidder, at the House of Mr. Weston, called the Fox and Crown Inn, in North-Aston, in the said County of Oxford, on Wednesday the 12th Day of September next between the Hours of Eleven o'Clock in the Forenoon and Five in the Afternoon, in the Manner directed by the Act passed in the thirteenth Year of the Reign of his present Majesty King George the Third, " For Regulating the " Turnpike Roads;" which Tolls Lett the last Year for the Sum of 600 l. and will be put up at that Sum.

Whoever happens to be the Best Bidder, must at that Time pay down one Month's Rent in Advance, and give Security, with sufficient Sureties to the Satisfaction of the Trustees of the said Turnpike Road, for Payment of the Remainder of the Rent agreed for, and at such Times as they shall direct.

By Order of the Trustees, JOHN WALKER, Clerk.
August 29*th*, 1787.

N. B. The Attendance of the Trustees is particularly requested, as no Business could be done at the Two last Meetings for Want of a sufficient Number of Trustees.

Figs. 13d and 13e. *Advertisements relating to Banbury to Oxford Turnpike.*

The Oxford and Adderbury Turnpike Road.
TOLLS TO BE LET.

NOTICE is hereby given, that a Meeting of the Trustees of the above-named Turnpike Road will be held at the Town Hall, Oxford, on Saturday the 6th day of November, 1875, at Twelve o'clock at noon, at which Meeting the Tolls to arise and become payable at the several Gates on the said Road, called the

KIDLINGTON GATE, or OLD MAN'S GATE;
And DEDDINGTON GATE;

will be LET by AUCTION, to the best bidder, in one or two lots as may be decided by the Trustees then present, for Ten Calendar Months, from the 1st day of January next at noon, and upon such conditions as shall be agreed upon by the Trustees then present, in manner directed by the Acts for regulating Turnpike Roads, and which Tolls are at present Let at the clear yearly sum of £545, and will be put up at £154 3s. 4d., being 10-12ths of such sum.

Whoever happens to be the best bidder must at the same time pay down such sum as the Trustees shall require, by way of deposit, and give security, with sufficient sureties, to the satisfaction of the Trustees, for payment of the rent monthly, so that one month's rent shall always be paid in advance.

GEO. P. HESTER,
16th October, 1875.   Clerk to the said Trustees.

The Buckingham to Hanwell Trust had a toll-house at Adderbury, just to the north of the commencement of this new road. The new trust built a toll-gate at a small bridge on the southern edge of Deddington open field. The southern end the road was controlled by a gate near Water Eaton known as Old Man's Gate. The surviving two storey toll-house between Kidlington and Oxford is built of stone[12] and dates from 1844 when the original house was demolished.

Old Man's Gate, near Water Eaton

A weighing engine was located on the opposite side of the road and the profits from fines imposed for overloaded wagons were leased with the toll-gate (Fig. 13f).

---

[12] *RUTV* 10.

OXFORD.

OXFORD AND ADDERBURY TURNPIKE ROAD.—The annual meeting of the Commissioners of this road was held on Wednesday week at Hopcraft's Holt Inn, and was attended by the following members :—Rev. B. S. Peel, Rector of Rousham, who occupied the chair; Revs. W. Green, E. Marshall, and J. Marshall, D. Hanley, Esq., Mayor of Oxford, Alderman Castle and Cavel., Messrs. Dore, Greenwood, Grimbly, Hookman, Houghton, Hutt, James, Rowland, Underhill, Parish, G. Ward, Walsh and Wing. Mr. G. P. Hester, Town Clerk of Oxford, who has been Clerk *pro tem.* since Mr. Henry Churchill's abrupt disappearance, was unanimously elected permanent Clerk to the Trust. It was announced that the last instalment of the debt due to Mr. Cave, a former Surveyor, had been defrayed, but that it would nevertheless be requisite to call on the several parishes through which the line extends to contribute their usual quotas towards the repair of the road. The weighing bridge at the toll-gate in the township of Water Eaton was directed to be put into an efficient state of repair, to the satisfaction of the Engineer of the Oxford Canal Company, and it was ordered that the toll-house there shall be repaired and lime washed. Committees to advise with the Surveor (who for some unexplained reason was absent) were appointed, that is to say for the south end of the line—Alderman Carr and Hughes, Messrs. G. Ward, Parish, and Rowland. Northend—Holford Risley, Esq., Revs. E. Marshall and J. Marshall, C. S. Peel, and W. Wing.

Fig. 13f. Advertisement (1870) relating to Banbury to Oxford Turnpike.

5. Oxfordshire to Northamptonshire Turnpikes

The roads connecting rural north Oxfordshire to the agricultural county to the north-east and north were turnpiked after the trunk roads from London. The more important of these roads was the ancient highway from Oxford to Northampton, which crossed the Birmingham to London road at Towcester. The second, from Banbury to Lutterworth crossed the Birmingham road at Daventry.

5.1 The Weston on the Green to Towcester Trust

5.1.1 Operation of the First Trust

This trust, created in 1757, was responsible for the road from the south end of the village of Weston on the Green, through Brackley to the Birmingham road at Towcester. It was turnpiked at almost the same time as the Oxford to Banbury Road, which, until 1781, administered the branch road as far as Gosford. The old road to Brackley followed the line of the ancient highway, across what was to become Middleton Park. It seems likely that the turnpike trustees respected (or were pressured to respect) the privacy of the local landowner and adopted the present line through the village of Weston. North of Ardley the road returned to the line of the old highway to Brackley and then followed the ridge to merge with the old Roman road south of Towcester. The section of the road from Towcester on to Northampton (the continuation of the modern A43) was not turnpiked until 1794.

The powers of the trust were continued in 1800 when William Hayto gave evidence on behalf of the trustees.[1] The earliest detailed records of the Weston to Towcester Trust date from the renewal Act in 1821. The trustees met "*at the house known by the sign of the Crown in the town of Brackley*" and most of the administration was exercised from here.

In the 1780s, there was a gate at Burcott Wood, where the old Roman road from Buckingham met the turnpike south of Towcester. A check-gate at the Soap Office was presumably nearer Towcester (Figs. 14a, 14b).[2] North of Brackley there were gates at Hoppersford Lane, near Syresham with a check gate at High Cross. An additional gate may have been built at Weston on the Green following improvements to the Bicester road in 1793. This trust did not allow a single ticket purchased at one gate to give free passages at all others: the gates were let in groups, with a ticket only valid within each group.

---

[1] *JHC* **55**, 826.

[2] Robert Weston, clerk to the trustees, was estate agent to the Cartwrights of Aynho from 1777 to 1814. See Cooper, Nicholas, *Aynho: A Northamptonshire Village*, BHS 20 (1984).

TURNPIKE TOLLS to be LETT,

NOTICE is hereby given, That the Tolls arifing at the Toll Gates upon the Turnpike Road leading from Towcefter through Silverftone and Brackley, in the County of Northampton, and Middleton Stoney to Wefton Gate, in the Parifh of Wefton on the Green, in the County of Oxford, called or known by the Names of Burcott Wood Gate, with the Check Gate near the Soap Office ; Hopper's Ford Gate, with the Check Gate at High Crofs ; and Middleton Stoney Gate, will be Lett by Auction to the Beft Bidders, at the Houfe of Tho. Crump, at Brackley, in the County of Northampton, on Wednefday the Eleventh Day of November next, between the Hours of Ten and Eleven in the Forenoon, in the Manner directed by the Act paffed in the Thirteenth Year of the Reign of his Majefty King George the Third, " for Regulating the Turnpike Roads ;" which Tolls produced the laft Year the following Sums above the Expence of collecting them, and will be put up at thofe Sums refpectively, viz.

Burcott Wood Gate, with the Check Gate near the Soap Office, — — — £. 127
Hopper's Ford Gate, with the Check Gate at High Crofs, — — — 112
Middleton Stoney Gate, — — — 52
£. 291

Whoever happens to be the beft Bidder, muft, at the fame Time, give Security, with fufficient Sureties, to the Satisfaction of the Truftees of the faid Turnpike Road, for the Payment of the Rents agreed for, and at fuch Times as they fhall direct,

ROBERT WESTON,
Clerk to the Truftees of the faid Turnpike Road,
Aynho, 12th October, 1789.

Figs. 14a and 14b. Advertisements relating to Weston to Towcester Turnpike.

TURNPIKE TOLLS TO BE LETT.

NOTICE is hereby given, That the Tolls arifing for one whole Year from the Ninth Day of December next, at the Toll-Gate called Burcott Wood Gate, with the Burcott Gate at the Soap Office, and at the Toll-Gate called Hopper's Ford Gate, with the Check Gate at High Crofs, upon the Turnpike Road leading from Towcefter through Silverftone and Brackley, in the County of Northampton, and Ardley and Middleton Stoney, to Wefton Gate, in the Parifh of Wefton on the Green, in the County of Oxford, will be LETT feparately by Auction to the beft Bidders, at the Houfe of Elizabeth Crump, called the Crown Inn, in Brackley, on Wednefday the Seventh Day of November next, between the Hours of Eleven and Four, in the Manner directed by the Act paffed in the Thirteenth Year of the Reign of his prefent Majefty " for regulating Turnpike Roads," No Bidder having offered at a former Meeting held for the Purpofe of letting the faid Toll, the fame will be put up at fuch Sums of Money as the Truftees think fit.

Whoever happens to be the beft Bidder muft at the fame Time give Security, with fufficient Sureties, to the Satisfaction of the Truftees of the faid Turnpike Road, for the Payment of the Rent agreed for, and at fuch Times as they fhall direct.

And Notice is hereby further given, That new Truftees will be elected in the room of fuch Truftees as are dead, and whofe Vacancies are not already filled up. Dated this Second Day of October, 1792.

ROBERT WESTON,
Clerk to the Truftees of the faid Turnpike Road.

Surviving minutes books cover the period after 1820 (Table 6). In 1821, Towcester, Burcott and Silverstone formed one group, Biddlesden Lane (near Syresham) and Hoppersford just north of Brackley were a second group, and

Middleton and Weston were a third group (Fig. 15) The working surveyors were also appointed to cover the same three sections of road. They were charged with laying the road with stones which were broken to pass through a two and a half inch ring, to make the carriageway sixteen feet wide and to maintain a fall of one inch to the yard from the centre. One of the surveyors no doubt got the blame when Joseph Underwood, the driver of the mail cart from Oxford to Northampton, claimed compensation from the trust *"for damage*

Table 6: Towcester to Weston on the Green Turnpike Trust

Trustees (active)	1820: Rev Thomas Causton, William Baty, John Yates, JH Butterfield, Rev WJ Palmer, Rev T W Fawcett, Phillip Sydney Pierrepoint, John Beauclaerk, Gregory Morgan, Jn Howard, Thomas Collier, Henry High Bennet, Thomas B Woodward, Rev W Baty, W Plantwright, Gilbert Flesher, RW Leonard, Geo Nelson, James Cockerton, Rev A Jones.
Toll gatherers or lessees	**Allen, William of Middleton Gate, toll collr** (Middleton & Weston 1826, 7, 8, 9, 30, 1, 1832, 3, 5, 7, 8, 9, 40, 1, 2, 3) **Brewerton, Wm, of Towcester, toll collr** (Towcester, Burcott, Silverstone 1821) Cave, George (Towcester, Burcott, 1833) Coggins (alias Badon), John of Halesowen, cordwainer (Towcester, Burcott, Silverstone 1826) Cumming, George of Camphill, Beds, (Towcester, Burcott, 1835) **Edwards, William of Gracesbury [Grimsbury?] Gate, Northants** (Middleton & Weston 1844) **Foxley, John of Souldern Gate, Oxon, toll collr** (Hoppersford & Biddesdon 1825) Gardner, Thomas of Towcester (Towcester, Burcott, 1847) Goodman, George of Northampton (Evenly 1835) Higgs, James (Towcester, Burcott, 1834; Middleton & Weston 1836) **Ingram, William, of Middleton, Toll collr** (Middleton & Weston 1821, 2, 3, 4) James, John of Syresham, labourer (Hoppersford & Biddesdon 1827, 8, 9, 30, 1, 2, 3, 4; Brackley & Biddlesden 1836, 7; Towcester, Burcott, 1839, 40, 1, 2) **James, Joseph of Brackley Bridge, toll collr** (Towcester, Burcott, 1838) James, Sarah, widow (Towcester, Burcott, 1843, 4) **Keene, Thomas, of Yarnton, toll collr** (Middleton & Weston 1834; Evenly 1834) Lines, Thomas of Chipping Warden, labourer (Brackley, Hoppersford, Biddlesden 1838) **Millard, John of Tingewick Gate, toll collr** (Towcester, Burcott, 1837) **Newport, Joseph of Fifield Gate, Northant, toll collr** (Middleton & Weston 1825) Pittam, Joseph, dealer of Woodend, Northants (Hoppersford & Biddesdon 1821, 2, 3, 4, 6, 35; Towcester, Burcott, Silverstone 1822, 5, 8, 9, 30) Street, Robert of Brackley, labourer (Brackley, Hoppersford, Biddlesden 1840, 1, 2, 3, 4) **Tidmarsh, Samuel of Adderbury Gate, toll collr** (Towcester, Burcott, 1831, 2,) **Tonge, James of Kingsbury Gate St Albans** (Towcester, Burcott, 1835, 6; Brackley, Hoppersford & Biddlesden 1839) Wilcox, John of Towcester, carrier (Towcester, Burcott, Silverstone 1823, 4)

sustained of his horse and cart by falling on a heap of stones left in the road". The trust complained to Mr Beesley, the mail contractor in St Mary Hall Lane, Oxford, that he might better provide for his carts since at the time of the accident this cart had only one lamp.

The trustees responded to changing patterns of traffic to maximise the toll income. The Weston Gate was moved in 1821 but the trust did not incur any cost since William Ingram, the current lessee, offered to build the house at his own expense save for the £15 it cost to haul the necessary stone. The trustees had resolved to remove the Burcott Wood Gate, south of Towcester, and build a new gate north of Silverstone. A temporary box and chain were put up at Silverstone in March 1821 and a new toll-house, 15 feet long, 9 feet 6 inches wide and 8 feet 6 inches high, was commissioned from the surveyor at a cost not to exceed £35. However, the income records show that both gates operated for several years in parallel and in fact the new Silverstone Gate was to be removed within a few years. In 1825 discussions were taking place over the enclosure of Silverstone Open Field and new bridges were required to carry the realigned roads over streams. One bridge was needed near the new road leading to Whittlebury and another over the rivulet at the bottom of Stonebridge Hill. The trust negotiated the removal of the toll-gate at Silverstone in return for the parish helping erect the bridges. The trust sold the materials from the Silverstone Toll-house for £12 in September 1828. It is likely that all the toll-houses were simple thatched buildings as, in 1829, Joseph Pittam was allowed £2 for the thatching of Towcester Turnpike House.

From the mid-1830s there were several alterations in the position of the toll-gates, particularly around Brackley (Fig. 11b, page 47). This arose from the opening of the railway that altered the pattern of traffic in the region. In 1833 William Allen, who was lessee of the Middleton Gate, built a new toll-house for the trust at Evenley, on the hill just south of Brackley. He did this at his own expense and was allowed the lease for the first year at £50; it was leased the following year for £250. In December 1835 this new gate was demolished, the materials sold for £4.10s. and a new toll-house built, by Messrs Mold & Willeman, lower down the hill at Brackley Bridge. The importance of traffic going to stations on the new railway led the trust to upgrade a mile of the road leading north towards Blisworth, the nearest station on the Birmingham to London line. In 1845 the trust agreed to allow the London to Worcester and Rugby to Oxford Railway Company to carry the road outside Middleton Stoney across their new line on an arch; this is still a constriction to modern traffic. In July 1849 the Buckingham Railway Company was allowed to remove the existing toll-house at Brackley Bridge, replacing it with a new toll-house near to the railway bridge; this was subsequently referred to as Brackley North End Gate. The old gate at Hoppersford seems to have been removed at this time but a sidegate was created on the lane to Hinton.

5.1.2 Merger with the Buckingham to Banbury Trust

The trustees were less than diligent in the 1840s and asked that their trust should be omitted from the Annual Bill for the renewal of turnpike powers. In December 1850 they wrote to Sir George Grey at the Home Office, which was responsible for the English turnpike system, saying that they then changed their minds. In the subsequent enquiry[3] it emerged that they had not lodged accounts since 1834 *"despite the fact that the clerk was paid £50/a and should be able to conduct with greater regularity"*. Of the £3,050 advanced by 32 subscribers in 1793, £2,830 was still outstanding. Furthermore, no interest had been paid since 1828 and so the accumulated debt had climbed to £7,414. The Mayor and Aldermen of Buckingham petitioned to have the toll-gate in the Parish of Buckingham removed, despite protests from the trustees that if it were moved near to Chackmore or Stowe, tolls would be reduced. In addition, a railway running almost parallel to the road had been opened from Buckingham to Brackley and the trustees expected that traffic would be *"annihilated"*.

The same group of gentlemen were trustees to the Weston to Towcester Turnpike and had a similar record of mismanagement here, although the main debt was only £2,000 owed to the Duke of Bridgewater and accumulated interest of £550. Mr Litchfield and Mr Bartlett had a discussion with Sir James McAdam about their position. The great surveyor was surprised that the Buckingham to Banbury Trust seemed to have *"petitioned to die"* in the way they had replied to the Home Office and he regretted it was now out of his hands. The final outcome was that, on the recommendation of Sir George Grey, the Weston to Towcester Trust was amalgamated with the Buckingham to Banbury Trust that crossed each other in Brackley. The merged Brackley Consolidated Trust met for the first time in November 1851.

The trustees set about restructuring the network of toll-houses that the new trust had inherited. On the old Banbury to Buckingham road they commissioned a new toll-house at Grimsbury Green, near to the junction of their road with the Daventry road and close to Banbury Bridge Gate (Fig. 11a, p.46). This was to be built by Thomas Bannard of Brackley, carpenter, to the same plan as Brackley North End Gate with an iron fence around it. At the eastern end of the Buckingham road they erected a new gate at Radclive, across the road leading to Stowe, and disposed of the old Buckingham Gate for £45 to George Nelson. A new side gate was built at Bufflers Holt, close to the Turweston Hill Gate, east of Brackley. The old Turweston Toll-house was considered beyond repair in 1856 and a new toll-house and gates were erected at the angle of the road leading to Evenley near the windmill.

---

[3] *PP* 48, 1851.

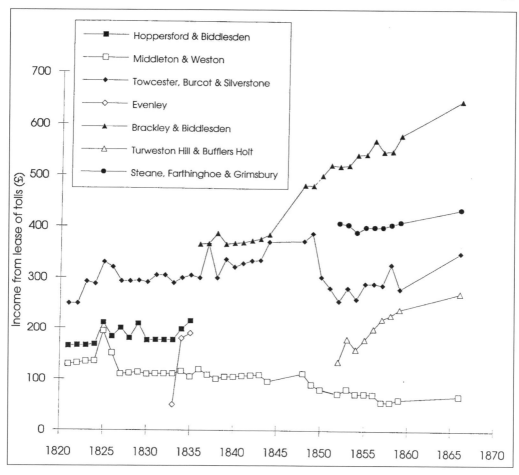

Fig. 15. Income from leasing indivdual gates: Weston to Towcester Turnpike.
Compare with Fig. 18, page 86.

The gates nearer Towcester had been the most profitable for the Weston to Towcester Trust (Fig. 15) but the advent of the railway led to a steady rise in income from the gates close to Brackley. The gates east of Brackley, closer to Buckingham, earned a greater toll income than those to the west, closer to Banbury. This again emphasises that these roads were principally serving Buckinghamshire and Northamptonshire more than Oxfordshire.

The trust attempted to keep its costs low and was in dispute over repairs to the bridges in this area. It tried to get the Bucks Railway to help in repair of the road over Skew Bridge and unsuccessfully tried to get the County Magistrates to pay for the lengthening of Shalstone Bridge.

5.2 Turnpikes through Bicester

In the latter half of the eighteenth century a web of turnpike roads were created around Bicester. The pattern suggests that these trusts were dealing with the pieces left between other turnpikes but may also indicate a growing status for Bicester as a transport hub in this period. The old line of Akeman Street from Aylesbury to Bicester had been turnpiked in 1770 but the through routes linking Bicester to Oxford, Banbury and Buckingham were not turnpiked until the 1790s (Fig. 10f; Section 3.5, pages 43-44, deals with the Bicester to Aynho road). Hedges[4] tells that originally the residents of Bicester had opposed the idea of the turnpike, "*but relented when they saw how much Middleton benefited from coaches. Bicester folk placed a sign-board at Weston declaring that their town was the nearest way to Buckingham and Northampton*"; the latter is untrue. An advertisement for coach service from Bicester appeared in papers in 1793, just after the road to Aynho had been turnpiked.

Bicester citizens had shown an early interest in turnpikes. In 1711, during the first phase of road improvement, a petition had been placed before Parliament to turnpike the ten miles of Akeman Street from Aylesbury to Bicester. However, there was vigorous opposition from the bailiff and burgesses of Buckingham[5] who claimed that "*the repairing of this highway would prejudice the trade of the town of Buckingham by turning the course of the road leading from Aylesbury through Buckingham to Brackley, Banbury, etc*". Further they asked that a Bill be passed to improve the Aylesbury to Buckingham road instead.

A cross road from Newport Pagnell, through Stoney Stratford and Buckingham to Bicester and on to Woodstock was created by an Act of 1768. Among the trustees were the Spencers from Woodstock and Sir James Dashwood, alongside whose estate at Kirtlington the road would run. The trustees were to hold their first meeting at the house of Master Thomas Potter, known by the sign of the King's Arms in Bicester. The Act specifically mentioned the need for a new bridge at Catersford in the parish of Leckhamstead, where in winter the ford was so deep that carriages could not pass.

The first meeting to put the Act into execution actually took place in July 1770. Subsequently, Henry Smith, one of the trustees, called a meeting of the trust at Middleton Stoney to discuss the Bicester to Stoney Stratford road.[6] A later meeting[7] considered extending the Kirtlington to Bicester road to

---

[4] Hedges, S., *Bicester wuz a little town*, Bicester Advertiser, Bicester (1968).
[5] *JHC* **17**, 186.
[6] *JOJ*, Apr. 1769.
[7] *JOJ*, Jan. 1772.

Buckingham so it appears that implementation was slow. This turnpike linked the two main roads from London to Birmingham but may have failed in attracting traffic since the Act was allowed to lapse. However, sections of the road were incorporated into three other turnpike trusts. The eastern end of this road between Buckingham and Newport Pagnell was re-turnpiked in 1814, whereas the western end was incorporated into trusts controlled from Bicester.

BICESTER and AYLESBURY TURNPIKE TOLLS.

NOTICE is hereby given, That a Meeting of the Trustees of the Turnpike Road from Bicester to Aylesbury, will be held at the King's Arms, in Bicester, on Friday the 13th Day of July next, at Eleven o'Clock, for the Purposes of appointing new Trustees in the Room of several dead, and of others who refuse to act, and to consult about erecting several Side Bars or Gates on or near the said Road, to wit, one Bar or Gate near the said Turnpike Road in the Town of Bicester, and across the common Road leading from thence towards Launton; two other Bars or Gates by the Side of the said Turnpike Road, in the Roads leading from Blackthorn to Launton, and from Blackthorn to Marsh Gibbon; one other Bar or Gate by the Side of the said Turnpike Road, in the Road leading from Waddesden to Quainton; one other Bar or Gate by the Side of the said Turnpike Road, near to a Lane called Gullet's Lane, in the Parish of Waddesden; and two other Bars or Gates by the Side of the said Turnpike Road, near to a certain Ground called Highway Ground, in the Road leading across the said Turnpike towards Quarenden. Also at this Meeting will be lett to Farm for one Year, from the 16th Day of July next, the Tolls to arise upon the said Turnpike Road at the several Gates called Wretchwick Gate, Launton Side Gate, Westcot Gate, and Stone Bridge Gate, with the Toll-Houses, Side Bars or Gates to the same respectively belonging; which Tolls will be lett according to the Directions of the Statute made in the Thirteenth Year of his present Majesty's Reign "For regulating Turnpike Roads," and produced in the last Year over and above the Charges of collecting, as follows;

Wretchwick Gate, and Launton Side Gate,	£121 0 0
Westcot Gate,	37 0 0
Stone Bridge Gate,	175 6 5

Which said Turnpike Tolls, with the said Toll Houses, Gates and Side Bars, will be put up to Auction at the several Sums above mentioned to have been lett; and whoever happens to be the best Bidder must immediately give Security to the Satisfaction of the said Trustees for Payment of the Rents agreed upon, and at such Times as the said Trustees shall direct.

BICESTER, HENRY CHURCHILL, Clerk to the
20th *June*, 1792. Trustees of the said Turnpike Road.

N. B. Any Person or Persons desirous of undertaking the Repairing and keeping in Repair the above Road, are requested to apply at this Meeting for that Purpose, when the Trustees will be ready to contract for the same, in three or more Divisions, as may be agreed upon.

Fig. 14c.

The roads from Bicester to two points on the Oxford to Birmingham road were put under a turnpike trust in 1793. The first branch went to the Cherwell crossing at Enslow Bridge near Woodstock, the other to the more northerly crossing at Heyford and on to the Rollright road at Enstone. A third branch of this road went south from Bicester to the junction of the Gosford road and the Towcester road at Weston on the Green. The final section of the old road from Bicester to the Buckingham Road at Finmere was eventually re-turnpiked in 1812 when it was incorporated into the Bicester to Aynho Trust (see Section 3.5 above).

Access to Bicester along the turnpike was controlled by gates at Sheep Street and Skimming Dish Barn on the Aynho road, at Wretchwick Gate on the Aylesbury road (Fig. 14c) and at Kings End Gate on the Heyford road (Fig. 14d).

Enstone, Heyford Bridge, Bicester, Weston-on-the-Green, and Kirtlington Turnpike Roads

NOTICE is hereby given, that a Meeting of the Trustees of the above-named Turnpike Roads will be held at the King's Arms Hotel, in Bicester, in the county of Oxford, on Wednesday the 19th day of November next, at Two o'clock in the afternoon, when the Trustees will proceed to LET by AUCTION, for one year, from the 1st day of January, 1874, the TOLLS arising at the several Gates on the said Roads, which have produced for the current year, over and above the expenses of collecting the same, the following sums respectively:—

Bicester King's End Gate £261
Heyford Town and Bridge and Barton Gates } 320
   (in hand) ....
Cuckold's Holt Gate 21
Kirtlington Gate 63

and they will be put up at these sums or such other sums as the Trustees may determine.

Whoever is declared to be the best bidder will be required to pay down one month's rent in advance, and enter, with satisfactory sureties, into an agreement for the punctual payment of the rent monthly in advance, and for the due performance of the several conditions to be contained in the said agreement. And such other general business will be transacted as the circumstances of the Trust require.

By order, WILLIAM HARDMAN MILLS,
Bicester, 22nd October, 1873.   Clerk.

Fig. 14d.

5.3 The Banbury to Lutterworth Trust

5.3.1 The First Parliamentary Act

A petition to Parliament in February 1765[8] was made by gentlemen, clergy, freeholders and other principal inhabitants of the Counties of Oxford, Northampton and Leicester. This set forth that *"the public road leading from the bridge, at or near the east end of Banbury in the County of Oxford, through the hamlets of Grimsbury in the parish of Chalcombe* [sic, actually in Banbury parish], *the town of Wardington, Chipping Warden, Byfield and Cherwellton in the Parish of Fausley and Badbury, the hamlet of Drayton and town and parish of Daventry and thence through the parishes of Welton, Ledgers Ashby and Kilsby to the Watling Street Road, at or near the north-east corner of Kilsby open fields, and thence along the same road about three miles to a place called The Gibbet, through the town and parish of Cottesbatch, through part of the parish of Lutterworth in the County of Leicester, are in many parts thereof in a founderous condition and, in the winter season in particular, almost impassable..."*. In evidence before a Committee,[9] Henry Bagshaw and David Prowth said that *"the statute work has been done, and in addition sixpence in the pound applied towards the repairs of some of this road, and has been found ineffective, and that the said roads are narrow in many places and cannot be properly widened and repaired by the laws in being"*.

Later evidence to the Committee by Mr William Wyatt[10] stated that *"the road leading out of the turnpike road in Banbury at or near a place called Parsons Lane, and down the same lane to the east end of the bridge at the east end of Banbury, is in a ruinous condition and cannot be effectively repaired and widened by the present methods provided by the Law"*. As a result provision was made in the Bill to include this section in the jurisdiction of the trust. The trustees could not collect tolls effectively from travellers on this western bank of the Cherwell, but the toll-gate to the east of the bridge would intercept all through traffic. The road along Parsons Lane funnelled travellers to the start of the main turnpike section and the trustees had a vested interest in seeing that it was well maintained, even though they could not levy travellers on it directly.

This had not been a major road in Tudor or Stuart times (Fig. 2a, page 9). The new turnpike crossed the Cherwell at Banbury Bridge and then met the old trackway that followed the eastern bank of the river as the Portway (Fig. 1, pp. 2-3), re-crossing the river at Wardington. From Wardington the road crossed

---

[8] *JHC* **30**, 144.
[9] *JHC* **30**, 180.
[10] *JHC* **30**, 158.

the northern end of the Cotswolds to Daventry and on over the watershed into the Midland Plain. North of here the turnpike adopted the line of Watling Street. Southern sections of this old Roman road had been turnpiked already, but this section from Northamptonshire into Leicestershire (Fig. 6, page 25) was no longer a trunk road. The route from Banbury to Lutterworth was not a particularly important through road but it intersected three large turnpikes carrying traffic from London to the West Midlands.

5.3.2 Implementation and Administration

The minutes book for the first twenty years of the trust gives details of how the trust operated (Table 7). The trustees began their work as soon as the Act was passed. The first meeting recorded in their minutes book was on June 14th 1765 at "*the house of Robert Clerke known by the sign of the White Swan in Daventry*". They met a week later at "*the house of William Baker* [Barker] *known by the sign of the Three Tuns in Banbury*"[11] and the week following at "*the house of Robert Smith, known by the sign of the Spread Eagle in Lutterworth*". It was decided to divide the road into two districts: Lutterworth to Badby Gap and Badby to Banbury. Thomas Holled was appointed clerk and treasurer to the first district and Henry Bagshaw Harrison was appointed to the corresponding offices in the second district. They were allowed £20 each per annum for their trouble, though both men were also the chief financiers of the improvements, loaning £350 each to the trust. A further £300 was lent by William Mayo of Great Brington and five years later William Cullingworth lent another £100. The trust paid annual interest at four and a half percent on these loans that were for the most part not redeemed during the life of the initial bondholder.

At the first meeting, Jeffery College of Kilsby, labourer, was appointed surveyor of the northern district at £20 per year: his son, Thomas, and grandson Thomas Jnr, were to be surveyors to the trust for periods until well into the nineteenth century. At the second meeting Richard D'Anvers of Wardington was selected rather than another candidate, William Wyatt of Banbury, as surveyor for the second district. D'Anvers had to retire in 1770 due to ill health.[12] The trustees also reminded landowners and occupiers of land worth more than £50/a and every owner of a team that they were still obliged to provide normal statute labour; the amount varied for the different parishes along the road from three days/a for parishes such as Byfield and Badby, through two days/a for Kilsby and Banbury to one day/a for Daventry.

---

[11] See Gibson, J., "The Three Tuns in the Eighteenth Century", *C&CH* **8**.1 (1979), 5.
[12] *JOJ*, May 1770.

Table 7: Banbury to Lutterworth Turnpike Trust

Trustees (active)	1765: Jno Godfree, Jas Riley, Wm Caldecott, F Montgomery, Wm Deacon, Robt Andrew, Wm Lovett, Charles Watkins, Tho Watson, Lumley Arnold, Knightley Holled, Saml Goddard, Richard Burford, John Cadman, William Bull, Jno Clay, Rd Hanwell, Wm Rose. 1771: Wm H Channey, Robt Rymile, William Bull, Rd Humphris, Charles Wyatt. 1772: Matthew Lamb, Elisha Heydon, Saml Sparrow, Charles Wyatt, Rd Burford. 1773: Robert Shawof Lutterworth in place of Oliver Wright, gent, dec. Samuel Mills in place of Revd John Cadman, dec. Rev Richard Welchman in place of Joseph Clarke, Esq., dec. Rev Hamlyn Harris in place of Thomas Grace, Esq., dec. Henry Hickman in place of William Hickman, dec. Earl of Denbigh in place of Sir Charles Shuckburgh, bart. 1778: D Knightley, WM Channey, Charles Fox, Matthew Lamb, Elisha Heydon, Rd Burford 1783: Richard Nicoll, John Loveday, Charles Fox, H Bartholomew, Wm Calcott
Toll gatherers or lessees	Claridge, William (1783, 4, 88, 91) Cocks, William (Welton, 1765) Dickens, William (Badby 1765, 9, 72, 3, 4) Fennel, Robt (Badby 1787) Lambert, John (Banbury Bridge, 1765, 9, 72, 3) Marriott, Simon (1778, 82, 3) Phillips, Mr (1786) Sheath, John (Dow Bridge, 1765)

The trustees made decisions on the best line for the road to be laid out under direction of the surveyor. The turnpike from Daventry to Lutterworth was to go from Wheatsheaf Corner, down Sheaf Street and Brook End and then by the west end of the Home Close of Mr Robert Andrew, along and over a place in the open fields of Daventry called Old Grove into the present public road called Rugby Road. General improvements to the road began in late June when Joseph Hill was allowed £1 per day *"for the use of four carts with standing pillars for eight hours work each day, drawing a tun and an half in every cart in carrying gravel to mend the road from the Horse Close Gate at the south end of Cottesback Town to the south end of New Quick in the Mill Field, this summer next"*. In the autumn the trustees instructed *"Jeffery College our surveyor to make a temporary road from the ground between Ashby Town and Leicester Lane through two closes of Mrs Ashley, in order to carry gravel from the gravel pit to repair the road and that draw rails with bridges be put up and made at the two new quickset hedges upon College's taking great care that no young trees be destroyed"*. They agreed to share with the trustees of the Warwick Road, the cost of making and raising a mound from Foxhill to Drayton Enclosure (just south of Daventry) and later, arranged through Richard Burford, a trustee on both roads, *"for £5 to be applied to repair such part of the turnpike road as lie between Banbury Bridge and the Oxford Turnpike Road up Parsons Lane*". The trust was not directly responsible for the bridges but did assist the County with repairs: in 1771 they contributed a quarter of the costs of repairs to Dow Bridge on the Watling Street. The main running costs of the road were for stone and gravel. Sufficient labour must have been provided by statute work but some unusual payments were made: in January 1776 the treasurer paid out 12s. for "*making a passage in the snow*".

Inhabitants of Banbury were given the liberty "*to bring any quantity of grass, hay, fodder, straw, corn or other produce of his farm or estate through the turnpike gate at Banbury Bridge to his dwelling or farm in Banbury for private consumption, without paying tolls*". The trustees were prepared to consider what was effectively a season ticket for regular users of the road. In July 1768, "*Thomas Bray, a miller of Welton, petitioned the Commissioners to compound for his going to his mill and back again in Welton Inclosure for a year from this time with one horse only*": the commissioners (trustees) agreed a price of 12s. The trust also allowed "*waggons or carriages going empty for coals and paying a toll to return toll-free with a load*".

5.3.3 Toll Collection

The collectors of tolls were appointed as a matter of urgency. They were nominated at the initial meeting of the trust and each required to give security of £40 to the trustees "*for his faithful discharging the trust*"; this against a salary of only £15 per year. At the second meeting William Dickens of Daventry was required to "*attend upon Badby Bridge from the first day of July next, all night and day, with a chain or line, to collect such tolls as are ordered by the said Act to be taken, until such time as a house can be built or rented to him*". John Lambert the younger of Banbury was similarly charged to attend "*at the turnpike gate to be erected at Banbury Bridge*". The two toll-gates on the northern section were dealt with a week later. The Welton Gate on the road "*leading out of Welton Lordship into Ashby Lordship where the roads meet coming from Rugby and Lutterworth to Daventry*" was assigned to William Cock of Daventry from July 8th 1765. John Heath of Leir in Leicestershire, a woolcomber, was appointed collector at Dow Bridge Gate and side bar, located by the Biggin Gate.

The contract to construct toll-houses was let at the June 28th meeting. John Wagstaff was "*appointed to build three toll-houses and three toll-gates and paint the same and twice over, according to the estimate and plan now delivered in the sum of £310.10s., as soon as possible but by Old Michaelmas at the furthest*".

In August John Bloxham was "*appointed to build a toll-house and toll-gate and paint the same three times*" near the east end of Banbury Bridge at a cost of £54, to be ready on or before November 1st 1765. Before the work began, in September, the trustees changed their minds about the location of the Badby

Gate, resolving that it should be at Badby Gap rather than on the bridge across the Nene. They also agreed that Mr Wagstaff should make the three houses a yard longer at an additional cost of five guineas for each property.

Banbury Bridge was the most valuable gate (Fig. 16). The original toll-gate at Banbury was at the eastern end of the bridge. When the canal was built in 1778, the bridge arch was modified so the gate had to be removed. It was relocated in the hamlet of Grimsbury, on the Banbury side of the junction with the Buckingham road, though the latter was not turnpiked until 1791. In 1794 the trust resolved to build a new gate between Wilscot Lane and Byfield (Fig. 7, page 27), subsequently known as Wilscot Gate.

NOTICE is hereby given, That a Meeting of the Trustees of the Turnpike Road leading from Banbury to Lutterworth, will be holden at the Red Lion, in Banbury, on Tuesday the 21st Day of October next, at Eleven o'Clock in the Forenoon; at which Meeting the Tolls to arise for one Year at Banbury Bridge Toll Gate will be LET to FARM by AUCTION to the best Bidder, in Manner directed by the Act of Parliament of the 13th Year of the Reign of his present Majesty, "for regulating Turnpike Roads," which Tolls produced the last Year the Sum of 264 l. over and above the Charges of collecting the same, and will be put up at that Sum. Whoever happens to be the best Bidder, must at the same Time give Security, to the Satisfaction of the Trustees, for the Payment of the Rents agreed upon, at such Times as they shall direct. And those Persons who reside in any of the Parishes, Townships, or Places through which the said Road doth lie, and occupy any Farms, Lands, and Estates, in any adjoining Parish, Township, or Place, and for the necessary Occupation of such Lands have Occasion to pass through the said Turnpike Gate, may, immediately before the Tolls are put up, compound for his or their Tolls at such Turnpike Gate, in Respect of such Farms, at such Sums as the said Trustees shall direct. And Notice is hereby further given, That at this Meeting the Trustees will take into Consideration the Propriety and Expediency of erecting a Ticket, or other Turnpike Gate, upon or across the Turnpike Road at some proper Place between Wilscott Lane and Byfield; and also the Propriety and Expediency of erecting a Side Bar, or Gate, at or near Wilscott Lane aforesaid, or some other Part of the said Turnpike Road between Wilscott Lane and Byfield. Dated the 15th Day of September, 1794.
By Order of the said Trustees,
H. B. HARRISON, their Clerk

Fig. 16. Advertisement relating to the Banbury to Lutterworth Turnpike.

5.3.4 Further Acts

The trustees applied to renew their powers in March 1785, incurring costs of £146.16s.6d. in fees for the parliamentary clerk. They argued that some of the money borrowed to make the original improvements was still outstanding. Mr Henry Bagshaw Harrison gave evidence that £1,876 remained due, although the exact amount was not clear until problems over the estate of Thomas Holled were resolved.[13] Holled, the chief financier of the northern section, had become bankrupt and at the time of his death the issues of interest on his loan to the trust had to be resolved as other trustees were buying out his commitments. Knightly Holled, probably his son, continued as a trustee.

Parliament again renewed the powers of the trust in 1807 and 1828. A further Act in 1840 placed under the powers of this trust, the road from Badby Bridge, through the parishes of Badby and Newnham to the Stratford and Dunchurch Road near Dodford Lane (Fig. 6, page 25). To administer these improvements, the trustees were to meet at the Griffin Public House in Chipping Warden.

---

[13] *JHC* **40**, 871.

6. Oxfordshire to Gloucestershire Turnpikes

The historic highway from London to Worcester ran north-west from Oxford through Chipping Norton (Fig. 2a, page 8). This route was one of the earliest turnpikes in the region (Fig. 5, page 22) administered by several separate trusts. The section from Woodstock to Rollright on the Birmingham road was turnpiked in 1730 and the branch from the junction at Chappel on the Heath to Bourton in 1731. Turnpiking of the roads along the Cotswold ridge did not commence until the 1770s. The Cotswold routes ran through an agricultural region and, in contrast to the earlier turnpikes, three of these roads had their terminus in Banbury itself. This suggests that these later roads were roads *to* Banbury and its markets rather than through-routes connecting major cities outside the region. The road north-westwards to Daventry and Lutterworth (dealt with above in 5.2) was the first of these routes to be turnpiked. The roads south-eastwards to Gloucestershire ran deep into the Cotswolds, to rural market towns such as Chipping Norton, Shipston and Burford and were among the last of the roads to be turnpiked.

6.1 The Chappel on the Heath to Bourton Trust

The turnpike road from the heath above the town of Chipping Norton to the edge of the Cotswolds scarp at Bourton was part of the ancient highway from London to Worcester and was referred to as the "Gloucester Road" when the petition was brought before Parliament in 1731. It covered *"several roads leading through the town of Moreton Henmarsh and includes that part of the road leading from Worcester to Oxford and London from the quarry above Bourton Hill to Chappel on the Heath as well as the road from Tidmington Bridge through Toddenham and the said town of Moreton Henmarsh"*. Evidence as to the very bad state of these roads was given by Henry Hunt, William Deacle and William Winslow. The Act stated that the trustees *"shall meet together at the sign of the Unicorn in morton Henmarsh aforesaid, on or before the seventh day of June 1731"*.

The powers of this trust were renewed in 1743. The petition[1] mentions that *"by reason of the deepness of the soil and many heavy carriages frequently passing through the same, the road is almost impassable in winter"*. John George said that he had travelled the road for thirty years and that before the first Act it was in such a *"bad and ruinous condition that carriages were obliged to go by Stow, 2 or 3 miles out of their way"*. Thomas Cooke and Robert Bright gave evidence that the trust had debts of £800 and on the second

---

[1] *JHC* **24**, 547.

debts of £800 and on the second renewal in 1765[2] Dr Thomas Butler said that the debt had risen to £1,200. In 1791[3] Joseph Knight justified the need to increase the debt beyond £2,400 so that improvements could be made to Salford and Little Compton Hills which *"are steep and the passage over the same inconvenient and unfit for carriage"*.

The trust had a toll-house at Chappel on the Heath, close to where the road branched off the Woodstock to Rollright road. There were further gates either side of Chipping Norton. Although the trust maintained one of the major roads to the south-west Midlands, it became relatively less important than the road to Birmingham.

6.2 The Banbury to Burford Trust

6.2.1 The Act

The petition to Parliament, in February 1770, for turnpiking roads to the south-west of Banbury was supported by gentlemen, clergy, freeholders, tradesmen and other inhabitants of Burford, Chipping Norton, Banbury, Deddington, Stow, Aynho and Brackley.[4] The roads covered by the Act were a network of intersecting highways *"from Burford through Chipping Norton to Banbury and to the end of a lane leading from Bourton on the Water to the foot of Stowe Hill in the parish of Maugersbury in the County of Gloucester where it joins the turnpike road through Stowe, and the road branching out of the road from Chipping Norton to Banbury, through Deddington to the river Cherwell"* (Fig. 6, page 25). These roads were described as very founderous and *"the passage over the said river and through a meadow, called Aynho Meadow, is at present only a bridle road and very dangerous and in floods is at some times impassable and it would be a public utility if the said several roads were made good carriage roads and a bridge built over the said river, and a public carriage road continued over the said meadow to the town of Aynho to join the road leading from Buckingham through Aynho to Banbury"*.

Mr Thomas Brooks provided evidence that the roads were in a poor condition.[5] Samuel Churchill (of Deddington) added that were *"a proper bridge built over the River Cherwell, it would be a great advantage to the inhabitants of Deddington and the adjacent places, as by that means an easy communication would be opened with the intended canal from Coventry to Oxford which will be carried within half a mile of the parish of Deddington and that without this communication the inhabitants of the parish will be obliged to go four or five miles, and possibly further, before they can come to any wharf upon the said canal"*.

---

[2] *JHC* **30**, 145.
[3] *JHC* **46**, 160.
[4] *JHC* **32**, 672.
[5] *JHC* **32**, 742.

The trust meetings were held at the White Hart in Chipping Norton, at the mid-point on the road, although the administration in the early years seems to have been dominated by Samuel Churchill, in Deddington. One of the first actions of the trustees was to seek loans, on the credit of the tolls that would be taken at the gates.[6] The trust was very protective of the valuable assets it was creating and offered a reward for information regarding the theft of the chain which had been placed across the road between Chipping Norton and Churchill (as a temporary toll-bar). Later, a notice[7] the trust published a statement that *"persons defacing milestones on the Burford to Banbury road will be prosecuted"*.

6.2.2 Toll-gates

The road was administered in three divisions each with a surveyor[8] and separate tolls. The Burford to Stow Division of the road had a gate at Gawcum on the top of the hill near Wyck Beacon. The gate at Fulbrook near Burford, on the north bank of the Windrush, was shared with the Burford to Chipping Norton Division. The latter Division's second gate was located on the southern side of Chipping Norton. The northern section, the Chipping Norton to Banbury Division, had a gate at Chappel on the Heath and at Saltway, where the old track crosses the main road (Figs. 17a, 17b and 17c). The Aynho branch was controlled by a gate at the junction at Swerford Heath.

The Burford Gates (Fulbook and sidegates on the Stow road) were the most valuable (in 1780 the income at Burford was £170, at Saltway £100, at Chipping Norton £60 and at Chapel Heath £50). Although their income was far from high, the trustees reduced the tolls at Fulbrook Gate in July 1782 and at Saltway in April 1783.[9] Traffic using the old tracks around Banbury must have been an irritation to the trustees and they resolved to erect a new pair of gates at Wycombe [Wickham or Wykham] Hill where the lanes to Broughton and Bodicote meet.[10] A new gate at Wykham replaced the old Saltway Gate and a weighing machine was installed here to check for over-weight wagons. The fines from this were kept by the lessee of the gate and in 1831 were worth £98.10s. At the beginning of the nineteenth century there was a gate at Bloxham but this was closed in 1828 and the tolls were subsequently increased at Chapel Heath.

---

[6] *JOJ*, Oct. 1770.
[7] *JOJ*, Sept. 1773.
[8] *JOJ*, Jan. 1771.
[9] *JOJ*, July 1782, April 1783.
[10] *JOJ*, Feb. 1789.

Burford, Chipping-Norton, Banbury, Stow, and Aynho Turnpikes.

NOTICE is hereby given, That a General Meeting of the Trustees of the above Turnpikes, will be held (by adjournment) at the White Hart Inn, in Chipping-Norton, Oxfordshire, on Monday the 10th day of July, 1775, by eleven o'clock in the forenoon.

Also, That the Tolls arising at the Burford and Chipping-Norton Toll-gates will be Lett by Auction, to the best bidder, at the place above-mentioned, on the said 10th day of July, between the hours of two and four of the clock in the afternoon, in the manner directed by the Act passed in the thirteenth year of the reign of his Majesty King George the Third, " for regulating the Turnpike Roads;" which Tolls, at the Burford Gates, produced the last year the sum of 161l. 10s. and at the said Gate called Chipping-Norton Gate, the sum of 60l. above the expences of collecting the same respectively. The Burford Gates will be put up together, at the said sum of 161l. 10s. and the Chipping-Norton Gate at the sum of 60l. Whoever happens to be the best bidder, must at the same time give security, with sufficient sureties, to the satisfaction of the Trustees, for the payment of the rent agreed for, at such times as they shall direct.

Also, That new Trustees will be elected.

SAMUEL CHURCHILL,
Clerk to the Trustees of the above Turnpike Roads,

Burford, Chipping-Norton, Banbury, Stow, and Aynho
TURNPIKES.

NOTICE is hereby given, That a General Meeting of the Trustees of the above Turnpikes will be held, by Adjournment, on Wednesday the Fourth Day of July next, at the White Hart Inn in Chipping-Norton, in the County of Oxford, at Eleven o'Clock in the Forenoon.

Also, That the Tolls arising at the Burford, Chipping-Norton, Chapel-Heath, and Saltway Gates, will be separately lett by Auction, to the best Bidder, at the Place above-mentioned, on the said Fourth Day of July, between the Hours of Two and Four o'Clock in the Afternoon, in the Manner directed by the Act passed in the Thirteenth Year of the Reign of his present Majesty King George the Third, for regulating the Turnpike Roads; which Tolls, at the Burford Gates, produced, the last Year, the Sum of 681 l. — at Chipping-Norton Gate, the Sum of 811. — at Chapel-Heath Gate, the Sum of 641. — and at Saltway Gate, the Sum of 105l. above the Expences of collecting the same; and will be put up at those respective Sums. — Whoever happens to be the best Bidder, must at the same Time give Security, with sufficient Sureties, to the Satisfaction of the Trustees, for the Payment of the Rent agreed for, and at such Times as they shall direct.

Also, That new Trustees will be elected in the Stead of those who are dead, or refuse to act; and that such other Business will be done and transacted at the said Meeting as by the said Act is required.

Deddington, SAMUEL CHURCHILL, Clerk to the Trustees
6th June, 1792. of the said Turnpike Roads.

Burford, Chipping-Norton, Banbury, Stow, and Aynho,
TURNPIKE ROADS.

NOTICE is hereby given, That a General Meeting of the Trustees of the above roads will be held, at the White Hart Inn, Chipping Norton, in the county of Oxford, on Monday the 25th of May instant, at Eleven o'clock in the forenoon. At which Meeting the Trustees will proceed to the election of a Treasurer or Treasurers of the said Roads, in the stead of Thomas Wapshot, Esq. who has signified his intention of resigning the office of Treasurer.

And at the same Meeting new Trustees will be elected, in the stead of those who are dead or refuse to act; and such other business transacted as the Acts require.

Deddington, By order of the Trustees,
May 7th, 1812. SAMUEL CHURCHILL, Clerk.

Figs. 17a, 17b and 17c: Advertisements relating to the Banbury to Burford Turnpike.

The Aynho Division met at the King's Arms, Deddington, to consider erecting another gate on the road between Swerford Heath Gate and Deddington.[11] This gate was erected west of the village of Deddington (Fig. 17d) whereas another gate for the Kidlington road was south of the village.

---

[11] *JOJ*, Sept. 1789.

Aynho Division of the Burford, Chipping-Norton, Banbury, Stow, Deddington, and Aynho
TURNPIKE ROADS.

NOTICE is hereby given, That a Meeting of the Trustees of the above Turnpike Roads will be held at the King's Arms Inn, in Deddington, in the county of Oxford, on Saturday the Sixteenth day of September next.

At which Meeting the Tolls arising at the Deddington and Aynho Gates will be LET by AUCTION, to the best bidders, between the hours of Twelve at noon and Three in the afternoon, in the manner directed by the Act passed in the 13th year of the reign of his late Majesty King George the Third, " For regulating the Turnpike Roads," which Tolls produced the last year the following sums, over and above the expences of collecting, (that is to say)—

	£
Deddington Gate	65
Aynho Gates	175

and will be put up at those sums respectively.

All persons who intend to be bidders for the Tolls of either of the said Gates are required to deliver, in writing, the names and places of abode of their intended sureties, at the Office of Messrs. Churchill and Field, solicitors, Deddington, at least seven days previous to the Meeting, otherwise they will not be allowed to bid; and every taker must pay down at the time of taking one month's rent in advance, and the remainder in such proportions, and at such times as the Trustees at the above Meeting shall direct.

And at the above Meeting new Trustees will be elected in the stead of those who are dead or refuse to act, and such other business transacted as by the several Acts is required.

SAMUEL CHURCHILL,
Clerk to the Trustees.

Deddington, August 16, 1820.

Fig. 17d

AYNHOE DIVISION OF ROADS.

NOTICE IS HEREBY GIVEN that a Meeting of the Trustees of the above Division of Roads, will be held at the CARTWRIGHT ARMS INN, in AYNHOE, in the County of Northampton, on WEDNESDAY, the 15th day of November next, at 12 o'Clock at Noon, for the purpose of LETTING BY AUCTION, from the first day of January next, the Tolls arising at all the Gates on the said Division of Roads, called Swerford Heath Gate, Deddington Gate, and Clifton Bridge Gate.

The Tolls are now in hand and will be put up at such sum and for such term as the Trustees present may decide upon.

WHOEVER is declared to be the best bidder will be required to pay down one months rent in advance, and enter, with satisfactory sureties, into an Agreement for the punctual payment of the Rent monthly in advance, and for the due performance of the several conditions to be contained in the said Agreement.

And such other business will be transacted as the circumstances of the trust require.

By order,
W. G. W. LOVELL,
Clerk.

Deddington.

Fig. 17e

As the canal wharf began to attract traffic, the trust created gates on either side of the Cherwell valley at Clifton Bridge and at Aynho Wharf (Fig. 17d). The only toll-house to survive is at Swerford Heath. It is a small two storey cottage built of stone; the space for the toll board has been converted into a window on the first floor.

Swerford Heath toll house.

6.2.3 The Divisions

Samuel Churchill spoke again on behalf of the trust when the Act was renewed in 1792.[12] He asked that terms of the Act be continued so that the £1,270 borrowed on the credit of the tolls could be repaid. The Chipping Norton and Aynho Divisions were financially more sound than the Stow Division. The Chipping Norton Division, covering the road from Banbury to Burford, had toll receipts of £814 in 1831 and paid out £569 for work on the road. The Aynho Division earned £267 and spent £126 but the Stow Division had an income of £300 with expenditure of £287. In 1832 the trustees again applied to renew and extend their powers, increase tolls and in addition, take into their jurisdiction a new section of road from Fulbrook, over Milton and Shipston Downs to another part of the existing turnpike where there was already a junction with the Charlbury Trust. Early drafts of the bill also included a proposal to turnpike one of the cross roads on the section between Chipping Norton and Banbury, "*where a certain highway called London Lane joins the (turnpike) in the Parish of Chadlington, to a place in the Parish of Daylesford, called Chipping Norton Gap, where the highway from Chipping Norton through the Parish of Cornwell joins the turnpike road to Stow, and also from a certain spot where the public highway leading from Chipping Norton towards Churchill crosses the end of London Lane and extending from thence to a certain place in the town of Chipping Norton*".

---

[12] *JHC* **46**, 159.

The trustees withdrew this provision from the final Bill and these lanes remain minor roads. It is a mystery why the many roads around Charlbury attracted so much attention from turnpike trusts.

This Act formally identified three Divisions of the trust, the main road from Burford to be the Burford to Banbury, the new branch to be the Stow Division and the existing branch from Swerford Heath to Aynho as the Aynho Division. Each Division had a separate clerk, treasurer and surveyor (Appendix 3.3, page 152). A day ticket on one Division did not give free passage on the others and money raised on one could not be applied to the others. The Stow Division created new side-gates at Lyneham Lane, Dog Kennel Lane, Little Rissington and Wick Rissington. Later, in 1849, the Stow Division was incorporated into the Stow & Moreton United Roads Trust whereas the Banbury and Aynho Divisions became almost separate organisations, advertising their meetings separately and being treated differently by the Parliamentary Commissioners dealing with the closure of turnpikes.

6.3 The Banbury, Brailes and Shipston Trust

6.3.1 The New Road

This road runs eastwards from Banbury to meet the Oxford, Woodstock to Stratford road at Shipston. In July 1793 Edward Cotterell wrote to Francis Canning[13] that "*the road from Banbury to Shipston has been quite abandoned and given up. The Shipston people apprehending it would be to their disadvantage to have a good road to Banbury, as it would totally decay their market. This appears to be very improbable but there is no accounting for men's opinions*". It appears that the argument of the progressives prevailed and within ten years of this correspondence a new turnpike was created, facilitating travel to Banbury markets.

An Act of 1802 created the trust to turnpike this road and in May of that year the trustees held their first meeting at the house of James Upton known as the George Inn in Lower Brailes, midway along the proposed road. The Act covered the road leading from "*the turnpike road in the Horse Fair in the town of Banbury in the County of Oxford through Swalcliffe in the County of Oxford and through Brailes in the County of Warwick, to the bridge across the River Stour in the Parish of Barcheston in the County of Warwick*". The trustees stated that the line of the road was to be "*from Banbury, along the present track of the road through the village and townships or places of Broughton, Lower Tadmarston, Upper Tadmarston and Swalcliffe and from Swalcliffe along the present line of the road to a place called Tynehill, from Tynehill to a place called Brailes, through Lower Brailes and Upper Brailes, then along the present line of the road to a place called Nollands Lane in the*

---

[13] Gloucestershire Record Office: Letter of Francis Canning [D2857/2/16].

Parish of Nonnington [Honington], *along Nollands Lane to Barcheston Grounds, along Barcheston Grounds to Barcheston Leasows, across Barcheston Leasows from Burrow Hill Gate to a bend or curve in the Hedge at a place called New Piece, and then along the present line of the road to the Bridge crossing the River Stour in the parish of Barcheston in the County of Warwick.*" The divergence of the road near Barcheston to the bridge at Shipston appear to pre-date the turnpike and was probably undertaken by the local justices.

The road ran for a similar distance through two counties and the trust created two districts, with the boundary on the Shipston side of Brailes. Timothy Cobb of Banbury, gent, and William Gillett of Upper Brailes, shopkeeper, were treasurers for the respective districts and Samuel Churchill the younger of Deddington, gent., and William Walford the younger of Banbury, gent., were to serve as the two clerks, without fee. Minutes books survive for the whole of the trust's existence.

Comparing this route with the road described by Ogilby in 1675 (Fig. 2a, page 8), it appears that the trust cut several new sections of highway. The roadway along the whole route was to be sixteen feet wide with stones, free from dirt, twelve inches deep in the middle and eight inches on each side. The individual parishes through which the turnpike ran were to provide between half a day and three days Statute Duty to assist in the maintenance of this main road. However, the major work needed to bring the road up to an adequate standard was contracted to John Pickering of Chipping Norton, road surveyor. The new road was to be made "*travellable*" by the start of August and all work completed by the 10th October at a cost of £2,057. However, at the next meeting of the trust in June it appears that the contract had been split so that the road would be travellable by the 5th July. John Smith was to make and widen the section from the Horse Fair to Sibford Ferris for £719; the rest was to be done by a consortium of Pickering and Charles Carter of Enstone, road surveyor, for £1,563. The work entailed building a new bridge over the branch of the Stour in Brailes, lowering the hill at Brailes and filling in the holloway in Breach [Bretch] Lane in the parish *[sic]* of Neithrop. Throwing down the 343 yard long bank in the holloway was done for 22 pence a yard. This work was not completed on time and the toll collector at Broughton, John Smith (also one of the contractors) was allowed £2 of his lease as a consequence of the road being unpassable by the throwing down of the hill near Long Breach. Once the new road was completed, in October 1804, John Pickering was contracted for £120 per annum, to keep in repair the whole length of the road using proper white stone. This arrangement lasted until 1821 when Mr Cave the surveyor reported adversely on the poor state of repair of Mr Pickering's district.

6.3.2 Toll-houses

The trustees quickly decided on the general location of the three toll-gates; one at the end of Broughton Lane, a second near Green End in Lower Brailes and a third near Shipston Bridge. By June 1802 the leases to collect tolls had been auctioned and the turnpike was in operation. The detailed location of the new toll-houses took some time to resolve. It was proposed that the Brailes toll-house should be at Hillocks Gate, upon the road leading out of the turnpike road to Winderton. The Broughton Toll-house was to be beside the house of Edward Marchy called or known by the name of the Twistleton's Arms.

Broughton toll-house.

The westerly toll-house was set at Leasows in Barcheston. However, there were frequent minor revisions to the plan and it was not until July 1804 that William Gillett was given approval to erect the new toll-house in the middle of Brailes Green. The cost to the trust was only £20 but they permitted him to have the newly erected turnpike-house at Brailes, in lieu. Mr Keen was to have the new toll-house on Brailes Green but relinquish the premises erected by the side-gate. It seems the original plan had been changed at some cost and a main gate and side-gate were created. In October 1804 the trustees resolved to build a new toll-gate near the Bull Bar in Banbury but this does not appear as a separate account in later documents.

There must have been concern about damage done by overloaded wagons because, in May 1808, the trust commissioned Mr Miles of Enstone, road surveyor, to erect a weighing machine near Broughton Gate; this had been removed by 1871 (Fig. 19d). The road near Broughton Gate was modified in 1834 allowing the trust to sell off 66 perches of the old road leading from the toll-house to Crouch Lane.

In 1823 the trust reduced by a quarter the tolls on horses drawing vehicles: as a result traffic must have increased since the following year the amount paid to lease the tolls actually rose by over ten percent!

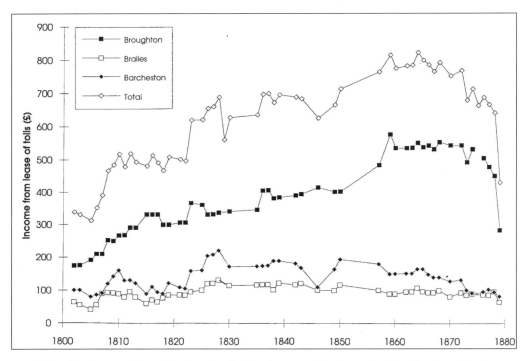

Fig. 18. Income from leasing individual gates: Banbury to Barcheston Trust.
Compare with Fig. 15, page 67.

The income from letting tolls (Fig. 18) indicates that Broughton was consistently the most valuable gate with the Barcheston gate near Shipston earning significantly less. This is evidence for greater economic activity at the Banbury end of the road. Arrangements were made for regular users of the turnpike to compound for an annual amount to give them freedom to pass through the gates; Richard Brain of Shipston had done this for his wagons, carts, carriage, horse and cattle in 1805. In 1834 a very large composition deal was struck with Samuel Hobley who was about to erect brick kilns in Neithrop. He was to pay £300 by way of compensation for tolls which would be payable for all traffic to and from the kilns. However, this arrangement ran into trouble in 1837 and again in 1842 when the trust threatened to put up a bar and collecting box across the road within a quarter mile of Banbury, on the Banbury side of Garrett's brickyard *"unless Joseph Garrett of Neithrop pays his arrears of composition money"*.

Meetings of the trust were held at Brailes, Broughton or Banbury (Figs. 19a, 19b; 19c and 19d, page 88). Although there were two clerks (Appendix 3.4), the two divisions of the road seem to have dealt with the whole road as a unit.

BANBURY, BRAILES, and SHIPSTON
TURNPIKE ROAD.

NOTICE is hereby given, That a Meeting of the Trustees of the above Turnpike Road will be held at the George Inn, in Brailes, in the county of Warwick, on Monday the 19th day of June next.

At which Meeting the Tolls arising at the Barcheston Gate and Side Gate will be LET by AUCTION, to the best bidder, between the hours of Twelve at noon and Four in the afternoon, in the manner directed by the Act passed in the 13th year of the reign of his late Majesty King George the Third, " For regulating the Turnpike Roads;" which Tolls produced the last year the sum of £122, over and above the expences of collecting them, and will be put up at that sum.

Whoever happens to be the best bidder must, at the same time, pay down one month's rent in advance, and give security, with sufficient sureties, to the satisfaction of the Trustees, for payment of the remainder of the rent, in such proportions and at such times as they shall direct.

And at the said Meeting new Trustees will be elected in the stead of those who are dead or refuse to act, and such other business done and transacted as by the Acts is required.

By order of the Trustees,
SAML. CHURCHILL,
WM. WALFORD, } Clerks.

May 18th, 1820.

Figs. 19a and 19b.

Banbury, Brailes, and Shipston Turnpike Road.

NOTICE is hereby Given, that the Annual General Meeting of the Trustees of the above Turnpike Road will be held at the house of Charles White Fowler, known by the sign of the Red Lion Inn, in Banbury, in the county of Oxford, on Friday, the twenty-sixth day of January next, at Twelve o'clock at noon, for the purpose of auditing the accounts of the trust for the past year, and transacting such other business as may be requisite.—Dated the 30th day of December, 1843.

W. WALFORD, Clerk to the Trustees.

Banbury, Brailes, and Shipston Turnpike Road.
SECOND LETTING.

NOTICE is hereby Given, that a Meeting of the Trustees of the above Turnpike Road will be held at the Twisleton Fiennes Arms Inn, in Broughton, in the County of Oxford, on Monday, the 7th day of October next, at Twelve o'clock at noon, at which Meeting, between the hours of Twelve at noon and Two in the afternoon, the Tolls arising at the Brailes Gates, on the said Road, will be LET by AUCTION, to the best bidder or bidders, for the term of two years from the 10th day of October next, in the manner directed by the Acts passed in the Third and Fourth years of the Reign of His late Majesty King George the Fourth, "For Regulating Turnpike Roads," which Tolls produced last year the sum of one hundred and twenty-one pounds, and will be put up at such sum or sums as the Trustees present shall think proper. Whoever happens to be the best bidder, must pay down immediately one months' rent in advance, and give security, with sufficient sureties, to the satisfaction of the Trustees for payment of the remainder of the rent monthly, so that at all times one months' rent shall be paid in advance. And new Trustees will be elected in the room of those who are dead or refuse to act, and such other business transacted as may be required.—Dated the 4th day of September, 1844. W. WALFORD, Clerk to the Trustees.

Figs. 19c and 19d.

Banbury, Brailes, and Shipston Turnpike Road.

NOTICE IS HEREBY GIVEN, that a meeting of the Trustees of the above Turnpike Road will be held at the Red Lion Inn, in Banbury, in the County of Oxford, on Monday, the 13th day of February, 1871, at 12 o'clock at noon, for the purpose of Electing New Trustees, Auditing the Accounts for the past year, and transacting such other business as may be requisite, and at which meeting, between the hours of Twelve at Noon and Two in the Afternoon, the Tolls arising from the several Gates upon the said Road, WILL BE LET BY AUCTION to the best bidder or bidders, for one, two, or three years; and in one or more lot or lots, as the Trustees present shall direct, from the First day of March next, in the manner directed by the Acts passed in the third and fourth years of the Reign of His late Majesty King George the Fourth, "For regulating the Turnpike Roads;" which Tolls produced at the last letting the sums following, over and above the expenses of collecting the same, and will be put up at those sums, namely.

Broughton Gate and Side Gate	£542.
Brailes Gate and Side Gate	£86.
Barcheston Gate and Side Gates	£128.

Whoever happens to be the best Bidder or Bidders, must pay down immediately one month's rent in advance, and give security with sufficient sureties, to the satisfaction of the Trustees, for payment of the remainder of the rent monthly, so that at all times one month's rent shall be kept paid in advance.

JOHN FORTESCUE,
Clerk to the Trustees.

Banbury, 11th January, 1871.

7. Running the Turnpike Trusts

The hierarchy within the trust reflected the social structure of eighteenth century England. Not surprisingly, the administration of the turnpike system was dominated by men (Tables 2 to 7); on a few occasions widows leased the tolls and a few toll collectors were female. Local aristocrats and landed gentry provided parliamentary support for the Act and then lent capital for the improvements. Minor gentry, local tradesman and the parish clergy were the active trustees who met to make decisions and help implement the plans of the trust. A local solicitor assisted in securing the Act and generally became the first clerk to the trust, dealing with all legal matters. Local businessman or the leading innholder in the larger towns would act as treasurer. The surveyors were normally men from the parishes who had working experience of the road. The collectors of the tolls were local people with rudimentary education. By the end of the eighteenth century it had become common practise to lease the right to collect the tolls. Initially local tradesmen took this opportunity to risk their capital to earn the profit from toll collection but by the nineteenth century, many of the leases were taken, either directly or indirectly, by professional toll collectors (Tables 2 to 7). These men often leased several gates and installed local collectors to attend the gates.

7.1 Finance and Capital

Loans, often of between £50 and £500, were raised against the security of the tolls and this capital then applied to improvements to the road, erection of milestones and construction of toll-gates. Most of the capital was raised soon after creation of a new trust but powers to borrow more money were frequently included in renewals of the Acts. This new capital was then used to finance major improvements such as easing steep slopes or building new bridges. Very few of the aristocratic supporters of the turnpike Act or the chief financiers such as Lord Warwick, Lord Bridgewater, the Earls of Guilford and Dartmouth (see Appx. 3, p.150), participated directly in the subsequent operation of the trust. Bondholders were prepared to forego interest payments until the trust had become well established and almost all trusts mentioned their inability to pay off the principal on the initial loans when seeking to renew their powers, generally 21 years after the initial Act. Loans were rarely repaid in the lifetime of the lender and interest was normally between four and five percent. Smaller trusts were often unable to make even these annual interest payments. In addition, when the trusts were finally closed, the heirs of these investors received back only a fraction of the capital. Although on a national scale some trusts overstretched themselves and failed to repay loans made in the mid-nineteenth century, the trusts around Banbury seem to have cleared most of their debts before they were wound-up (Appx. 2).

The return on turnpike bonds contrasts markedly with investment in canals where it is said that the Coventry to Oxford Canal paid a dividend of up to thirty percent in good years.[1] Turnpike trusts were a safe investment, which in most cases continued to give a steady but unspectacular return over several lifetimes. The original bondholders were presumably motivated by a sense of patrician duty and local pride so their returns did not have to be exclusively financial. For instance, in 1853, when proposing to write off some of the debt, the clerk to the Drayton to Edgehill Trust argued that most of the bondholders were local landowners who presumably would have to pay rates to the parishes if the turnpike had not existed. Later investors included several clergymen, widows and spinsters who were looking for small, low risk investments which gave a reliable income.

The active trustees were the local worthies in towns such as Banbury and Brackley. One of the trustees acted as chairman at meetings, but the job often seems to have fallen to one person of some authority. For instance in 1830, the Banbury to Burford Trust complemented the Rev. A.W. Ford for his role as chairman over the previous twelve years. The trustees treated these activities as a civic duty, though they clearly benefited from the improvement in trade which good roads brought. They worked hard to make their town important in other ways; for example Mr Douglas was complemented by the trustees of the Drayton to Edgehill Trust for his *"great exertions in attaining the Mail coach through this county, the same having a great public accommodation to this town and neighbourhood."*

Innkeepers were prominent among the active supporters of the trusts. They were obvious beneficiaries of increased traffic but also acted as local financiers and money lenders and so were suitable treasurers. For instance, Francis Edge acted as treasurer for the Drayton to Edgehill Trust and was an original trustee of both the Drayton to Edgehill and the Ryton Bridge Trusts, formed in 1753 and 1755 respectively. He was landlord of the Three Tuns in Banbury[2] and had interests in the "Old Stage Coach" which ran the principal service between Birmingham, Warwick, Banbury and London.[3] He later moved to Potterspury on the Watling Street[4] and William Barker, a London vintner, took over the Three Tuns and later treasurership of the trust.

---

[1] Cooper, N., *Aynho*, Banbury Historical Society **20**, and Leopard's Head Press (1984), 261.
[2] Gibson, J., "The Three Tuns in the Eighteenth Century", *C&CH*.**8**.1 (Autumn 1979), 5-12.
[3] *JOJ*, 1753.
[4] *JOJ*, May 1756.

However, in May 1771[5] Barker was declared bankrupt and gave up the inn and his responsibilities to the trust. James Haddon, Edge's son-in-law, took on the Three Tuns for a while[6] but in 1782 he moved to West Bromwich, leaving William Pratt at the Red Lion to take on the role as leading innkeeper. Pratt and his successor at the Red Lion, William Edwards, leased toll-gates on the local turnpikes (Tables 2 to 7).[7]

7.2 Clerks and Surveyors

The main expenditure for the trust was associated with the construction and maintenance of the roadway. A further significant cost was the salaries of officials, notably the clerk who acted as chief administrator and the surveyor who organised the labour and materials for work on the road. The clerk to the trust was generally a local attorney. Several of these individuals were also active in promoting the creation of the turnpikes but if they took up paid positions on the trust, such as clerk, they could not be trustees. For instance, Samuel Churchill, an active supporter of turnpiking, had to resign as a trustee when he became clerk to the Aynho Division in 1829. Some attorneys, such as the Churchills, were clerks to several trusts. Two Samuel Churchills (Snr and Jnr) of Deddington, acted as clerks to the Deddington to Kidlington Trust, the Bicester to Enstone Trust, the Bicester to Aynho Trust and the Banbury to Shipston Trust. A letter kept in the records of the latter trust records Samuel Jnr's regret in having to give up his responsibilities when he moved to Summertown, near Oxford, in March 1839. He records that his father was the projector of the road and had advanced money on security of the tolls (about £50). Samuel himself had helped secure the Act and became clerk to the trust, alongside William Walford, in 1802. Subsequent generations of the Churchill family were not so diligent and in 1871 the trustees of the Oxford to Adderbury Turnpike were inconvenienced by *the abrupt disappearance* of Mr Henry Churchill their clerk (Fig. 13f, p.61). Enthusiasm for the business of the trusts faded as the initial novelty wore off and meetings of trustees were frequently adjourned because they were not quorate. For example in advertising a meeting of the Deddington to Adderbury Trust,[8] John Walker stated that *"trustees are specifically desired to attend as no business could be done at the last two meetings for want of sufficient number of them"*.

---

[5] *JOJ*, May 1771.

[6] *JOJ*, July 1780.

[7] For the Red Lion, see Wood, V., *The Licensees of the Inns, Taverns and Beerhouses of Banbury*, Oxon. FHS (1998), 85-87. and Gibson, J., "An Historic Photograph Discovered", *C&CH*.**10**.6 (Summer 1987), 147-50. William Edwards is not named as a licensee by Wood.

[8] *JOJ*, Aug. 1770.

The job of surveyor became important as the traffic using the road increased in the late eighteenth century. Professional road surveyors were given more responsibility under contracts to keep the road in good repair and make use of the Statute Labour. In 1819 the trustees of the Drayton to Edgehill Turnpike proposed that a single, professional surveyor be employed by all the trusts around Banbury. After consultation with the great road engineer McAdam, they chose George Cave of Bodicote, who was already surveyor on the Towcester to Weston Turnpike at £2/week. He also acted for the roads through Brackley and for the Banbury to Wykham section of the Banbury Division. He had been *"employed under the direction of Mr McAdam"* whose technique for creating an inexpensive but effective highway was to have well drained foundations and form a water repellent surface by compacting small angular stones. Cave eventually became surveyor for most roads in the area ensuring that common standard was applied across this part of the Cotswolds. George was succeeded as surveyor by Charles Cave who continued in this post until his death in 1856, after which George and Charles junior took on the work.

The Cave family were also wharfingers and coal merchants on the Coventry canal at Banbury, so that they could supply many of the materials which were needed for repair of the road. Several trusts showed a preference for Hartshill stone which was imported into the area along the canal. For instance the Drayton to Edgehill Trust paid £300 for Hartshill stone in 1853 and £480 the next year, at 9s. per ton. In 1869 they bought 300 tons at 5s.6d. per ton and 1s.2d. per ton haulage cost.

7.3 Toll Collection

A person had to be present at the gate to collect the tolls from travellers. Payments to the toll-gatherer appear in several minutes books. Most of the other incidental costs of operation were lost in the combined accounts but there is one entry for the printing of *"tickets for the Gates £1.8s."* by Charles Hide of Banbury. The Chappel on the Heath to Bourton Trust paid 10s. for 4,000 tickets to be printed in 1760.

Initially the trusts themselves employed men to collect the tolls. For example, after its creation in 1755, one of the first actions of the Ryton Bridge Trust was to appoint three gate keepers at a salary of 4s. per week. These gate keepers also seem to have acted as surveyors for their respective sections of road. By 1759 payments for *"use of the road"* are made to John Burgess, collector at Ladbrooke, William Glaze, collector at Hardwick, and Robert Webb, collector at Stretton.

Employees may not have been diligent toll collectors, but in 1770 Jonathan Burgess and William Glaze were each given 5s. *"for their care and trouble in seizing supernumerary horses"*. (Limiting the number of horses on a wagon was intended to exclude very heavy wagons that would damage the road unduly.) The collectors paid their takings to the treasurer of the trust each week but by the 1760s individual collectors were occasionally leasing the gates for several months at a fixed rent, keeping any excess income themselves.

In 1766, John Trinder at Middleton Gate, Richard Morris at Moreton Gate and Richard Pickering at Salford Gate were each paid 5s./week as toll collectors for the Chappel on the Heath to Bourton Trust. On the Drayton to Edgehill Turnpike, created in 1753, tolls were initially taken by salaried collectors employed by the trustees. However, in 1772 these trustees also adopted the policy of putting the lease of the tolls up to auction. This road seems to have stagnated as the salaries paid to collectors on the occasions when the collection was taken in hand by the trust had fallen to only 3s.6d. per week in 1804.

Like other eighteenth century trusts, the Banbury to Lutterworth trust, created in 1765, administered the collection of tolls itself, but in 1768 they decided to lease out the collection of tolls. Advertisements for the lease of tolls were placed in the Northampton, Coventry and Oxford newspapers at a cost of £1.18s. in 1773. By the 1780s, most trusts were advertising the sale of leases for toll collection. These auction notices give details of the amount paid for the lease of the preceding period and are an important source of information on the changes in the relative value of individual toll-gates and the overall income to particular trusts (Appendix 2).

The Banbury to Barcheston Trust, created in 1803, adopted the policy of auctioning leases from the beginning. The auctions were normally held at one of the larger hostelries on the turnpike and the trust paid for limited entertainment of those bidding. A small trust such as the Drayton to Edgehill expended 10s. for punch, much less extravagant than larger trusts would provide. The Bicester to Aynho trust paid Edward Deakins £2 for entertainment of the "bidders for tolls" at the King's Arms at Bicester. A general Turnpike Act specified that the bidding should be managed with a minute glass, which was to be turned three times before a final offer was accepted. The lease was normally put up at the value paid the previous year and bids generally ran upwards from here. In 1833, at the auctioning of the gates on the Banbury to Burford road, the Wykham Gate was put up at £321. Thomas Keene, an important farmer of tolls, took the bidding up to £344 but the gate was finally taken by Samuel Tidmarsh at £371.

Keene took the bidding for the Chapel Gate from £182 to £232 but lost to Harris at £233. In other instances no bids were received at the offer price and the gate was taken in hand by the trustees (e.g. this happened at Burford Gate in 1822) or a lower, private offer was accepted by a group of trustees after the auction.

During the late eighteenth century the existing gate-keepers and surveyors seem to have taken responsibility for individual gates on the Weston to Towcester Turnpike. These were generally local men and they may have lived in the toll-house. William Allen leased the Middleton Gate for almost twenty years, occasionally taking a lease on other gates on roads around Bicester and Brackley. As the amount of money handled by the trusts increased, new investors were drawn into bidding for leases (Tables 2 to 7). Thomas Thomson, a shagweaver of Banbury, is an example of an investor without an obvious involvement in road transport. William Ingram was probably a local investor who employed the old gatekeepers to take the tolls, hoping to make a profit by holding costs well below the income received at the gate. By the early nineteenth century a new class of professional toll collector had emerged. William Edwards seems to have been based at the Red Lion in Banbury but leased gates on the Stokenchurch and Fyfield Turnpikes. William Avinall of Burford leased gates on the Fyfield road as well as on the Edgehill road. Thomas Keen of Yarnton was a major toll-collector in the area. He leased a number of gates each year in southern Oxfordshire including those on major roads such as the Stokenchurch and the Henley Turnpikes. Based on the home address of lessees, several of them operated nationally. Joseph Tonge leased gates as far afield as Manchester and Hertfordshire, Adam Williams operated on the Watling Street and Bicester Roads and Thomas Gardner leased gates in Exeter and Oxfordshire. These men clearly amassed considerable amounts of capital. Keene was also able to act as guarantors for other gatekeepers (e.g. on the Burford to Banbury road), to loan capital to trusts when they were set up and to help finance the activities of minor gatekeepers.

The professional farmers of tolls could not collect the tolls nor reside at all the gates that they leased. Hence they employed pikemen or collectors who lived at the gate and actually took the tolls. The residents at most of the toll-houses at the time of the 1851 census (Table 8, page 95) were almost all employees of the lessee. They appear to be family people who would appreciate the accommodation that came with the job. A basic proficiency in writing and arithmetic would have been essential for this type of work.

Table 8: Occupiers of Toll-houses at time of 1851 Census (lessees marked *)

Toll-Gate	Collector	Age	Residents	Birth Place
Adderbury, Twyford Lane	Edward Catch	51	3	Adderbury
Adderbury	James Goode	46	5	Broughton
Neithrop, Hardwick	John Edwards	40	1	Adderbury
Neithrop, Wykham	William Mason	50	2	Alderminster
Bicester, Wretchwick	John East	49	1	Weston
Middleton Stoney	George Sharman	35	3	Shotswell (Warks)
Swerford	Susannah Smith	36	5	Dorn (Worcs)
Broughton	William Cox	34	2	Woodhurst
Grimsbury Green	Sarah Bagley	54	4	Adderbury
Banbury Bridge	Sarah Polton	35	8	Swerford
Williamscott	Hannah Ward	47	3	Wardington
	Ann Jackman	35	8	Deddington
Bicester, Sheep Street	John Cuming *	48	3	Walkhampton (Devon)
Fritwell Bar	Fanny Godfrey	39	4	Souldern
Fringford	Frederick Eyles	64	5	Stratton Audley
Weston 1	Elizabeth Brain	34	2	Weston
Weston 2	Hannah Clarke	24	4	Weston
Fulbrook	John Franklin	63	1	Burford
Deddington, Oxford Road	Richard Busby	47	5	Curbridge
Deddington, Chipping Norton Road	Thomas Shreives	56	5	Pasenham
Gosford	Thomas Hughes	36	2	Gt Marlow
Finmere, Bacon Wood	William Baxter	25	2	Stretton (Derby)

8. Traffic through Banbury: Coaches and Passengers

The toll charges on each of the turnpikes illustrate the variety of vehicles and animals using these roads (Fig. 20). These users fall into three broad categories: (i) passengers' transport; (ii) goods carriers; and (iii) drovers' animals. The first of these classes includes private individuals on horse back, private post-chaises and public transport, particularly stage coaches. The second class covers wagons and wains carrying merchandise between major towns as well as carts and vans operated by local carriers and tradesmen. The third category includes sheep and cattle being driven from farm to market and then on to urban areas for slaughter.

The Tolls. For every Coach, Berlin, Landau, Chariot, Chaise, or Calash, drawn by Six Horses or Mares, the Sum of One Shilling;

For every Coach, Berlin, Landau, Chariot, Chair, Calash, or Chaise, drawn by Four Horses or Mares, the Sum of Nine Pence.

For every Coach, Berlin, Landau, Chariot, Chaise, Calash, or Chair; drawn by Two Horses or Mares, the Sum of Six Pence, or drawn by One Horse or Mare, the Sum of Three Pence.

For every Waggon, Wain, Carr, Cart, or Carriage, drawn by Five or more Horses or Oxen, if belonging to a common Carrier, the Sum of Eight Pence; if to a Farmer, not usually carrying for Hire, the Sum of Four Pence; and drawn by Four Horses or Oxen, the Sum of Three Pence; and drawn by Two or Three Horses or Oxen, the Sum of Two Pence; and drawn by One Horse or Mare, the Sum of One Penny.

For every Horse, Mare, Mule, or Ass, laden or unladen, and not drawing, the Sum of One Penny.

For every Drove of Oxen, Cows, or Neat Cattle, the Sum of Ten Pence a Score; and so in Proportion for every greater or less Number.

For every Drove of Calves, Hogs, Sheep, or Lambs, the Sum of Four Pence a Score; and so in Proportion for any greater or less Number.

Fig. 20a. Typical toll charges on Turnpikes: Woodstock to Rollright Lane, 1751.

Banbury was on one of Ogilby's main highways from the Midlands to London and so benefited from traffic that passed through the town as well as traffic that originated in the locality. In 1637 there were three carrier services per week passing through this area and another eleven originating within it. The road appears to have remained difficult into the mid-eighteenth century since, in 1738, one of the carriers from Stratford was still using packhorses. The number of services grew slightly in the early eighteenth century but by 1790 (Table 12, pages 116-17), when the turnpike network was established, there were actually fewer carrier services per week (six from beyond the area and potentially six from within it).

For every Horse or other Beast or Cattle drawing any Coach, Stage Coach, Omnibus, Barouche, Landau, Chariot, Chaise, Phaeton, Curricle, Hearse, Break, Litter, Chair, Gig, Cart upon Springs of any Kind, or other Four or Two wheeled Carriage of the like Description, by whatever Name called or known, the Sum of Four-pence :

For every Horse or other Beast or Cattle drawing any Waggon, Wain, Cart, or other Carriage of the like Description, having the Fellies of the Wheels thereof of the Breadth of Six Inches and upwards at the Bottom or Soles thereof, the Sum of Four-pence :

For every Horse or other Beast or Cattle drawing any Waggon, Wain, Cart, or other Carriage of the like Description, having the Fellies of the Wheels thereof of the Breadth of Four and a Half Inches and less than Six Inches at the Bottom or Soles thereof, the Sum of Five-pence :

For every Horse or other Beast or Cattle drawing any Waggon, Wain, Cart, Caravan, or other Carriage of the like Description, having the Fellies of the Wheels thereof of less Breadth than Four and a Half Inches at the Bottom or Soles thereof, the Sum of Sixpence :

For every Coach, Chaise, or other Carriage whatsoever with Four Wheels affixed to any Waggon or Cart, the Sum of Eight-pence :

For every Carriage with Two Wheels affixed to any Waggon or Cart, the Sum of Four-pence :

For every Coach, Waggon, or other Carriage, of whatever Description, propelled, drawn, or moved by Steam or Machinery, or any other than Animal Power, the Sum of Eight-pence :

For any Dog or Goat drawing any Cart or Carriage, Truck, Barrow, or other Thing, the Sum of Two-pence :

For every Horse, Mule, or Ass, laden or unladen, and not drawing, the Sum of Two-pence :

For every Drove of Oxen, Cows, or Neat Cattle, not drawing or laden, the Sum of Ten-pence *per* Score, and so in proportion for any less Number :

For every Horse, Mule, or other Beast drawing any Coach, Chariot, Landau, Berlin, Vis-a-vis, Barouche, Phaeton, Curricle, Calash, Chaise, Chair, Gig, Whiskey, Taxed Cart, Caravan, Hearse, Litter, or other such Carriage, the Sum of Sixpence :

For every Horse, Mule, or other Beast drawing any Waggon, Wain, Cart, or other such Carriage, having Wheels of the Breadth of Nine Inches in the Fellies or Sole thereof, the Sum of Four-pence :

For every Horse, Mule, or other Beast drawing any Waggon, Wain, Cart, or other such Carriage having Wheels of the Breadth of Six Inches, and less than Nine Inches in the Fellies or Sole thereof, the Sum of Sixpence :

For every Horse or other Beast of Draught drawing any Waggon, Wain, Cart, or other such Carriage, having Wheels of less Breadth than Six Inches, the Sum of Nine-pence :

For every Horse, Mule, or Ass, not drawing, the Sum of Two-pence :

For every Drove of Oxen or Neat Cattle, the Sum of One Shilling and Three-pence *per* Score, and so in Proportion for any greater or less Number : And,

For every Drove of Calves, Hogs, Sheep, or Lambs, the Sum of Ten-pence *per* Score, and so in Proportion for any greater or less Number.

Figs. 20b, 20c. Toll charges: Weston to Towcester, 1820; Woodstock to Rollright Lane, 1846

For every Coach, Sociable, Berlin, Landau, Chariot, Vis-à-Vis, Barouch, Chaise Marine, Calash, Curricle, Chair, Gigg, Whisky, Caravan, Hearse, Litter, or other such like Carriage, drawn by more than Four Horses or other Beasts of Draught, the Sum of Two Shillings ; and drawn by Four Horses or other Beasts of Draught, the Sum of One Shilling and Sixpence ; and drawn by Two Horses or other Beasts of Draught, the Sum of One Shilling ; and drawn by One Horse or other Beast of Draught, the Sum of Sixpence :

For every Drug so constructed as that the Distance between the Axletrees shall be more than Nine Feet, and laden otherwise than with a single Piece or Block of Timber or Stone, the Sum of One Shilling and Sixpence, over and above the Toll or Duty payable for each of the Horses or Beasts of Draught drawing the same :

For every Horse, Mare, Gelding, Mule, Ass, Ox, or Bullock, drawing any Waggon, Wain, Drug, Cart, or other such like Carriage, the Sum of Four-pence :

For every Horse, Mare, Gelding, Mule, or Ass, laden or unladen, and not drawing, the Sum of One Penny Halfpenny :

For every Drove of Oxen or Neat Cattle, the Sum of Ten-pence *per* Score, and so in Proportion for any less Number : And,

For every Drove of Calves, Swine, Sheep, or Lambs, the Sum of Five-pence *per* Score, and so in Proportion for any less Number :

Fig. 20d. Toll charges: Banbury to Lutterworth, 1840.

Nevertheless, in the nineteenth century the services were operated by wagons so that each vehicle would have had a greater carrying capacity than the carts or packhorses used by earlier carriers. Based on the evidence in London trade directories, the route through Banbury failed to capture the growing stream of both carrier and coach traffic that flowed from the Midlands to London along the Watling Street and roads through Oxford. This disparity was more apparent with coach traffic so that a particularly high proportion of the advertised services along the Banbury road was carriers and wagoners.

Table 9: Carriers and Coachmasters recorded in Banbury and Buckingham Areas

SURNAME	FIRST NAME	Town	Trade	Decade	Records
Stokes	Henry	Banbury	carrier	1620	will
Jordon	John	Banbury	wagoner	1680	Dir
Christmas	Leonard	Banbury	carrier	1690	will
Jordan	widow	Banbury	wagoner	1690	Dir
Westcare	Thomas	Banbury	carrier	1690	Dir
Dance	Thomas	Banbury	coachmaster	1700	Advert
Church	William	Banbury	coachmaster	1700	Advert
Bull	Samuel	Banbury	carrier	1700	OUCar
White	John	Banbury	carrier	1700	OUCar
Judd	Isaac	Banbury	carrier	1700	OUCar
Edge	Francis	Banbury	coachmaster	1750	Advert
King	William	Banbury	wagoner	1760	will
Barker	W	Banbury	coachmaster	1760	Advert
Garfield	Richard	Banbury	wagoner	1760	Advert
Judd	William	Banbury	wagoner	1760	Dir
Cooke	Samuel	Banbury	wagoner	1760	Papers
Allam	William	Banbury	wagoner	1770	Advert
Hill	John	Banbury	coachmaster	1770	Advert
Drinkwater	Francis	Banbury	wagoner	1770	Advert
Barrett	John	Banbury	wagoner	1770	Advert
Gulliver		Banbury	carrier	1780	OUCar
Clarke		Banbury	carrier	1780	OUCar
Mills		Banbury	carrier	1780	OUCar
Pratt & partners		Banbury	coachmaster	1780	Advert
Bennet		Banbury	wagoner	1790	Dir
Drinkwater	J	Banbury	coachmaster	1810	Advert
Drinkwater	George	Banbury	coachmaster	1810	Advert
Stone	Henry	Banbury	wagoner	1810	Dir

SURNAME	FIRST NAME	Town	Trade	Decade	Records
Parker		Banbury	wagon	1830	Advert
Green		Banbury	wagon	1830	Advert
Chamberlin	Edmond	Adderbury	carrier	1720	OUCar
Drinkwater	Benjamin	Deddington	wagoner	1770	Advert
Ewins	Richard	Bicester	wagoner	1680	Dir
Phillips	William	Bicester	carrier	1780	Dir/Ins
Bowden		Bicester	wagoner	1790	Dir
Kirby	Richard	Bicester	wagoner	1790	Dir
Edmonds	William	Bicester	carrier	1850	will
Willes	William	Charlbury	wagoner	1690	Dir
Willis		Charlbury	wagoner	1680	Dir
Eagles	Ezra	Cropredy	carrier	1780	Insur
Barrett	John	Hook Norton	wagoner	1690	Dir
Borsbury	John	Hook Norton	carrier	1840	will
Hammond	Thomas	Over Norton	coachmaster	1750	will
Morgan		Woodstock	wagoner	1690	Dir
Bellinger	Adam	Woodstock	carrier	1710	Insur
Garfield	William	Woodstock	wagoner	1750	Advert
Alcock	William	Woodstock	coachman	1760	will
Lord	William	Woodstock	coachman	1810	will
Holmes	Charles	Woodstock	coachmaster	1820	Advert
Higgins	John	Woodstock	carrier	1830	will
Webster	John	Buckingham	carrier	1680	Dir
Webster	Philip	Buckingham	carrier	1680	Dir
Webster		Buckingham	carrier	1730	Papers
Meads	Zachary	Buckingham	carrier	1740	Papers
Jones		Buckingham	carrier	1740	Papers
Watson	John	Buckingham	coachmaster	1760	Advert
Eagles	Hannah	Buckingham	carrier	1780	Insur
Stuckbury		Buckingham	wagoner	1790	Dir
Rogers & Malens		Buckingham	carrier	1800	Dir
Cole	Thomas	Marsh Gibbon	carrier	1680	Dir
West		Marsh Gibbon	carrier	1690	Dir
Hemmons	William	Brickhill	carrier	1690	Dir
Bedford	Robert	Brill	carrier	1680	Dir

Insur = Sun Insurance policy; Papers include Purefoy papers; OUCar= Registered University carrier: Dir = Thomas deLaune 1681/91; Universal Directory 1790; Bates Directory 1836; Adverts in Oxford Journal and Reading Mercury; Rusher's Banbury List.

Table 9 (pages 98-99) lists individual carriers and coachmasters from around Banbury and Buckingham. None of these businesses was of national importance but several generations of carriers earned a respectable living transporting goods along the turnpike network between Warwickshire, Oxfordshire, Buckinghamshire and London. [1]

8.1 Coach Services

The 1681 London directory lists one coach service per week from Warwick to London; this presumably ran through Banbury (Table 10b). An advertisement of 1705 clearly routes the Stratford to London coach through Kineton, Banbury and Aylesbury. This service left Stratford at four in the morning and *"if God Permits"* performed the service to London in two days. A note on this advertisement states that the coach from Banbury took just one day. This is confirmed by an advertisement published four years later. Charles Stokes was landlord of the Three Tuns, on Horse Fair, and his brother-in-law Daniel Style was at the Unicorn in the Market Place.[2]

Table 10a: Coach Services using Roads around Banbury
Services originating in and around Banbury: **Coaches to London**

Year	Operator	Starts	Via	London Inn	Schedule	Journey	Source
1705	Stoakes & Style	Banbury	Aylesbury	Black Bull, Holborn	Twice per week,	1 day	Advert (WRO)
1709	Stoakes, Dance & Church	Three Tuns Banbury	White Hart, Aylesbury	Black Bull, Holborn	Twice per week,	1 day in summer, 2 in winter	Advert (WRO)
1760	Sandeford & Jenken	Three Tuns Banbury	Star, Oxford	Oxford Arms, Warwick Lane	Twice per week,	One & a half days	Advert (JOJ)
1790	Stamp & Co	Banbury	Buckingham	Bell & Crown, Holborn	Thrice per week		Univ Brit Dir
1790	Pratt & Co (The Expedition)	Red Lion, Banbury					Advert (JOJ)
1836	Hearn & Co (The Union)	Banbury	Aylesbury	King's Arms, Snowhill	Thrice per week		Bates

By May 1731 a stage coach service had begun between the Swan Inn, Birmingham, and London, through Warwick, Banbury and Aylesbury. The advertisement shows a vehicle pulled by six horses with no outside passengers

---

[1] For the Jordan family, see page 115. For Leonard Christmas (d.1692/3) see Gibson, J., "Christmas come but once...", *C&CH* **10**.6 (1987), 151-2.

[2] See Gibson, J. "A Century of Tavern-Keeping, 1: The Stokes family at the Unicorn and Three Tuns.", *C&CH* **7**.4 (1977). Charles Stokes' grandfather Henry (d.1628) was the carrier listed on page 98.

and a postillion on the lead horse. It was operated by Nicholas Rothwell and took two and a half days, leaving Birmingham at 6 a.m. on Monday and reached the Red Lion, Aldersgate, London on the morning of Wednesday.[3] The fare from Warwick to London was 18s. The Birmingham and Warwick Flying stage coach, advertised in 1753,[4] set out from the White Swan in Birmingham at 3 a.m. to spend the night at the New Inn, Oxford before going on to London the following day. It passed through Stratford and Banbury, where Francis Edge at the Three Tuns[5] was one of the proprietors. The advertisement added that *"To oblige such gentlemen and ladies as find it inconvenient to rise so early"* (sic), there was another stage coach which left at 6 a.m., taking three days to reach London, spending the first night at Banbury, and the second at the White Hart, Aylesbury.

Table 10b: Coach Services using Roads around Banbury
Important Services originating beyond Banbury: **Coaches to London**

Year	Operator	Starts	Via	London Inn	Schedule	Journey	Source
1681	Richard Newcombe	Stratford	Banbury	Belle Savage, Ludgate Hill	Once per week (coach & wagon; wagon only in 1691)		De Laune
1705	Stokes, & Style	Swan, Stratford	Kington, Banbury, Aylesbury	Bell, Holborn	Once per week,	2 days in winter	Advert (WRO)
1731	Rothwell	Swan, Birmingham	Warwick, Banbury, Aylesbury	Red Lion, Aldersgate		2½ days	Advert (Potts)
1753	Peyton, Edge, Turner, Turner	White Swan, Birmingham	Warwick, Banbury, Oxford	Bull & Mouth, Aldersgate	Twice per week	Two days	Advert (JOJ)
1775	Payton & Manning	Swan, Warwick	Stratford	Bull & Mouth, Aldersgate	Four times per week		Advert (JOJ)
1790	Mountain & Co	Chester & Kidderminster	Banbury, Aylesbury	Saracen's Head, Snowhill	Daily		Univ Brit Dir
1836	Hearn & Co (Royal Mail)	Stourport	Birmingham, Banbury	King's Arms, Snowhill	daily		Bates
1836	Hearn & Co, (The Sovereign)	Leamington	Aylesbury	King's Arms, Snowhill	Daily		Bates

---

[3] Potts W. 2nd ed. rev. Clark E.T., *A History of Banbury*, Gulliver Press, Banbury, 1978, 225.
[4] *JOJ*, 1753.
[5] See Gibson J. "The Three Tuns in the Eighteenth Century", *C&CH.***8**.1 (Autumn 1979), 5.

Fig. 21. William Barker's billhead whilst he was landlord at the Three Tuns,
  Banbury, some time between 1756 and 1768 [Bodleian MS North, c.21].

By the middle of the eighteenth century, improvements in the roads were making it possible for operators to replace the heavy vehicles illustrated in Fig. 23 (page 104) with lighter and faster *machines*. In 1760 the Banbury Machine was running from the Three Tuns, Banbury,[6] to London for a fare of 16s for an inside seat (Fig. 22a). The proprietors were Mr Barker at Banbury (Three Tuns), Mr Sandeford of the Star in Oxford where the coach "lies" the first night and Mr Jenken of the Green Man & Still, the London terminus.

In 1773 the Machine reached London in one day, along the turnpikes through Buckingham and Winslow. A service from Warwick through Oxford to London is assumed to have passed through Banbury in 1775 (Fig. 22b).

---

[6] As footnote 5.

BANBURY MACHINE to LONDON,

In One Day and a Half, by Way of Oxford,

SETS out from Mr. Barker's, the Three Tuns in Banbury, on Friday next, the 30th of May Inst. and will continue to go from the same Place every Monday and Friday at One o'Clock; lies at the Star in the Corn-market Oxford, and is in London the next Day: Likewise sets out from the Oxford-Arms, in Warwick-lane, London, every Monday and Friday at Five o'Clock, and is in Banbury the next Morning. —— Places taken at the Three Tuns in Banbury, and at the Oxford Arms in Warwick-lane London. Price Sixteen Shillings; Ten Shillings to be paid on taking the Places. Each Passenger allowed 20lb. and for all above to pay a Penny a Pound.

Performed by W. BARKER, in Banbury.
R. SANDEFORD, in Oxford; and
E. JENKEN, at the Green Man and Still, the Corne of Swallow-Street, Oxford-Road, London.

N. B. They will not be answerable for Money, Bills, or Plate, unless Notice be given and paid for as such.

Fig. 22a. The Banbury Machine to London, 1760.

WARWICK, OXFORD, and LONDON MACHINE,
In One Day.

THIS is to acquaint the Gentlemen, Traders, and others, of Warwick, that a CARRIAGE was forwarded to and from Stratford, and will continue going four times a Week, viz. every Monday, Tuesday, Thursday, and Friday, for the purpose of conveying Passengers and Parcels between London and Warwick. Those who are inclined to encourage this undertaking, will please to observe, that they may engage their places for London at the Swan Inn in Birmingham, on Monday and Friday evenings in the Post-Coach; and on Tuesday and Thursday evenings in the Machine; and from the Bull-and-Mouth Inn, in Bull-and-Mouth-street, London, every evening for Warwick, either in the Machine, Post-Coach, or Diligence, and will be forwarded from Stratford with the utmost expedition, to the Swan Inn, in Warwick.

Performed by their obedient humble Servants,
JOHN PAYTON, Stratford,
SAMUEL MANNING. London.

N. B. Fare from Warwick to London, viz. in the Post-Coach 1 l. 4 s.—Machine 1 l. 1 s.—Diligence 1 l. 1 s.

Parcels, &c. taken the greatest care of.

N. B. The Proprietors will not be answerable for Money, Plate, Jewels, or other Things of Value, unless entered as such, and paid for accordingly.

Fig. 22b. The Warwick, Oxford and London Machine, 1775.

Fig. 23a. Early eighteenth century passenger vehicles.

Fig 23b. The equivalent in the early nineteenth century.
The Blenheim coach outside the Star Inn, Oxford, 1826.

By the 1789 the Red Lion, owned by William Pratt, had become the principal coaching inn in Banbury. *The Expedition*, the first coach going direct from Banbury to London, began running in December 1790, performed by Pratt & Partners.[7]

Local coach services were run by Mr Drinkwater whose coach from Banbury to Oxford, advertised in 1789, went through Woodstock, taking five hours and costing 5s. (Fig. 22c). By 1792, the ticket for Drinkwater's service from the Catherine Wheel had risen to 7s.[8] Francis Drinkwater had operated the Banbury, Woodstock to Oxford stage wagon until 1773 and Benjamin Drinkwater ran a stage wagon service from Deddington to London in 1776. Their coaching operation was run from Hopcroft's Holt (fig. 24, page 107), a convenient staging inn halfway between Oxford and Banbury. However, in 1819 they sold this to J.W. Churchill and may have used the receipts to finance extending their Post Coach Service, *The Regulator*, to Warwick and Birmingham (Figs. 22d, 22e).

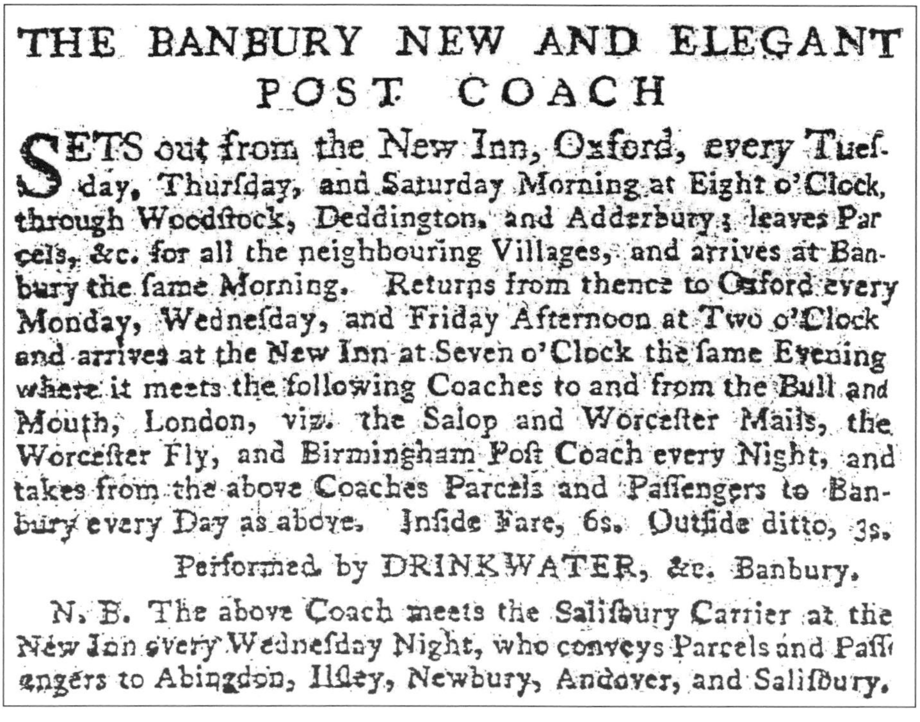

THE BANBURY NEW AND ELEGANT POST COACH

SETS out from the New Inn, Oxford, every Tuesday, Thursday, and Saturday Morning at Eight o'Clock, through Woodstock, Deddington, and Adderbury; leaves Parcels, &c. for all the neighbouring Villages, and arrives at Banbury the same Morning. Returns from thence to Oxford every Monday, Wednesday, and Friday Afternoon at Two o'Clock and arrives at the New Inn at Seven o'Clock the same Evening where it meets the following Coaches to and from the Bull and Mouth, London, viz. the Salop and Worcester Mails, the Worcester Fly, and Birmingham Post Coach every Night, and takes from the above Coaches Parcels and Passengers to Banbury every Day as above. Inside Fare, 6s. Outside ditto, 3s.

Performed by DRINKWATER, &c. Banbury.

N. B. The above Coach meets the Salisbury Carrier at the New Inn every Wednesday Night, who conveys Parcels and Passengers to Abingdon, Ilsley, Newbury, Andover, and Salisbury.

Fig. 22c. Banbury to Oxford via Woodstock, 1789.

---

[7] *JOJ*, Dec. 1790.
[8] As footnote 3, Potts/Clark, *A History of Banbury*.

The routes through Banbury were in competition with other roads for the lucrative through-traffic. For instance the services from Birmingham to Oxford could use the road through Enstone and Stratford and coaches for Warwick were able to use the Watling Street. Banbury was on the important stage coach route in the eighteenth century and was fortunate in attracting one of the prestigious Mail routes through the town. However, it appears that it was less favoured by the high speed coaches of the nineteenth century.

> # Regulator Post Coach.
> ## G. & J. DRINKWATER
> RESPECTFULLY inform their friends and the public in general, that they have started their COACH every day from the ANGEL INN, OXFORD, through BANBURY, SOUTHAM, LEAMINGTON, and WARWICK, to BIRMINGHAM. This Coach meets a Warwick Coach that starts immediately through Coventry, Bedworth, Nuneaton, Hinkley, and Earl Shilton, to the Three Cranes, LEICESTER, where it arrives positively at Eight o'clock the same evening.
>
> N. B. The above Coach returns every day from Birmingham, at Eight o'clock, on its way to Oxford

Fig. 22d.. Drinkwater's and Churchill's operations.

HOPCROFT's HOLT.

JOHN WILLIAM CHURCHILL

BEGS leave to acquaint the Nobility, Gentry, and the Public, that he has (in addition to the House Business) taken to the POSTING, which has till lately been carried on by Mr. GEORGE DRINK-WATER, and humbly hopes for a continuance of those favours which have been conferred on his predecessor. His friends and those who may please to honour him with their support, may depend on having neat Post Chaises, with able horses, and steady drivers.

Hopcroft's Holt is situated on the road leading from Oxford to Leamington—

Distance from Oxford, ... 12 Miles.
Banbury, ... 11 ditto.
Chipping-Norton, 11 ditto.
Bicester, ... 8 ditto.

To those who have already proved their friendship by their favours conferred, J. W. C. begs leave to return his sincere thanks, and can only assure them that a continuance will be most thankfully acknowledged.

Fig. 22e. Drinkwater's and Churchill's operations.

Fig. 24. Hopcroft's Holt, described by John Byng in 1785 as 'a little, single public house of comfortable accommodation...'.[9] [British Library. Gough MSS. 15546/2].

---

[9] See Gibson, J., "Travellers' Tales", Part 2, *C&CH* **5**.8 (1974), 152.

RUSHER'S BANBURY LIST, 1815.

COACHES.

From the George and Dragon, to

Oxford, every Day, at 4 o'Clock; passing through Wood-stock and Oxford, to the Golden Cross, London.

From the Red Lion, to

London, every Sunday, Wednesday, and Friday Morn-ings, at Five o'Clock; through Brackley, Buckingham, Aylesbury, and Uxbridge, to the Bell and Crown Inn, Holborn.

Birmingham, every Sunday, Wednesday, and Friday Mornings, at half past Nine o'Clock; through Leaming-ton and Warwick, to the Saracen's Head Inn, Snow Hill.

Leicester, every Sunday, Wednesday, and Friday Morn-ings, at a quarter before Ten o'Clock; through South-am, Coventry, Nuneaton, and Hinkley, to the Stag and Pheasant Inn.

From the White Lion, to

Kidderminster: comes from the Black Horse Inn, Kid-derminster, at Eight o'Clock, every Morning, except Sunday, through Bromsgrove, Alcester, and Stratford-on-Avon; and arrives at the White Lion Inn, Banbury, at Five o'Clock in the Afternoon; from thence through Bicester and Aylesbury, to the Old Bell Inn, Holborn, London; where it arrives the following Morning, at Seven o'Clock:——Returns every Evening, at Seven o'Clock, (Sunday excepted,) arrives in Banbury at Seven o'Clock the following Morning, and at Kidder-minster by Five o'Clock the same evening.

Fig.25a. Rusher's 'Banbury List', 1815. 'Coaches'.

---

4   COACHES,

Carrying Four Insides only.

~~~~

From the Flying Horse Commercial Inn.

To London —The Royal Mail, every Night, at half-past Ten o'Clock, through Aynho, Bicester, Aylesbury, Tring, Berkhamstead, and Watford, to Griffin's Green Man and Still, 335, Oxford Street, and King's Arms, Holborn Bridge, London, at Six o'Clock every Morning, Returns from London every Evening at Half-past Seven o'Clock.

To Birmingham.—The Royal Mail, every Morning, at a Quarter past Four o'Clock, through Southam, Leamington Spa, Warwick, Knowle, and Solihull, to the Albion Hotel, Birmingham. Returns every Afternoon at Half-past Four o'Clock.

To Birmingham.—The Regulator, every day, (Sunday excepted) at ¼-before Twelve o'Clock, through Southam, Leamington, War-wick and Knowle, to the Castle and Saracen's Head Inns. Returns every day (Sunday excepted) at Half-past Eight o'Clock.

To Leicester.—The Regulator, every Morning, at a Quarter before Twelve o'Clock, through Southam, Dunchurch, Rugby, and Lutter-worth, to the George Inn. Returns every Morning (Sunday excepted) at Seven o'Clock.

To Northampton,—The Accommodation, every Tuesday, Thursday, and Saturday, at a Quarter before Twelve, through Southam and Daventry, to the Dolphin Inn. Returns Tuesday, Thursday, and Saturday Mornings, at Eight o'Clock, and arrives at Banbury at Half-past Two o'Clock.

To Oxford—The Regulator, every Afternoon (Sunday excepted) at Three o'Clock, through Deddington and Woodstock, to the Angel Inn, where it meets Coaches to London, Cheltenham, and Gloucester, the same Evening. Returns every Morning. at Half-past Eight o'Clock.

From the Red Lion Inn:

The Union Post Coach, to London every Morning (Sunday excepted) at Eight o'Clock: Monday, Wednesday, and Friday, by Adderbury and Aynho; Tuesday, Thursday, and Saturday, by Brackley:—through Buckingham, Winslow, Aylesbury, Amersham, and Uxbridge, to Griffin's Green Man and Still, Oxford-street; the Bell and Crown, and King's Arms Inns, Holborn, London. Returns from the City, Mornings at Eight o'Clock, and the Green Man and Still, at Half-past Eight o'Clock.

The above Coach meets at Buckingham immediate Coaches to Towcester and Northampton.

From the White Lion Inn:

Every Monday, Wednesday, and Friday Mornings, at Twelve o'Clock; through Bicester, Aylesbury, Tring, Berkhamstead, Watford and Edgeware, to the Old Bell, Holborn, London, at Nine o'Clock.

Every Tuesday, Thursday, and Saturday Afternoons, at a Quarter before Three o'Clock; through Edge-Hill, Stratford-on-Avon, Alcester, Redditch, and Bromsgrove, to the White Lion Inn, Kidder-minster, at Ten o'Clock.

Fig.25b. Rusher's 'Banbury List', 1830. 'Coaches'.

By 1830 the Flying Horse, in Parsons Street, appears to have taken over from the George and Dragon, in Horse Fair.

COACHES,

From the Flying Horse Commercial Inn:—

To London.—The Royal Mail, every night, at half-past ten o'clock, through Aynho, Bicester, Aylesbury, Tring, Berkhamstead, and Watford, to Griffin's Green Man and Still, 335, Oxford-street, and King's Arms, Holborn-bridge, London, at six o'clock every morning. Returns from London every evening at half-past seven o'clock, and arrives in Banbury at four o'clock every morning.

To London.—The Sovereign, every Monday, Wednesday, and Friday mornings, at eleven o'clock, the Mail route, to Griffin's Green Man and Still, at half-past six o'clock, and King's Arms, Holborn-bridge, at seven o'clock. Returns Tuesday, Thursday, and Saturday mornings, at nine, and arrives in Banbury at six o'clock.

To London.—King William, every night, (Sunday excepted,) at eleven o'clock, the Mail route, to Griffin's Green Man and Still, and King's Arms, Holborn-bridge. Returns every afternoon at four o'clock, and arrives in Banbury at a quarter before two every morning.

To Birmingham.—The Royal Mail, every morning, at a quarter-past four o'clock, through Southam, Leamington Spa, Warwick, Knowle, and Solihull, to the Albion Hotel, Birmingham, at half-past nine o'clock. Returns at half-past four, and arrives in Banbury at half-past ten o'clock every night.

To Birmingham.—The Regulator, every day, (Sunday excepted) at a quarter-before 12 o'clock, through Southam, Leamington, Warwick, Knowle, and Solihull, to the Castle and Saracen's Head Inns, at six o'clock every evening. Returns at half-past eight o'clock, and arrives in Banbury every afternoon at half-past two o'clock

To Leicester.—The Regulator, every morning (Sunday excepted), at a quarter-before twelve o'clock, through Southam, Dunchurch, Rugby, and Lutterworth, to the George Inn, at six o'clock. Returns at eight o'clock, and arrives at Banbury every afternoon at half-past two.

To Oxford.—The Regulator, every afternoon (Sunday excepted), at three o'clock, through Deddington and Woodstock, to the Angel Inn, at six o'clock, where it meets Coaches to London, Cheltenham, and Gloucester, the same evening. Returns every morning at half-past eight, and arrives in Banbury at a quarter-before twelve o'clock.

To Oxford.—The Triumph, every day (Sunday excepted), at half-past ten, to the Angel Inn. Returns every afternoon at 3 o'clock.

To Kidderminster.—King William, every morning, (Sunday excepted,) at two o'clock, thro' Kineton, Stratford-on-Avon, Alcester, Redditch, and Bromsgrove, to the Black Horse Inn.

To Warwick.—The Triumph, every evening (Sunday excepted), at a quarter-before six, through Southam and Leamington, to the Castle Hotel. Returns every morning at half-past seven.

To Leamington.—The Sovereign, every Tuesday, Thursday, and Saturday evenings, at six o'clock, through Southam, to the Bath Hotel, Bath-street, at half-past eight. Returns Monday, Wednesday, and Friday mornings, at a quarter-before nine, and arrives in Banbury at eleven.

From the Red Lion Inn :—

The Union Post Coach, to London, every morning (Sunday excepted). at eight o'clock: Monday, Wednesday, and Friday, by Adderbury and Aynho; Tuesday, Thursday, and Saturday, by Brackley:—through Buckingham, Winslow, Aylesbury, Amersham, and Uxbridge, to Griffin's Green Man and Still, Oxford-street, at half-past five; the Bell and Crown, and King's Arms Inns, Holborn, at half-past six o'clock. Returns from the City, mornings at eight o'clock, and the Green Man and Still, at half-past eight o'clock, and arrives in Banbury at half-past six o'clock every evening. The above coach meets at Buckingham immediate coaches to Towcester and Northampton.

Fig.25c. Rusher's 'Banbury List', 1834. 'Coaches'.

In 1834, the Flying Horse is dominating the trade...

COACHES,

From the White Lion Inn:—

To London.—The Royal Mail, every night, at half-past ten o'clock, through Aynho, Bicester, Aylesbury, Tring, Berkhamstead, and Watford, to Griffin's Green Man and Still, 335, Oxford-street, and King's Arms, Holborn-bridge, London, at six o'clock every morning. Returns from London every evening at half-past seven o'clock, and arrives in Banbury at four o'clock every morning.

To London.—The Sovereign, every Monday, Wednesday, and Friday mornings, at eleven o'clock, the Mail route, to Griffin's Green Man and Still, at half-past six o'clock, and King's Arms, Holborn-bridge, at seven o'clock. Returns Tuesday, Thursday, and Saturday mornings, at nine, and arrives in Banbury at six o'clock. During the summer every day except Sunday.

To Birmingham.—The Royal Mail, every morning, at a quarter-past four o'clock, through Southam, Leamington Spa, Warwick, Knowle, and Solihull, to the Albion Hotel, Birmingham, at half-past nine o'clock. Returns at half-past four, and arrives in Banbury at half-past ten o'clock every night.

To Birmingham.—The Regulator, every day, (Sunday excepted) at a quarter-before 12 o'clock, through Southam, Leamington, Warwick, Knowle, and Solihull, to the Castle and Saracen's Head Inns, at six o'clock every evening. Returns at half-past eight o'clock, and arrives in Banbury every afternoon at half-past two o'clock.

To Leicester.—The Regulator, every morning (Sunday excepted), at a quarter-before twelve o'clock, through Southam, Dunchurch, Rugby, and Lutterworth, to the George Inn, at six o'clock. Returns at eight o'clock, and arrives at Banbury every afternoon at half-past two.

To Oxford.—The Regulator, every afternoon (Sunday excepted), at three o'clock, through Deddington and Woodstock, to the Angel Inn, at six o'clock, where it meets Coaches to London, Cheltenham, and Gloucester, the same evening. Returns every morning at half-past eight, and arrives in Banbury at a quarter-before twelve o'clock.

To Leamington.—The Sovereign, every Tuesday, Thursday, and Saturday evenings, at six o'clock, through Southam, to the Bath Hotel, Bath-street, at half-past eight. Returns Monday, Wednesday, and Friday mornings, at a quarter-before nine, and arrives in Banbury at eleven. Every day during the summer months, except on Sunday.

From the Red Lion Inn:—

The Union Post Coach, to London, every morning (Sunday excepted), at eight o'clock: Monday, Wednesday, and Friday, by Adderbury and Aynho; Tuesday, Thursday, and Saturday, by Brackley:—through Buckingham, Winslow, Aylesbury, Amersham, and Uxbridge, to Griffin's Green Man and Still, Oxford-street, at half-past five; the Bell and Crown, and King's Arms Inns, Holborn, at half-past six o'clock. Returns from the City, mornings at eight o'clock, and the Green Man and Still, at half-past eight o'clock, and arrives in Banbury at half-past six o'clock every evening. The above coach meets at Buckingham immediate coaches to Towcester and Northampton.

To London.—The Hero, every Monday, Wednesday, and Friday, at 12 o'clock, by way of Brackley, Buckingham, Aylesbury, and Uxbridge, to Griffin's Green Man and Still, at half-past 8, and the King's Arms, Holborn, at 9 o'clock. Returns Tuesday, Thursday, and Saturday, mornings at 6 o'clock, and arrives at Banbury at 3 o'clock.

To Kidderminster.—The Hero, every Tuesday, Thursday, and Saturday, at a quarter-past three, through Kineton, Stratford-on-Avon, Alcester, Redditch, and Bromsgrove; to the Lion Hotel, Kidderminster, at nine o'clock at night.

The above coach meets coaches to Bath, Bristol, Cheltenham, Hereford, Bridgenorth, Bewdley, Liverpool, Cladbury, Wolverhampton, Ludlow, Aberystwith, Birmingham, &c.

Fig.25d. Rusher's 'Banbury List', 1835. 'Coaches'.

...but in 1835 it is clear that the White Lion has taken over.

The mail service to Birmingham was re-routed through Oxford in 1808, and although a few years later the new mail service to Kidderminster was initially run through Banbury, in 1835 William Jones of Drayton Gate sought compensation of £20 on account of his *"great loss by the Kidderminster coach having discontinued to go on this road since the commencement of the contract"* (his leasing of the tolls). For many years the driver of the Kidderminster coach was Tom Bowden.

The main coach services were operated by London-based companies such as James Hearn & Co of the King's Arms Snow Hill or Edward Sherman & Co of the Bull & Mouth, St Martin's-le-Grand.[10] Waddells of Oxford had an interest in some of the main routes and co-operated with the Banbury coach proprietor, John Drinkwater. Fig. 26, showing traffic flow, uses information[11] on licensed coach services between London and the West Midlands in 1836, just before competition from railways caused major changes.

Nineteen coach services and two mail coaches approached Oxford from London each day and fourteen services and two mail coaches ran through Daventry and Coventry from London. In contrast, although Banbury was on one of the principal mail coach routes, it had only four regular services from London and one coach service coming up from Oxford (Table 11, page 114). Southam to the north was as important as Banbury as a stop on through-coach services to the West Midlands. Other records of the coach services make it apparent that there were frequent changes in the operators, routes and coaches.

The relative importance of the routes through Buckingham and Bicester into Banbury changed over the coaching era. The road through Aynho to Buckingham was the first of the roads in the area to be turnpiked and so, it may be assumed, was the most important road from Banbury towards London in the early eighteenth century. About 1750, Henry Purefoy wrote in his diary[12] that the Aylesbury stage coach left the Bell Inn, Holborn every Tuesday at 6 a.m., arrived at Aylesbury the same evening and travelled the next day to its terminus at the Cobham Arms in Buckingham. An alternative route from Banbury through Brackley to Buckingham was created in 1770 and the road from Aynho to Bicester (what was to be the main A41) was turnpiked in the same year. It was the Aylesbury, Bicester, Aynho road that had become the dominant coach road into Banbury by the 1830s and was the route used by the mail coach. Nevertheless the road through Buckingham retained some traffic with John Lomax & Co running a service from the Red Lion, Banbury, to connect with the London service from the Cobham Arms in 1779. Until it closed in 1848, the Cobham Arms was the main coaching inn and post office

---

[10] *RUTV* 11.

[11] Bates, A., *Directory of Stage Coach Services, 1836*, David & Charles, Newton Abbot (1969).

[12] Elliott, D. J., *Buckingham - the loyal and ancient borough*, Phillimore, Chichester (1975).

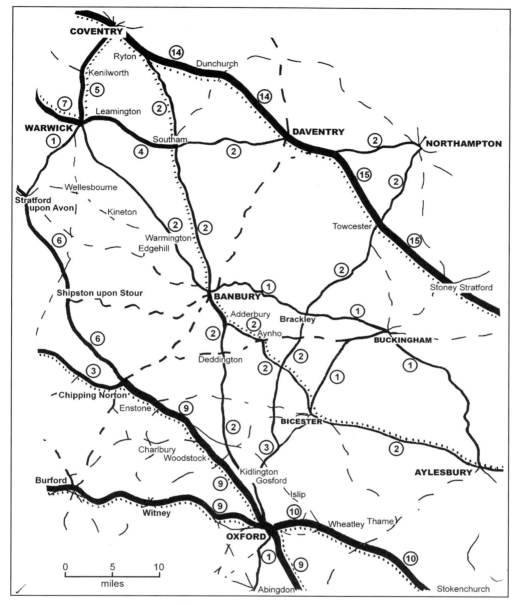

Fig. 26. Main coach services in 1836.
Dotted lines: mail coach routes. Circled numbers: scheduled coaches per day.

in Buckingham:[13] the Baxter family were the postmasters for many years.[14] By the early nineteenth century the Buckingham road was of only minor importance although *The Union* from Banbury to London and *The Rising Sun* from Oxford to Northampton passed through the town.

---

[13] As footnote 12.
[14] Shem 1720-1776; Dunney 1776-1810.

Table 11: Coach Services through Banbury

Year	Route	Coach	Operator	@ Banbury
1816 & 1819	Oxford, Banbury, Southam, Leamington, Warwick, Birmingham.	The Regulator	Drinkwater	
1830	Kidderminster, Banbury, Aylesbury, London.	The Britannia		White Lion
	Oxford, Banbury, Southam, Birmingham.	The Regulator		Flying Horse
	London, Aylesbury, Bicester, Deddington.	Post coach		
1836	London, Buckingham, Banbury.	The Union	Hearn	Red Lion
	London, Bicester, Banbury, Warwick, Birmingham.	The Union	Hearn	
	London, Bicester, Banbury, Leamington	The Sovereign		
	London, Oxford, Banbury, Southam, Warwick.	The Hope		
	London, Banbury, Warwick, Birmingham, Stourport.	Royal Mail		Flying Horse
	Oxford, Banbury, Warwick.		Drinkwater	
1844	Banbury, London	The Sovereign	Drinkwater & Fowler	Red & White Lion
	Banbury, Cheltenham	The Lion	Fowler & Churchill Parker	Red Lion
	Leamington, Banbury, Bicester, Aylesbury, London	Sovereign	Drinkwater & Waddell	White Lion
	Banbury, Oxford, Gt Western train to London	The Favourite, The Rival & The Regulator		Red & White Lion
	Banbury, Brackley, Wolverton, train to London.	The Union	Fowler & Drinkwater	Flying Horse
	Banbury, Weedon.	The Star	Cave	

9. Traffic through Banbury: Carriers

9.1 Wagon Services

It may be assumed that the stage wagon services followed similar routes to those of the coach services but travelled at a lower speed. The earliest directory of common carriers into London lists services from Banbury, Buckingham and Kineton.[1] It is probable that these were performed by either carts or packhorses (Table 12, pages 116-117). By 1681 the directory published by de Laune states that John Jordan of Banbury[2] and William Ricketts of Kineton were both using wagons to provide carrier services to London, whereas the services from Brackley and Buckingham may still have used carts. John Jordan 'senr.' died in May 1689. His probate inventory (totalling £245) included "Horses, waggon, and other things as belongs to a carrier, £40", and £84 in "good debts". His son John Jordan 'junr.', his successor as carrier, died only nine months later, and his inventory reveals that there were "twelve horses, one waggon" etc. still worth £40, whilst "debts sperate and desperate" came to £50.[3]

The 1731 coach advertisement mentioned earlier (page 100) includes information on a stage wagon that took a week to complete the round trip from Birmingham to London. Wagons were operated from Banbury by Samuel Cooke of Drayton, who died in 1764, and William King, who died in 1765. The Richard Garfield who sold his wagons in 1767 may have been related to William Garfield who ran a wagon service from Woodstock in the 1750s. John Baker of Woodstock is recorded as taking over a wagon service from John Arne in 1775[4] (Fig. 27). His wagon ran from Oxford, Deddington, Banbury and Warwick to Birmingham, taking two and a half days.

BIRMINGHAM Old Stage Waggon.
JOHN BAKER, of Woodstock, in the county of Oxford, having taken the Stage Waggon from Birmingham to Oxford, (late Arn's) hereby gives Notice, that he began on Tuesday the 16th of May last, at six o'clock in the morning, to set out from the Roe-Buck, in the Corn-Market, Oxford, through Deddington, Banbury, and Warwick, and arrives at Birmingham on the Thursday following, at two o'clock in the afternoon; returns from thence on Friday morning, and arrives at Oxford on Monday, by two o'clock in the afternoon. Those who please to favour him with the carriage of their goods, &c. may depend on having the greatest care taken of them, and the strictest punctuality in the delivery thereof.

Fig. 27. The 'Old Stage Waggon' from Oxford through Banbury to Warwick., 1775.

---

[1] See the introductory discussion and Table 9 on pages 96-100 above.

[2] John Jordan, senr., carrier, buried 10 May 1689; John Jordan, junr., carrier, buried 11 Feb 1689/90. James Jordan, carrier, buried 8 June 1701. Banbury Parish Register [BHS 9, 1968].

[3] Oxfordshire Record Office, MS Wills Peculiars, 44/1/8 and 44/1/9.

[4] Potts W. 2nd ed. rev. Clark E.T., *A History of Banbury*, Gulliver Press, Banbury, 1978, 225.

Table 12: Carrier Services using Roads around Banbury
Carriers & Wagons to London

Year	Operator	Starts	London Inn	Journey per week	
1637	carrier	Banbury	George, Holborn Bridge	Three	Carriers Cosmol
1637	Carrier	Buckingham	Saracen's Head, Carter Lane	Twice	Carriers Cosmol
1637	Carrier	Buckingham	King's Head, Old Change	Twice	Carriers Cosmol
1637	Carrier	Kineton	Bell, Friday Street	Once	Carriers Cosmol
1681	Joseph Sare	Dreyton	Mermaid, Carter Lane	Once	De Laune
1681	John Jordon (wagon)	Banbury	Belle Savage, Ludgate Hill	Once	De Laune
1691	Widow Jordon (wagon)	Banbury	Ram, Smithfield	Once	De Laune
1691	Thomas Westcare	Banbury	Saracen's Head, Carter Lane	Once	De Laune
1681	Ralph Harlow	Brackley	Mermaid, Carter Lane	Once	De Laune
1691	William Cook (wagon)	Brackley	Oxford Arms, Warwick Lane	Once	De Laune
1681 & 1691	William Ricketts (wagon)	Kineton	George, Smithfield	Once	De Laune
1681	Philip Webster & Son	Buckingham	George, Smithfield	Once	De Laune
1691	John Webster	Buckingham	George, Smithfield	Once	De Laune
1738	Carrier	Banbury	White Swan, Holborn Bridge	Once	Intellig
1738	Carrier	Banbury	Ram, Smithfield	Once	Intellig
1738	Carrier	Buckingham	Bell, Warwick Lane	Once	Intellig
1738	Carrier	Buckingham	Oxford Arms, Warwick Lane	Once	Intellig
1738	Carrier	Buckingham	George, Smithfield	Twice	Intellig
1738	Carrier	Buckingham	Bear & Ragged Staff, Smithfield	Once	Intellig
1738	Carrier	Birmingham via Banbury	George, Snowhill	Once	Intellig
1738	Packhorses	Stratford via Banbury	Ram, Smithfield	Once	Intellig
1738	carrier	Tingewick	Peacock, Clare Market	Once	Intellig

Year	Operator	Starts	London Inn	Journey per week	
1738	Carrier	Brackley	Oxford Arms, Warwick Lane	Once	Intellig
1790	Eagles (wagon)	Buckingham	George, Snowhill	Twice	Univ Brit Dir
1790	Jane Eagles, (wagon)	Brackley	Oxford Arms, Warwick Lane	Twice	Univ Brit Dir
1790	Stuckbury (wagon)	Buckingham	Oxford Arms, Warwick Lane	Once	Univ Brit Dir
1790	Bennet, (wagon)	Banbury	Oxford Arms, Warwick Lane	?	Univ Brit Dir
1814	William Judd	Banbury			Rusher
1816	John Golby	Banbury			Rusher
1818	Richard Judd	Banbury			Rusher
1823	Henry Stone	Banbury	Bell, Warwick Lane	daily	Rusher
1825	Parker & Green	Banbury			Rusher
1830	Thomas Golby	Banbury			Rusher

Table 12 *continued*: **Carrier Services using Roads around Banbury: Carriers and Wagons to London**

By 1764, William Judd[5] operated two wagon services from the George in Digbeth, Birmingham, probably through Stratford to London. One service went via Banbury and Aylesbury, the other through Oxford. In the same year William Webster also operated two wagon services from Moor Street, Birmingham, one through Oxford to Southampton, the other through Banbury, Bicester, Buckingham and Aylesbury to London. By 1803, Webster's service had been transferred to William Phillips but Judd ran his services until the 1820s (both Judd and Phillips were turnpike trustees).

Fig. 28. Early eighteenth century vehicles - for goods...

---

[5] See Renold, P., "William Judd and Banbury Corporation", *C&CH* **12**.2. (Spring, 1992). However, Judd is perhaps mistakenly identified as having been born in 1750, son of a Horley farmer. See also fn.17. There had been Banbury carriers named Judd around 1700 and in the 1760s (Table 10, page 98).

Fig. 29. ....and the equivalent early nineteenth century transport:
a typical stage wagon.

Stage wagons of the late eighteenth century were enormous vehicles with very wide wheels and a high canvas cover. They carried substantially more goods than the packhorses and carts that carriers had used prior to the road improvements brought about by turnpiking (Fig. 29). The old gateways into Banbury impeded the passage of the large vehicles and in 1785 Mr Judd was given permission for one of his wagons to pull down the South Bar[6] to give easier access along the Oxford road. In the 1820s the North Bar was also demolished to allow Golby's wagon freer passage towards Birmingham.[7]

Fig. 30. South Bar, Banbury

---

[6] As footnote 2, Potts/Clark, *A History of Banbury*, 44; *Banbury Past through Artists' Eyes*, BHS **30**, 23.

[7] Beesley A., *History of Banbury*, 208, which states it was still standing around 1817.

In 1798, William Judd was operating twice weekly wagon services from Banbury to London, one through Deddington, Buckingham and another through Islip and along the Stokenchurch road, and also to Birmingham.[8]

RUSHER'S BANBURY LIST, 1812.   9

WILLIAM JUDD AND SONS' London Fly Market Waggons, leave Banbury every Monday, Wednesday, and Saturday Mornings, at Ten o'Clock, through Buckingham, Winslow, Aylesbury, &c. arrive (in 40 Hours) in London every Wednesday, Friday, and Monday Mornings, for Market; return the same Days, and arrive in Banbury, every Friday, Sunday, and Wednesday Mornings.—The Monday's Waggon to the Bell Inn, and the Wednesday and Saturday's Waggon to the Oxford Arms, Warwick Lane.

Their Waggon through Deddington, Aynho, Buckingham, &c. loads every Friday Morning, at Ten o'Clock, and arrives at the Bell Inn, Warwick Lane, London, every Monday Morning, for Market; returns the same Day, and arrives in Banbury on Wednesday at Noon.

Their Birmingham Fly Waggons, from their Warehouse, New Street, Birmingham, (from whence Goods are forwarded to all parts of the North) every Monday, Wednesday, and Saturday Night, arrive in Banbury (on their Road for London, to the White Horse, Cripplegate,) every Tuesday, Thursday, and Sunday Nights: arrive at, and return from London, every Tuesday, Thursday, and Saturday, and arrive at Banbury (on their Road through Warwick to Birmingham) every Thursday, Saturday, and Monday Mornings.

Their Banbury Waggons load for Birmingham every Saturday and Monday Evenings; the Monday's Waggon by way of Kineton, Welsborne, Stratford, &c. arrives at their Warehouse, New Street, every Tuesday and Thursday; returns the same Nights, and arrives at Banbury every Thursday and Friday.

Their Oxford Waggon, which is met by regular Carriers, to and from Reading, Wallingford, Newbery, Winchester, Salisbury, Witney, Bristol, and Southampton, and to all the intermediate and adjacent Places, Goods

10   RUSHER'S BANBURY LIST, 1812.

are forwarded regularly from Southampton to Portsmouth, the Isles of Wight, Guernsey, and Jersey, (through Woodstock) loads at Banbury every Saturday Morning; arrives at the Star and Garter Inn, Oxford, returns the same Day, and arrives at Banbury on the Day following. Also Wednesday Morning's, to Oxford, from the above places, returns on Thursday Mornings. The Waggon out of London on Wednesday, returns thro' Deddington on Friday.

WILLIAM JUDD AND SONS' CANAL CONVEYANCE. Their Boats load for Oxford every Monday and Thursday, and return every Wednesday and Saturday. These Boats are met at Oxford by regular Land Carriers to and from Reading, Newbury, Winchester, Salisbury, Southampton, Portsmouth, and all the intermediate and adjacent Places. Vessels sail regular from Southampton to the Isles of Wight, Guernsey and Jersey.

Also every Wednesday and Saturday for Warwick and Birmingham, and return every Tuesday and Friday. By these Boats Goods are regularly forwarded for Bromsgrove, Worcester, &c. Kidderminster, Stourport, Bewdley, &c. Stourbridge, Dudley, Tipton, West Bromwich, Bilston, Walsall, Wolverhampton, Shrewsbury, and all North Wales. Likewise Derby, Nottingham, &c. Chesterfield, Sheffield, &c.

CONSIGNMENTS.

From Oxford, per Judd and Sons' Boat, (their own Establishment)

Warwick,	ditto	ditto	ditto
Birmingham,	ditto	ditto	ditto
Bromsgrove, per Judd and Sons' Boat, from Birmingham,			
Worcester,	ditto	ditto	ditto.
Kidderminster,	ditto	ditto	ditto
Stourport	ditto	ditto	ditto
Bewdley	ditto	ditto	ditto

Fig. 31a. Rusher's 'Banbury List', 1812

Richard Judd took over the service after his father in 1815 and by 1818 he was in partnership with Henry Stone, operating wagons to London, Birmingham and Shrewsbury.[9] However, the partnership did not prosper and Judd ceased to advertise after 1818 and by 1822 Stone was bankrupt (although still advertised in 1823).

[8] As fn. 5, Renold, "William Judd...", *C&CH* **12**.2
[9] Gibson J.S.W. "The immediate route from the metropolis to all parts", *C&CH*.**12**.1, 10-24.

10   RUSHER'S BANBURY LIST, 1815.

Warmington, W. 6, Mitchell, Plow, and to Messrs.
    Judd's, Tuesday and Thursday
    Plumber, Rein Deer, Monday and Thursday.
Warwick, see Judd's Banbury, and Woodley's Kineton.
Woodford, N. 12, Hiam, Catherine Wheel, Thursday,
    and to Daventry.
    Mumford, Bull's Head, Thursday.
Wroxton, O. 3, Holland, Windmill, Thursday.

R. R. JUDD AND CO.'s
BANBURY & LONDON WAGGONS,

Load on Monday Morning, and Tuesday and Friday
Evenings; and arrive in London, at the Bell Inn,
Warwick Lane, by way of Buckingham, Aylesbury,
&c. on the following Wednesday, Friday, and Monday
Mornings, in time for each Day's Market; from whence
they return the same Mornings, and arrive in Banbury
on Friday Evening, Monday Morning, and Wednesday
Evening.
N. B. They call at the Green Man and Still, Oxford
Street, both going in and coming out of London.

RICHARD JUDD's BIRMINGHAM WAGGONS,

Load at his Warehouse, New Street, every Monday,
Wednesday, and Saturday Evenings, and arrive in
Banbury, at the Warehouse of R. R. Judd and Co. on
Tuesday and Friday Evenings, and Monday Morning;
where they load on Wednesday and Thursday Evenings,
and Monday Morning, for Warwick, &c.
N. B. The Wednesday's Waggon from Banbury, by way
of Kineton and Welsbourne, also the Monday's Waggon
from Birmingham; the others by Way of Gaydon Inn.

Mr. William Welch, London Salesman, attends at the
Red Lion, every Thursday.

10   RUSHER'S BANBURY LIST, 1823.

H. STONE's LONDON VANS AND WAGGONS,

Load daily, and arrive in London, at the Bell Inn,
Warwick Lane, by way of Adderbury, Deddington,
Aynho, Buckingham, Aylesbury, Uxbridge, &c. in
time for each Day's Market. Return every Morning.

HENRY STONE's LIVERPOOL, MANCHESTER,
AND BIRMINGHAM VANS AND WAGGONS,

Load at his Warehouse in Banbury, every Monday,
Wednesday, and Friday Mornings, and arrive at his
Warehouse, Dale End, Birmingham, every Tuesday,
Thursday, and Saturday Mornings; where they load
every Saturday, Tuesday, and Thursday; arrive in
Banbury, Monday, Wednesday, and Friday, by way
of Gaydon Inn, Warwick, Knowle, Solihull, &c.
Warwick Waggon loads every Tuesday Evening,
through Kineton, Welsbourn, &c. &c.

J. GOLBY's BANBURY & LONDON WAGGONS,

Load at his Warehouse, Banbury, on Monday, Thursday,
and Saturday Mornings; and arrive in London, at the
Bell Inn, Wood Street, on Wednesday, Saturday, and
Monday Mornings, by Five o'Clock, for Market: the
Monday and Thursday's Waggon through Aynho,
Buckingham, Aylesbury, Tring, Berkhamstead, Wat-
ford, Edgware, &c. and the Saturday's by way of
Bicester, Aylesbury, Missenden, Uxbridge, &c. Re-
turn by the same Roads early on Monday Morning,
Wednesday Evening, and Saturday, and arrive in
Banbury on Tuesday and Saturday Mornings.

J. GOLBY's BIRMINGHAM WAGGONS,

Load at his Warehouse, in Banbury, on Tuesday and
Saturday; arrive at the Red Lion, Digbeth, Birmingham, on Wednesday and Monday Mornings. Return
from thence on Wednesday and Saturday; and arrive
at Banbury on Monday and Thursday Mornings.
☞ Both Waggons through Southam, Leamington, &c.

R. PARKER's LONDON VANS AND WAGGONS,

Load daily, through Oxford and Wycombe; leave the
Buck and Bell Inn, Banbury, every day at Noon, and
arrive at his Warehouse, No. 17, Old Change, Cheap-
side, the next Morning, in time for the Markets; leave
London, every Evening at Six, and arrive at Banbury
the following Morning.
His Vans also leave Banbury daily, for Leamington,
Warwick, Coventry, and all places adjacent.

Fig. 31b. Rusher's 'Banbury List', 1815, 1823.

A competing service run by John Golby operated wagons from London
to Birmingham, through Banbury and Warwick, from 1816. Parker &
Green began to advertise their services with Golby in 1825 but each seems
to have operated independently in subsequent years.

10   RUSHER'S BANBURY LIST, 1826.

———

GOLBY's BANBURY & LONDON WAGGONS,

Load at his Warehouse, Banbury, on Monday, Wednesday, Thursday, and Saturday Mornings; and arrive at the Bell Inn, Wood Street, Cheapside, London, on Wednesday, Friday, Saturday, and Monday Mornings; return the same days, and arrive at Banbury, on Friday, Monday, (Monday two Waggons), & Wednesday Mornings.

GOLBY's BIRMINGHAM WAGGONS,

Load at his Warehouse, in Banbury, on Monday, Wednesday, and Friday Mornings, and arrive at 52, Dale End, Birmingham, on Tuesday, Thursday, and Saturday Mornings. Return the same Evenings, and arrive at Banbury, on Wednesday and Friday Evenings, and Monday Mornings.

———

PARKER AND GREEN's LONDON WAGGONS,

Load at their Warehouse, late Stone's, every Monday, Wednesday, Thursday, and Saturday Mornings, and arrive in London, at No. 17, Old Change, Cheapside, every Wednesday, Friday, Saturday, and Monday Mornings, early for each day's Market, by way of Deddington, Woodstock, Oxford, Tetsworth, Wycomb, &c. &c. Return and arrive in Banbury, every Monday, Wednesday, Thursday, and Saturday Mornings.

———

T. HORTON's BIRMINGHAM WAGGONS,

Load at the Waggon and Horses, on Monday and Thursday Mornings; to the Red Lion Inn, Warwick, and arrive at the Red Lion, Digbeth, Birmingham, every Monday and Friday. From Wellesbourne, Birmingham, Solihull, Knowle, Warwick, Barford, and Kineton, Monday and Thursday.

———

PHILIP CAMBRAY,

Woodstock, Chipping-Norton, Banbury, Deddington, Oxford, and Wycomb Carrier, to London, see Woodstock.

Fig. 31c. Rusher's 'Banbury List', 1826

Evidently Parker's had taken over Stone's bankrupt business.

T. Horton of Birmingham (to 1828), and Philip Cambray, of Woodstock (1826 only), were also offering services.

By 1830, Thomas Golby of the Cow Fair, Banbury, was running a wagon from London through Buckingham and Banbury, going on through Warwick to Birmingham.

His competitors, Parker & Green, had a warehouse in High Street, Banbury. They used the Deddington route to London through Woodstock and Oxford. By the 1840s, Mr Parker of Fish Street had become the main wagon master operating from Banbury (Figs. 32a, below, and 32b, page 123).

J. H. PARKER,

LONDON, BANBURY, AND LEAMINGTON

CARRIER.

J. H. P. begs to inform the Public in general, that his FLY VANS and WAGONS leave his Office, FISH STREET, BANBURY, (as usual) every Tuesday, Wednesday, Friday, and Saturday, arriving in London for the early markets, and leave the KING'S ARMS, SNOW HILL, every Monday, TUESDAY, Thursday, and Saturday, delivering Goods at Banbury, every Wednesday, THURSDAY, Saturday, and Monday. Dairymen and Butchers will find Tuesday and Friday, a great accommodation, as Meat, &c., will arrive in London for the early markets the following morning.—A Van for the conveyance of Furniture, Glass, &c., leaves London every Friday morning.

W. TAYLOR, Agent for Banbury.

N.B.—DEALER IN LINSEED OIL CAKE.

Fig. 32a. J.H. Parker, carrier, operating from Banbury in the 1840s.

Fig. 32b. Parker's carrier service from Banbury to London.

9.2 Traffic Type

In the absence of detailed records it is impossible to establish the proportion of traffic falling into each of the main classes. However, in the nineteenth century, since none of the trunk routes between London and other great cities passed through the town, the roads into Banbury probably carried a high proportion of local traffic. Banbury Market and the Banbury Fairs meant that large numbers of travellers used roads into the town. Locals may have known ways around the toll-gates but traders and their customers along with farmers and merchants must have been important clients for the toll-gate keepers. The seasonal nature of this pattern of travel resulted in fluctuations of income from tolls during the year and no doubt during each week .

The weekly accounts of toll income shown in Fig. 33 (page 124) illustrate that traffic varied considerably over the year and between gates. During the winter, toll income was generally low, presumably because travel was difficult and only essential journeys were made.

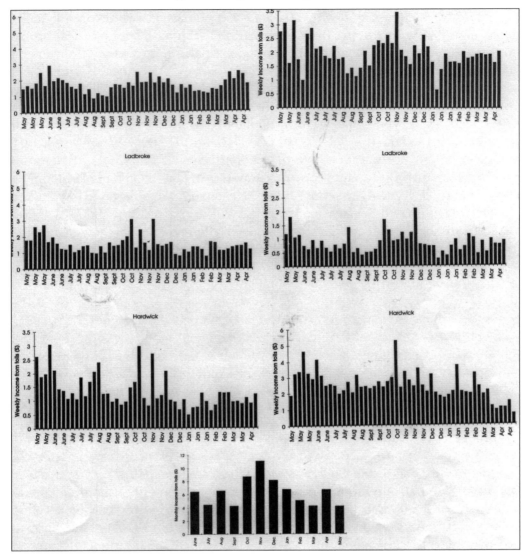

Fig. 33. Weekly income from tolls at Stretton, Ladbroke and Hardwick Gates on the Ryton to Banbury Turnpike (a-c) 1769/70and (d-f) 1800/1; and (g) the Wilscot Gate on the Banbury to Lutterworth Turnpike 1809/10.

In 1760, the income at the Moreton Gate showed a sharp increase in April, corresponding to the time when the main coach services began to "fly" again after the winter. The figures for 1769/70 show (Figs. 33a-c) that at the Hardwick Gate, just north of Banbury, there were slight but definite peaks of income in late May and mid-October. Neither of the other gates showed such distinct changes in a single week. In 1800/1, the peak in income at Hardwick during late May and early June are still apparent (Figs. 33d-f) but the peak in mid-October is dramatic, rising to twice the average weekly income. This sharp peak is obvious in subsequent years, up to at least 1806 when the surviving records cease. These short term peaks are the result of traffic bound into Banbury for the main fairs in Summer and at Michaelmas. It is interesting to note that the effects of fair traffic are not so apparent at Ladbrooke or Stretton Gates suggesting that the fair was drawing most of its (toll paying) visitors from within a few miles of the town. Furthermore, the relatively greater magnitude of the effect in 1800 compared with 1769 suggests that the Michaelmas fair became more important in the nineteenth century, at least for those with vehicles and animals paying a toll.

The pattern of income at Gawcum and Little Rissington gates on the Burford to Stow road shows a peak in November and to a lesser extent in June: again this may reflect attendance at Fairs, particularly Michaelmas. An analysis of the tolls taken at Wilscot Gate in 1809/10 (Fig. 33g) indicates that the amount of money handed to the treasurer during November, and therefore taken in October, was substantially greater than in any other month. This is further evidence of the additional traffic stimulated by the Michaelmas Fair.

Surveys taken in 1845 to support a case for the Oxford to Worcester, Rugby and Wolverhampton Railways give useful information (Table 13, page 126) on the composition of traffic, just before the railways totally changed road travel. The route carrying the most coach passengers was that from Oxford to Banbury with 59 coaches per week (note that about half these can be accounted for as public stage coach services in Fig. 20a-c). There were less than half this number through Southam and only three coaches per week ran along the Stratford road. The Bicester to Aylesbury road carried the greatest amount of freight although the Southam to Banbury road also received a high proportion of its toll income from vehicles carrying merchandise. The vast majority of travellers crossing Banbury Bridge were on foot but about one in eight were on horseback and so paid a toll. There were more vehicles carrying merchandise than carrying passengers although it should be noted that this route to Daventry or Brackley was not one of the principal routes for long distance commercial traffic through the town.

Table 13: Estimates of traffic through Banbury
(based on a survey made for the Oxford to Wolverhampton Railway in 1845)

	Passengers per year						Vehicles per week							
	Posthorse	Flys & Gigs	Vans & Cart	Gen Merch	Agric Prod	Coaches	Posthorse	Flys & Gigs	Vans & Cart	Gen Merch	Agric Prod	Coaches	Total Veh	% Pass veh
Banbury to Stratford	286	2202	3224	1118	1508	156	3	21	31	11	15	3	83	32
Banbury to Southam	442	3900	6812	3458	1508	1200	4	38	66	33	15	23	178	36
Banbury to Buckingham				2704		470				26		9		
Banbury to Bicester	390	3432	3042	1534	1352	806	4	33	29	15	13	16	109	48
Bicester to Aylesbury	286	3354	8970	6318	1040	806	3	32	86	61	10	16	208	24
Oxford to Bicester	52	3770	4498	1742	312	1226	1	36	43	17	3	24	123	49
Oxford to Banbury	832	3926	5018	2626	1482	3060	8	38	48	25	14	59	192	54
Oxford to Aylesbury	52	1690	2132	988	702		1	16	21	10	7	0	54	31
Oxford to Birmingham	520			1040		1901	5			10		37		

Annual income from toll on horses (£)

	Posthorse	Flys & Gigs	Vans & Cart	Gen Merch	Agric Prod	Coaches	Total £	Actual £	
Banbury to Stratford	14	55	81	56	75	16	297		
Banbury to Southam	22	98	170	173	75	120	658		
Banbury to Buckingham				135		47	182		
Banbury to Bicester	20	86	76	77	68	81	406	536	Bicester-Aynho-Finmere Turnpike
Bicester to Aylesbury	14	84	224	316	52	81	771	996	Aylesbury-Bicester Turnpike
Oxford to Bicester	3	94	112	87	16	123	435		
Oxford to Banbury	42	98	125	131	74	306	777	870	Kidlington-Deddington Turnpike
Oxford to Aylesbury	3	42	53	49	35	0	183		
Oxford to Birmingham	26			52		190	268		

Crossing Banbury Bridge	horses/veh	toll £/a	actual £
pedestrians	1008	0	
horses not drawing	132	1	50
carts & waggons	55	3	248
private carriage	36	3	162
beasts	372		112
		571	843 for all

9.3 Competition from the Canals

The turnpikes increased travel and improved the speed and efficiency with which goods could be carried to distant markets. However, toll charges were substantial and boats were better suited than horse drawn vehicles for carrying delicate or bulky wares. In the south Midlands, there is no network of large rivers to provide natural waterways for trade. Nevertheless, the building of canals in the mid-eighteenth century created an important alternative to road transport, just as the turnpike network was being formed. Canal barges were the most economic method for carrying heavy goods over long distance, but the canals were not serious competitors for passenger traffic and long distance passenger vehicles favoured the turnpikes.

The accounts of the Ryton Bridge to Banbury Turnpike Trust illustrate the degree to which competition from a new canal affected road traffic. Income from the toll-gates between Coventry and Banbury was fairly constant over the first decade of operation from 1755 (Fig. 12, page 52). In 1767 the toll income from all the gates rose, particularly that from Ladbrooke Gate. Income from Ladbrooke halved in 1776 and that from Hardwick halved in 1778 whereas that at Stretton declined slowly between 1776 and 1779. The Ladbrooke and Hardwick Gates continued to stagnate until 1790, after which they rose steadily.

These changes reflect competition from the Coventry to Oxford Canal that ran parallel to the turnpike through Banbury (Fig. 34, pages 128-129). The new cut was close beside the turnpike road for much of the way from Coventry and so during construction of the canal there would have been an increase in traffic from the navigators. Once the canal opened, boats were a much more economical means of carrying heavy goods such as coal. As a result road traffic, from the coal pits around Coventry, fell once the canal provided an alternative means of transport. The canal was opened as far as Banbury in 1778[10] and the drop in revenue from the Hardwick Gate illustrates the degree to which haulage decreased. It may be inferred that, by 1776, the canal was opened beyond Ladbrooke, perhaps to the locks at Napton on the Coventry side of the watershed, or even as far as the summit near Fenny Compton. The canal was not open all the way to Oxford until January 1790,[11] after which the underlying increase in general traffic and passenger coaches restored the fortunes of the turnpike. Stretton Gate benefited from the general increase in business close to Coventry and from locally extracted minerals. For instance in 1790 the toll receipts record an income of £2.8s. from carts carrying material from the local lime kiln; this rose to £5.15s. in 1795. However, after 1795 improved links in the canal network to the West Midlands may account for the serious decline in income at this gate.

---

[10] Crossley, A., *VCH Oxon*, **10** (1972), 12; Compton, H.J., *The Oxford Canal*, David & Charles (1976).

[11] *JOJ*, Jan. 1790.

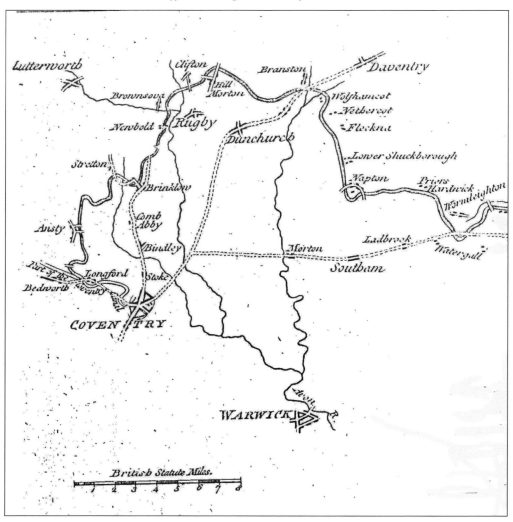

Fig. 34a. The Coventry to Oxford Canal (north): a map published in the "Gentleman's Magazine" of 1771 when construction was just beginning.

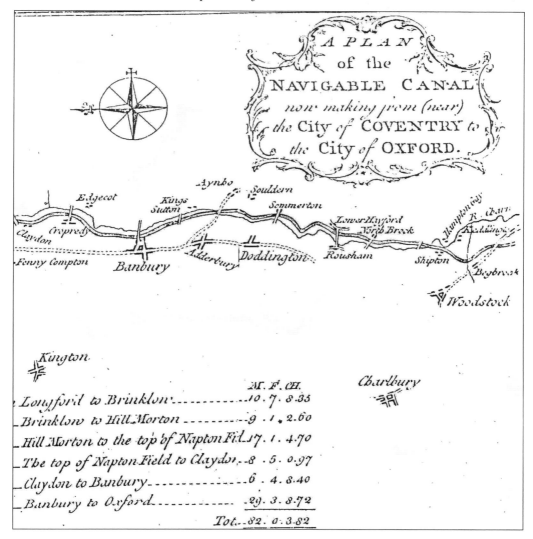

Fig. 34b. The Coventry to Oxford Canal (south): a map published in the "Gentleman's Magazine" of 1771 when construction was just beginning.

Income from turnpike gates south of Banbury also illustrate the effects of new wharves on the canal. The Weeping Cross Turnpike and the Deddington to Kidlington Turnpike had incomes of over £500/a and £600/a between 1779 and 1785. However, in 1787 toll incomes fell to £350 and £500 respectively. *Jackson's Oxford Journal* noted in March 1787 that *"the canal from Banbury to Oxford is now complete for navigation between Deddington and Aynho where coal has been landed and trade opened"*. Hence competition from the Aynho wharf seems to have cut north/south traffic by about a quarter. The Aynho Division of the Burford to Banbury Trust would have been a beneficiary since it was able to erect new toll-gates either side of the new wharf.

9.4 Competition from the Railways

Railways were to be a much more significant source of competition which attracted both passenger and goods traffic off the main roads.[12] Since traffic through Banbury was not dominated by through-services to London, the opening of the railways did not have the disastrous consequences that were experienced by the turnpike roads through Coventry and Oxford.[13] The London to Birmingham railway line was opened as far as Tring on October 16th 1837 and to Birmingham by September 1838; in the short term this presented more opportunities to coach operators. Local services carried passengers to the station, paying tolls as they passed though the turnpike gates. Contemporary maps show that Brackley was 15 miles from Bilsworth Station, Banbury was 19½ miles from Weedon Station and Bicester 21 miles from Wolverton Station. Early rail services even allowed coaches to be loaded directly onto the railway wagons and some public coaches offered combined tickets to cover the road and rail journey.

These opportunities were extended when the Great Western opened as far as Steventon in 1840[14] and in 1843 Mr Beesley was able to offer a coach service from Banbury to the new station (Fig. 35a). Drinkwater and Fowler were still running *The Sovereign* coach from the Red Lion and the White Lion, Banbury, to London in 1843 and early 1844 at the same fare as in the eighteenth century, 16s. (Fig. 35b).

---

[12] *RUTV* 12.

[13] *RUTV* 8; figures (in Appendix 2).

[14] *RUTV* 12.

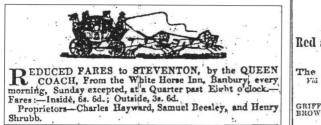

Figs. 35a and 35b. 1843: services to the new railway; cut-price to London.

At the same time Churchill and Fowler operated *The Lion* coach from the Red Lion, Banbury, to Cheltenham (Fig. 35c).

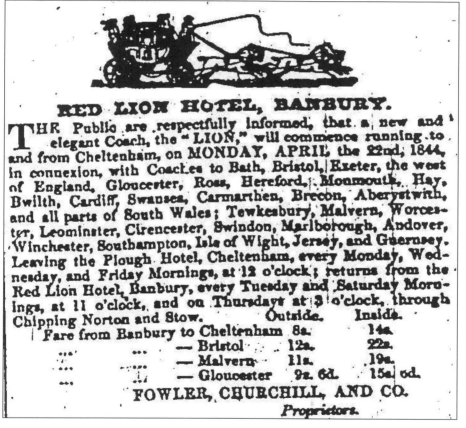

Fig. 35c. By "The Lion" to Cheltenham.

A significant change was to emerge after June 1844 when the railway branch from Didcot to Oxford was opened. Drinkwater & Waddell operated three coaches, *The Favourite*, *The Rival* and *The Regulator*, as feeder services to Oxford station (Fig. 35d),

Fig. 35d. *To the railway at Oxford, 1844.* Fig. 35e. *To the railway at Wolverton, 1844.*

while Fowler & Drinkwater used *The Union* to provide a service to the stations at Wolverton and Aylesbury (Fig. 35e). Later in October 1844 competition between coach operators and the railways intensified and both Drinkwater and Parker operated a coach called *The Sovereign* through Oxford to London (Fig. 34f); the former was *The Original Sovereign*.

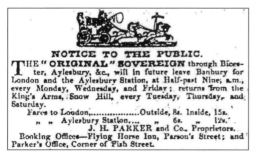

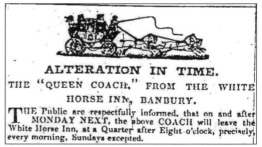

Fig. 35f. *To London by coach, 1844.*   Fig. 35h. *To Oxford by coach, 1844.*

Other operators, including Mr Cave, began to run services to feed passengers to the new main line stations; *The Star* ran to Weedon and *The Queen*, operated by Beesley, joined the services to Oxford (Figs. 35g and 35h).

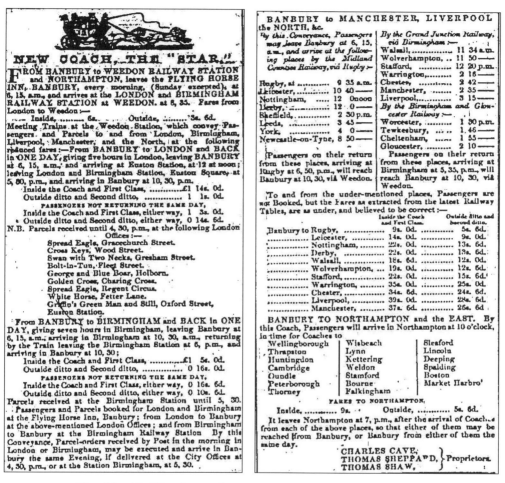

Fig. 35g. To Weedon railway station and Northampton, 1844.

Traffic to stations increased the income to some turnpikes. As a result turnpikes around Banbury and Brackley (Fig. 15, page 67) saw a rise in annual income in the 1840s at a time when the main trunk routes such as the Watling Street experienced a collapse of revenue (Fig. in Appendix 2).

The inexorable growth of the rail network continued and, after a great debate the northward extensions of the line from Oxford was eventually agreed; in 1850 the railway was opened through Banbury to Rugby. All residual long-distance coach services collapsed but the local traffic to Banbury market and vehicles carrying passengers to the stations meant that tolls were still taken at gates on the turnpikes into Banbury. Moreover, the Banbury turnpikes, though not in the top league for income prior to 1830, entered the last half of the nineteenth century as some of the financially more sound trusts in the region (Appendix 2).

10. The End of the Banbury Turnpikes

10.1 Winding up the Trusts

The domination of rail over road as the preferred means for long distance transport made turnpikes less significant in the later nineteenth century. The growth of local government and finance through local taxation removed the need for turnpike trusts, which had been criticised for inefficiency and corruption. The trusts around Banbury were wound up along with many others, in the 1870s (Appendix 1, page 143).

The Drayton to Edgehill Trust had been in financial difficulty as early as 1853. The debt was £2,120 and the trustees had been unable to pay the five percent interest on this during the previous 24 years. The trust was increasingly dependent on the parishes to contribute highway rates. The Home Office suggested that a single payment of a proportion of the unpaid interest was made to the *"landowners in the neighbourhood"* who were the principal debtors and that the road reverted to a parish highway. Nevertheless, the Act was renewed again and it survived until 1871 when several of the turnpikes through Banbury were closed.

The trustees had a final responsibility to dispose of assets, pay off residual loans and prepare for the roads to be handed over to the relevant local Highways Boards. The main assets were the toll-houses and gates. Several tollhouses were taken over directly by the Highways Boards and immediately demolished to widen the road. A few were sold at auction to private buyers for conversion into homes or businesses. In June the Banbury and Lutterworth Trust called for Mr Cave to review all remaining claims on the trust (Fig. 36a).

> ## BANBURY AND LUTTERWORTH TURNPIKE ROAD.
>
> ALL Persons who have any claims or demands upon the Trustees of that part of the above-mentioned Turnpike Road extending between Banbury and the hamlet of Drayton, in the parish of Daventry, are requested to send the particulars thereof forthwith to Mr. Charles Cave, the surveyor of the said road, Bridge Street, Banbury, in order that they may be examined and if found correct, discharged; and Notice is hereby given that the said Trustees will not recognise or be responsible for any claims or demands of which they shall not receive notice on or before the 24th day of June, instant.
>
> E. C. BURTON,
> Clerk.
>
> *Daventry, 6th June, 1871.*

Fig. 36a. Closing down the Trusts: Banbury and Lutterworth Turnpike, 1871.

Mr Cave was also responsible for arranging the sale of materials from the (demolished) toll-houses on the Buckingham to Hanwell upper Division (Fig. 36b),

CROUGHTON AND TINGEWICK.
RUSSEL & SON,

Are instructed by the Trustees of the Buckingham and Hanwell Turnpike Trust (upper division),

TO SELL BY AUCTION,

ON Tuesday, 24th October, 1871, at Two o'clock, upon the premises, in two or more Lots, the whole of the MATE-RIALS comprising the Croughton TOLL HOUSE, with all the fittings, posts and gates, &c.

And on the same day, at Tingewick, at Four o'clock, the GATES and POSTS of the Tingewick TOLL HOUSE.

Full particulars will be given in handbills, to be obtained of Mr. C. Cave, Surveyor, Banbury, or of the Auctioneers, Brackley.

Fig. 26b. Closing down the Trusts: demolition of Croughton toll house.

though the toll-house at Tingewick may have been sold intact. In late 1871 the lower Division was wound-up (Figs. 36c and 36d) and the gates on the Towcester to Weston Turnpike were also demolished and the materials sold.

Buckingham and Hanwell Turnpike Trust, Lower Division.

NOTICE IS HEREBY GIVEN that by virtue of "The Annual Turnpike Acts Continuance Act 1871," the Local Act for the above trust will expire on the First day of November next, and that the Trustees will in persuance of the direction of Mr. Secretary Bruce, make the necessary arrangements for pulling down and removing the several Tollgates, Bars, &c., and if required, the Tollhouses also, and for disposing of the Trust properly, previously to such date.

AND NOTICE IS HEREBY FURTHER GIVEN, that a Meeting of the Trustees of the said Lower Division of the said Road will be held at the Town Hall, in the borough of Banbury, in the County of Oxford, on Tuesday, the Seventeenth day of day of October instant, at 12 o'clock at noon, for the purpose of proceeding with the above mentioned arrangements.

Dated this Second day of October, 1871.

B. W. APLIN,
Clerk to the Trustees.

Fig. 36c. Closing down: winding up of Buckingham to Hanwell Trust (Lower Division).

BUCKINGHAM and HANWELL TURNPIKE ROAD.
Lower Division
TOLL HOUSES, LAND AND GATES, FOR SALE.
TO BE SOLD BY AUCTION, BY
MR. JAMES HALL,

AT the Red Lion Inn, in Adderbury, in the County of Oxford, on Monday, the 30th day of October, instant, at 4 o'clock in the Afternoon (by direction of the Trustees of the said Road, the Trusts of which will expire on the 1st day of November next) under Conditions to be then produced, unless previously disposed of by private contract, of which due notice will be given.

LOT 1.—
The Materials of all that MESSUAGE or TENEMENT at Adderbury aforesaid, and the Buildings thereto belonging, now used as the Toll House for the Adderbury Turnpike Gate on the main road leading from Banbury to Aynho.

LOT 2.—
The Turnpike GATES with the POSTS and Sidings on each side of the said Toll House.

LOT 3.—
The Materials of all that MESSUAGE or TENEMENT and Buildings thereto belonging, now used as the Toll House for the Twyford Lane Turnpike Gate on the road leading from Banbury to Adderbury.

LOT 4.—
The Turnpike GATE with the POSTS and Sidings adjoining Lot 3.

N.B.—The Materials of each Lot will have to be taken down and removed by the purchaser at his own expense within a time to be named in the Conditions of the time of Sale.

Further particulars may be obtained, and a Plan of the Land seen at the Offices of Mr. Aplin, and of the Auctioneer, in Banbury.

NOTICE IS HEREBY GIVEN that the PIECE of LAND, forming Lot 5 of the Property advertised to be Sold by Auction by Mr. James Hall, at the Red Lion Inn, in Adderbury, on Monday, the 30th October, 1871, IS WITHDRAWN FROM THE SALE.

B. W. APLIN.

Banbury 24th October, 1871.

Fig. 36d. Closing down: demolition of Adderbury and Twyford Lane toll-houses., 1871.

The Drayton to Edgehill trustees instructed Henry Kirby to superintend the taking down of the Drayton Toll-house before the materials were auctioned by Mr Hall. Drayton Toll-house was definitely demolished (Figs. 36e and 36f) and it must be assumed that the Edgehill Toll-house was similarly removed. The toll-board from the latter may have been saved at the Sun Rising Inn until its value was recognised and it was donated to Banbury Museum.

DRAYTON AND EDGEHILL TURN-PIKE TRUST.

NOTICE is HEREBY GIVEN that by virtue of " The Annual Turnpike Acts Continuance Act 1871," the Local Act for the above Trust will expire on the first day of November next, and that the Trustees will in pursuance of the direction of Mr. Secretary Bruce make the necessary arrangements for pulling down and removing the several Tollgates, Bars, &c., and if required the Toll-houses also, and for disposing of the Trust Property.

And Notice is Hereby further given that a meeting of the Trustees of the said Road will be held at the Office of Mr. Fortescue in Banbury, on Monday, the thirteenth day of November next, at 12 o'clock at Noon, for the purpose of proceeding with the above-mentioned arrangements.

Dated this 25th day of October 1871.

JOHN FORTESCUE,
Clerk to the Trustees.

Figs. 36e and 36f. Closing down: demolition of Drayton and (probably) Edgehill toll-houses, 1871.

DRAYTON AND EDGE HILL TURNPIKE ROAD.
Toll Houses and Gates for Sale.
TO BE SOLD BY AUCTION, BY

JAMES HALL,

AT the Roe Buck Inn in Drayton, in the County of Oxford, on Friday, the 24th day of November instant, at 4 o'clock in the afternoon, by direction of the Trustees of the said Roads, under conditions to be then produced, in convenient Lots. The materials of the Drayton, Edge Hill, and Hornton Toll, also the Turnpike Gates with the Posts and sidings.

The above will be expressed in Catalogues to be had at the Roe Buck, Drayton, the Castle, Edge Hill, and of the Auctioneer, Banbury.

Other trusts were dissolved over the following years. In November 1873, when the Brackley Consolidated Trust was dissolved, it was ordered that all toll-houses be removed and auctioned by Mr Russell of Brackley. The Deddington to Kidlington Trust sold its assets in 1876 (Fig. 36g); although the weighing engine at Water Eaton was removed, the two-storey stone toll-house at Old Man's Gate (page 60) still survives. The Bicester, Aynho and Finmere Trust was dissolved in 1877 and the Sheep Street Gate was taken down. However, at least one gate was sold as a residence: the old Souldern Toll-house (page 45) still stands at the junction of the modern road and the lane into the village. It is a fairly substantial two-storey cottage built of local stone. Two other surviving toll-houses, at Swerford Heath (page 82), and at Broughton (page 85), are also of local stone. The latter is clearly a high quality, purpose built cottage, the former a rather less prestigious structure but still clearly designed to accommodate a toll collector.

> **DEDDINGTON AND KIDLINGTON TURNPIKE TRUST.**
>
> THE Trustees invite TENDERS for the purchase of the Gates, Side-Gates, Posts, and Weighing Machines at the Toll House at Water Eaton; and also for the purchase of the Gates, Side-Gates, and Posts at Deddington; such Tenders may be for the whole or any part of the above.
>
> Any person whose Tender may be accepted must remove the materials and securely re-make and restore the road during the daytime of Wednesday, the 1st November, 1876.
>
> The Trustees do not bind themselves to accept the highest or any Tender.
>
> Tenders to be delivered to the Clerk, marked outside "Tender," on or before Friday, the 27th day of October instant.
>
> The Trustees request any persons, who may have any claims or demands upon the Trust, to send particulars thereof to the Clerk before the first day of November, 1876, up to which time and no longer the Trust is continued.
>
> By order,
>
> JOHN HESTER,
>
> 117, *St. Aldate's-street, Oxford.* Clerk.

Fig. 36g. Closing down: Deddington and Kidlington Trust sale of assets, 1876.

10.2 Remaining Evidence

Besides a few toll-houses, the most lasting pieces of road-side furniture from the turnpike era are the distance makers that the trusts were obliged to place every mile along the road. Initially these would have been carved stone[1] but, during the nineteenth century, most of the trusts in this region seem to have put cast iron plates on the stones, rather than having the letters recut regularly.

---

[1] *RUTV* 10.

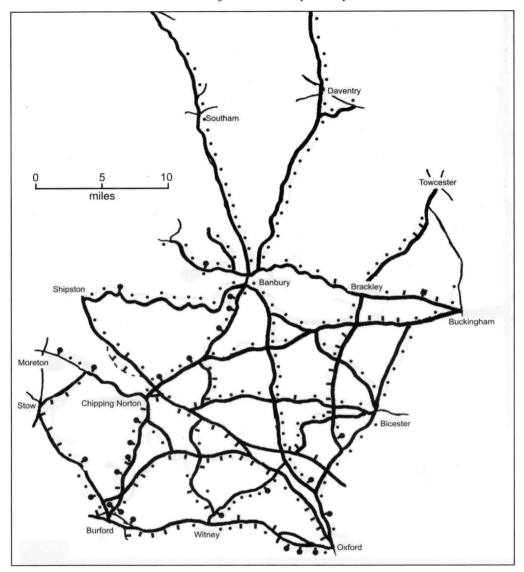

Fig. 37. Milestones surviving on old turnpike roads around Banbury.

Key   ♀ readable condition   ▪ defaced or unreadable stone   • missing stone
          ♣ restored since 1976   based on OCC and OS maps

A carved milestone survives in Wroxton[2] (Fig. 38a), having been recut after many years hidden in the hedge.

Fig. 38a. Wroxton milestone in 1969.

In 1819 the Drayton to Edgehill Trust ordered that *"proper milestones be provided which are to have cast iron faces market in with figures describing their perceptive* [sic] *distances from London"*. The Towcester to Weston Trust agreed to put up a direction post at Brackley but had hesitated to replace all the milestones in 1835 due to the cost. The quotations for iron mileposts had been 30s. each from Banbury Ironworks but only 24s. each from Messrs Barlow at Northampton.

Unfortunately, unlike the roads in Berkshire, those in north Oxfordshire and the adjoining counties retain very few of their milestones. Over-zealous destruction of wayside markers to confuse potential invaders during the second World War, and the ease with which the cast iron plates could be removed by souvenir hunters, robbed the area of these tangible reminders of the turnpike age.

Figs. 38b, 38c, and 38d: Bicester to Aynho; Brackley Consolidated Trust; Banbury to Shipston.

---

[2] Lawrence, K. "Turnpike Roads in Oxfordshire". Museum Service **5**. (1969, 1977).

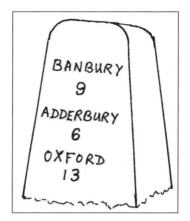 

Figs. 38e and 38f: Kidlington to Deddington; Banbury to Shipston.

The best surviving series of markers is that from Burford to Banbury (Fig. 38f), and even this is incomplete. A few milestones have been restored since Oxfordshire surveyed them in the mid 1970s; one of the best, taken from the Banbury Road, is displayed outside the County Offices in Oxford. Ironically, the oldest milestone in Oxfordshire is in this area, at Wroxton (Fig. 38g). Although this is technically a direction marker, the stone cross set up by Francis White in 1686, well before the creation of the turnpikes, directs travellers from London to Droitwich and Banbury to Stratford.

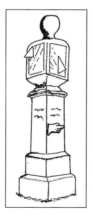

Fig. 38g. Wroxton Direction Post.

The toll board from Edgehill is preserved in Banbury Museum and some papers survive, chiefly in County Record Offices at Northampton and Warwick. However, the best and most lasting memento of the turnpike system around Banbury is the modern road network, which was laid out by the public-spirited gentlemen who formed the turnpike trusts in the eighteenth century.

Appendix 1:
Dates of Turnpike Acts for roads around Banbury.
(exp indicates expiration and closure)

1. Woodstock to Rollright Lane
1730	3 Geo II c21
1751	24 Geo II c21
1758	31 Geo II c48
1784	24 Geo III s2 c61
1804	44 Geo III c79
1822	3 Geo IV c126
1823	4 Geo IV c95
1824	5 Geo IV c69
1825	6 Geo IV c94
1846	9/10 Vic c7
1877	41/2 Vic c62 (exp)

2. Chappel on the Heath to Bourton Hill
1731	4 Geo II c27
1743/4	17 Geo II c10
1765	5 Geo III c80
1790/1	31 Geo III c111
1816	56 Geo III c1
1849	12/13 Vic c46
	to Stow & Moreton United Rd
1867/8	31/2 Vic c99
1870	33/4 Vic c73 (exp May 71)

3. Buckingham to Warmington (later Hanwell)
1743/4	17 Geo II c43
1769	9 Geo III c52 shortened to Hanwell
1792	32 Geo III c134
1811	51 Geo III c2
1831/2	2 Will IV c34
1867/8	31/2 Vic c99
1871	34/5 Vic c115 (exp Nov 71)

4. Drayton to Edgehill
1753	26 Geo II c
1779/80	20 Geo III c67
1801	41 Geo III c84
1822	3 Geo IV c90
1852	16/17 Vic c135
1853	17/18 Vic c58
1870	33/4 Vic c73
1871	34/5 Vic c115 (exp Nov 1871)

5a. Finford to Banbury
1755	28 Geo II c46
1779	20 Geo III c69
1801	42 Geo III c14
1822	3 Geo IV c95
1859	22/23 Vic c92
1878	41/2 Vic c62 (exp Nov 78)

5b. Kidlington to Deddington
1755	28 Geo II c46
1797	37 Geo III c170
1819	59 Geo III c122
1875	38/9 Vic c194

6. Towcester to Weston on the Green
1756/7	30 Geo II c48
1777/8	18 Geo III c87
1801	41 Geo III c50
1820	1 Geo IV c73
1851	14/5 Vic c61 (amalgamated)
1873	36/7 Vic c90 (exp Nov 73)

7. Banbury to Lutterworth
1765	5 Geo III c105
1785	25 Geo III c128
1807	47 Geo III c91
1828	9 Geo IV c86
1840	3 Vic c38
1867	31/2 Vic 99
1870	33/4 Vic c73 (exp May 71)

8. Stoney Stratford to Woodstock
1768/9 8/9 Geo III c88

9. Edgehill, Upton, Kineton to Wellesbourne
1770   10 Geo III c63
1792   32 Geo III c116
1812   52 Geo III c61
1833   3/4 Will IV c41
1867/8 31/2 Vic c99
1872   35/6 Vic c85 (exp Nov 72)

10. Bicester to Aylesbury
1770   10 Geo III c72
1791   31 Geo III c101
1813   53 Geo III c199
1833   3/4 Will IV c24
1863/4 27/8 Vic c75
1864/5 28/9 Vic c107
1874/5 38/9 Vic c194 (exp)

11. Burford to Banbury
1770   10 Geo III c101
1790/1 31 Geo III c128
1810   50 Geo III c210
1831/2 2 Will IV c16
1867   31/2Vic c99
        (Stow & Moreton United Rds)
1871 34/5 Vic c115 (exp May 77)
1872   35/6 Vic c85
        (Aynho div exp Nov 72)

12. Gosford
1781   21 Geo III c87
1801   41 Geo III c137
1821   1/2 Geo IV c86

13. Bicester to Aynho
1790   31 Geo III c103
1812   53 Geo III c200
1856/7 20/1 Vic c9
1876   39/40 Vic c39 (exp Nov 77)

14. Buckingham, Brackley, Banbury
1790/1 31 Geo III c105
1810   50 Geo III c 133
1820   1 Geo IV c200
1851   14/5 Vic c61 amalgamated
1873   36/7 Vic c90 (exp Nov 73)

15. Enstone, Heyford to Bicester
1793   33 Geo III c180
1813   53 Geo III c133
1851   14/5 Vic c38
1855   18/9 Vic c98
1856   19/20 Vic c49
1857   20/21 Vic c9
1858   21/22 Vic c63
1876   39/40 Vic c39 (exp)

16. Banbury, Brailes to Barcheston
1802   42 Geo III c38
1823   4 Geo IV c105
1872   35/6 Vic c85 (exp)

17. Southam to Kineton
1852   15/16 Vic c55
1874   37/8 Vic c95 (exp Nov 74)

Appendix 2: Financial Details of Turnpike Trusts

Table A2.1: Outstanding debts of turnpike trusts around Banbury

Trust	Debt before 1800 (£)	Debt in 1835 (£)	Ratio of debt to income 1835 *	Debt in 1870 (£)
3a. Buckingham - Hanwell, Upper div	475 (1768)	805	1.4	120
3b. Buckingham - Hanwell, Lower div		0	0	0
4. Drayton - Edgehill		4,787	23.7	800
5a. Finford - Banbury	1,700 (1800)	2,895	2.6	1,020
5b. Kidlington - Deddington		1,600	1.8	1,100
6. Towcester, Brackley, Weston		2,000	2.5	
7a. Banbury - Lutterworth, North div.		250	0.4	0
7b. Banbury - Lutterworth South div.	1,876 (1785)	652	0.7	0
9. Kineton - Wellesbourne	1,300 (1771)	2,040	8.3	0
10. Bicester - Aylesbury	3,300 (1791)	3,300	3.3	1,250
11. Burford, Chipping Norton, Banbury	1,270 (1792)	870	0.6	0
13. Bicester, Aynho, Finmere		0	0	0
14. Buckingham, Brackley, Banbury	3,070 (1793)	2,830	4.0	3,800
16. Banbury, Brailes, Barcheston		2,740	4.3	3,664

* for income to pay for interest on debt at 5%/a the ratio needs to be less than 20

Table A2.2: Typical toll charges on Turnpikes
(where the basis of charging is per vehicle, an estimate has been made of the toll per horse)

Year	Trust	coach horse	wag-gon horse	horse not drawing	cattle per score	sheep per score	Steam	tolls per day
1730	Woodstock - Rollright	3d	1.5d	1d	1s-3d	10d		
1731	Chappel on the Heath - Bourton	~3d	~3d	1d	10d	2d		
1747	Buckingham - Warmington	3d	~2d	1d	5d	5d		
1751	Crickley Hill - Campsfield (to Botley)	4d (3d)	4d (3d)	2d (1d)	10d (10d)	5d (5d)		
1751	Woodstock - Rollright	~2d	~2d	1d	10d	4d		
1753	Drayton - Edgehill	~2d	~2d	1d	10d	5d		
1755	Finford - Banbury Adderbury - Oxford/Weston	3d 3d	~2d ~2d	1d 1d	10d 10d	5d 5d		1/brch
1756	Towcester - Weston	3d	3d	1d	10d	5d		
1765	Banbury - Lutterworth	3d	~3d	1d	10d	5d		
1768	Stoney Stratford - Woodstock	6d	6d	2d	10d	5d		
1770	Banbury - Burford	6d		2d	1s-3d	10d		1/brch
1790	Bicester - Buckingham	4d	3d	1d	10d	5d		
1802	Banbury - Shipston	4d		1.5d				
1802	Finford - Banbury	5d	5d	1.5d	1s-8d	10d		
1804	Woodstock - Rollright	4d		1.5d	10d	5d		
1807	Banbury - Lutterworth	6d		1.5d				
1811	Buckingham - Hanwell	6d		2d				
1819	Gosford	3d	3d	1d	10d	5d		
1819	Bicester - Aynho	6d	6d	2d	1s-3d	10d		up to 2
1820	Towcester - Weston	6d	4d	2d				
1821	Crickley Hill - Campsfield	6d		2d	1s-8d	10d		
1822	Finford - Banbury		5d	1.5d				
1822	Drayton - Edgehill	3d	3d	1d	10d	5d		
1828	Banbury - Lutterworth	6d	6d	1.5d	10d	5d		up to 5

Year	Trust	coach horse	wag-gon horse	horse not drawing	cattle per score	sheep per score	Steam	tolls per day
1832	Buckingham - Hanwell	6d		2d				
1832	Burford - Banbury	6d		2d				
1834	Barrington - Campsfield	6d	6d	2d	1s-8d	10d	2s	
1840	Banbury - Lutterworth	6d	6d	1.5d				
1846	Woodstock - Rollright	4d	4d	2d	10d	5d	8d/wh	
1859	Finford - Banbury	6d	5d	1.5d			1s/wh	

Table A2.3: Trust income from lease of specific gates.

1. Woodstock to Rollright

Gates	1802	1812
Woodstock	£405	£775
Sansom's	£120	£295
Enslow Bridge		
Burgess's	£485	£600
Kiddington	£155	

2. Chappel on the Heath to Bourton

Gate	1760	1802	1823
Chipping Norton			£452
Salford Hill	£92		
Moreton	£92	£240	£463
Bourton	--	--	

3a. Buckingham to Hanwell (Upper Div)

Gate		1819
Dropshort		
Tingewick & Astwick		£458
Finmere Warren		
Croughton		

3b. Buckingham to Hanwell (Lower Div)

Gate	1792	1820	1844
Weeping Cross	£440	--	--
Adderbury		£575	
Twyford Lane			£1151
Neithrop		£253	

4. Drayton Lane to Edgehill

Gate	1790	1830	1850
Drayton Lane	£90	£200	£200
Edgehill	£35		

5a. Finford to Banbury

Gate	1760	1790	1823
Stretton	£70	£130	£124
Frankton	--	--	
Long Itchington	--	--	£291
Ladbrooke	£25	£40	
Bourton	--	--	£376
Hardwick	£55	£70	

5b. Adderbury to Kidlington

Gate	1780	1802
Deddington	£610	£556
Old Man's		

6. Towcester to Weston

Gates	1779	1830	1865
Weston		£120	£80
Middleton	£44		
Brackley Bridge			
Evenley			
Brackley Town			
Brackley North End			
Hoppesford	£89	£160	£650
Biddlesden Lane			
Silverstone			
Burcot Wood	£105	£300	£300
Towcester			

7a. Banbury to Lutterworth

Gate	1794	1823
Mill Field		
Dowbridge		
Welton		
Badby		
Byfield		£108
Wilscot		£85
Banbury Bridge	£264	£446

9. Edgehill to Wellesbourne

Gate	1839	1856
Great Kington	£191	£194
Wellesbourne	£85	£54

10. Bicester to Aylesbury

Gate	1792	1802
Stone Bridge	£175	£199
Westcott	£87	£100
Wrenchwick	£121	£193
Launton		

11. Burford to Banbury

Gates	1780	1830	1850
Gawcum		£87	£33
Rissington		£64	£32
Burford/ Fulbrook	£170	£309	£290
Chipping Norton	£60	£126	
Chapel Heath	£50	£182	
Swerford Heath			
Wykham		£321	
Saltway	£100		
Deddington		£65	
Clifton		£175	
Aynho			

12. Gosford

Gates	1782	1823	1860
Gosford	£98	£420	£157

13. Bicester to Aynho

Gates	1802	1830	1850
Skimming Dish Barn			
Bicester Sheep Street	£177	£332	£380
Launton Lane			
Souldern	£80	£221	
Fringford			

14. Buckingham, Brackley, Banbury

Gates	1850	1865
Buckingham		
Radclive		
Buffler's Holt Turweston Hill	£150	£260
Steane Farthinghoe Grimsbury Green	£400	£440

15. Enstone, Bicester, Weston

Gates	1820	1873
Cuckold's Holt		£21
Barton		£320
Langford Lane		
Heyford Bridge		
Chesterton		£261
Bicester King's End	£347	
Kirtlington	£81	£63

16. Banbury, Brailes, Barcheston

Gates	1810	1830	1850
Broughton	£250	£320	£380
Brailes	£90	£100	£105
Barcheston	£120	£150	£160

Towcester to Cotton End

Gate		1823
Tiffield		£148
Blisworth		£21
Far Cotton		£137

Appendix 3: Administration of Turnpike Trusts - (information from Minutes Books and Parliamentary Papers) (1)

Trust	Clerk	Treasurer	Surveyor	Bondholders	Meetings Venue
01. Woodstock to Rollright Lane	George Bulley (1775-1812) Henry Francis Mavor (1820) Benjamin Holloway of Woodstock (1832-1849)	Pearson & Co (1835)	Thomas Cheney (1835)		Bear, Woodstock (1779, 92, 94, 1805, 32, 49) Talbot, Enstone (1782, 94) Litchfield Arms, Enstone (1775) Marlborough Arms, Woodstock (1800, 02, 12, 20, 23)
02. Chapel on the Heath to Bourton Hill	Groves Wheeler, Chipping Norton (1772) Robert Chamberlayne (1774) Joseph Knight (1775, 88, 1802)	John Jones (1731-67) Rev Thomas Biggs			White Hart, Moreton (1775) Unicorn, Moreton (1784, 1802, 23)
03a. Buckingham to Hanwell (Upper Div)	Robert Miller (1775, 85) Thomas Hearn of Buckingham (1819-35)	Edward Parrott (1835)	George Cave (1835) Charles Cave (1871)		Cobham Arms, Buckingham (1775, 1819, 23)
03b. Buckingham to Hanwell (Lower Div) (Weeping Cross Turnpike)	Richard Bignell of Bicester & Thame (1775- 93 and 1820-44) BW Aplin of Banbury (1844-71)	Gillet & Tawney (1835)	George Cave (1835)		Three Tuns, Banbury (1775, 82) Red Lion, Banbury (1785, 92, 93) Town Hall, Banbury (1820, 23, 44, 71)
04. Drayton to Edgehill	John Makepeace (1753-1756) Charles Hide (1756-1766) Christopher Aplin of Adderbury (1766-94) William Walford of Banbury (1822-1845) John Fortescue (1853-1871)	Francis Edge (1753-1755) John Makepeace (1755-56) Charles Hide (1756-1766) Wm Barker (1766-1770) Christopher Aplin (1770-) Charles Wyatt (1785-) Charles Tawney of Banbury, banker (1822-24) Henry Tawney (1824-35)	Samuel Welchman (1753-) John Hayes (1808-) George Cave (1835)	1753/5 Earl of Guilford, Sir John Willes, Lord Chief Justice Dutchess of Argyll, Edward Burford, Earl of Dartmouth. 1801 Lady Maria North, Lord Dartmouth, Jno Willes, Jno Burford.	Red Lion, Banbury (1771, 84, 88, 92) Town Hall, Banbury (1794)

Appendix 3: Administration of Turnpike Trusts - (information from Minutes Books and Parliamentary Papers) (2)

Trust	Clerk	Treasurer	Surveyor	Bondholders	Meetings Venue
05a. Finford (Ryton Bridge) to Banbury	John Spicer (1755-1772) John Newcombe (1772-1792) Henry Rolls (1792 -1835) Richard Hry Rolls of Banbury (1844, 5) DP Pellatt of Banbury (1871-5)	T.S. Wright (1835)	1755/6 Joseph Parker 1757-64 Jonathan Burgess 1804 George Burgess Snr Richard Gould (1835)		Craven Arms, Southam (1844, 71)
05b. Deddington to Kidlington	Richard Bradgate (1755) John Walker (1779-88) Samuel Churchill (1797-Churchill & Field (1835) Henry Churchill (-1871) Geo P Hester (1871, 4) John Hester (1876)	Parsons & Co (1835)	Edwin Wagstaff (-1756) Richard Gould (1835) Charles Cave (1871)		Fox & Crown, North Aston (1755 - 1788) Town Hall, Oxford (1875)
06. Towcester to Weston (Brackley Consolidated Roads)	Robert Weston of Brackley (1779, 84, 88, 92, 1802, 20, 34, 35)	Dr Causton (until 1825) Edward Bartlett of Buckingham (1825, 34, 35-)	Mr Cave (till 1822) Charles White (1822-) William Holland of Silverstone (1823) John Weston of Hunton (1823) John Maynard (till 1831) George Cave of Bodicote (1831, 4, 5) Charles Cave of Banbury (1856-)	Lord Bridgewater Earl Brownlow	Crown Inn, Brackley (1779, 84, 80, 92, 1802)
07a. Banbury to Lutterworth. (Banbury to Daventry Div.)	Henry Bagshaw Harrison (1765-94) Edward S Burton, of Daventry (1835) E C Burton of Daventry (1871)	John Loveday (1835)	Jeffery College (1765-68) Thomas College (1768-1800) Thomas College Jnr (1802-Richard D'Anvers (1765-) George Cave (1835)		Red Lion, Banbury (1784, 94, 1823)

Appendix 3: Administration of Turnpike Trusts - (information from Minutes Books and Parliamentary Papers) (3)

Trust	Clerk	Treasurer	Surveyor	Bondholders	Meetings Venue
07b. Banbury to Lutterworth. (Badby to Lutterworth Div.)	Thomas Holled (1765-) Edward S Burton, of Daventry (1835) E C Burton of Daventry (1871)	Revd Thomas Smith (1835)	George Cave (1835)		Wheatsheaf, Daventry (1823)
10. Aylesbury to Bicester	Joseph Burnham (1779) Henry Churchill (1781 - 1802) R Smith & Henry Walford of Bicester (1819, 20) James James of Aylesbury (1832-73)	John Parrot (1835)	William Cross (1835)		Kings Arms, Bicester (1779, 90. 92, 1802, 20) White Hart, Aylesbury (1819, 44)
09. Great Kington to Wellesbourne	K Greenway of Warwick (1835) Gennis & Docker of Birmingham (1857)	Robert Green of Corbrook (1770) Josiah Woodley (1835)	William Jones of Gt Kington (1770) George Cave (1835) Taylor & Fitzpatrick of Edgebaston (1857)	1770-4: Robert Child Esq Robert Green, Lord Willoughby de Broke, Lord Warwick, Charles Henry Talbot, Thomas Woodward, Thomas Greenway, John Welchman, Margaret Claridge, Lord Guilford, Lady Maria North, 1793: Elizabeth Court 1823: Marquis of Bath, Earl of Guilford, Revd Wyatt, Revd Leonard, W Walford 1829: Marchioness of Bute	
11. Burford, Chipping Norton to Banbury	Samuel Churchill (1770-90, 2, 1812, 19) Weston Aplin of Chipping Norton (1829, 31, 35) John North Wilkins of Bourton (1829, 35) Samuel Churchill Field of Deddington (1829, 35) WGW Lovell of Deddington (1871)	Peter Brooks (1770) Rev Stone (1771) Rev Jones (1779) John Matthews (Chipping Norton), Jackson Clark (Stow) & Timothy Rhodes Cobb (Banbury) (1833, 35)	Mr Cave (1821) George Cave of Banbury (1819, 33, 35) Thomas Saul of Milton (Stow) (1833, 35) William Jeynes (Ch Norton) (1823) John Edwards Maynard (Swerford) (1823)		White Hart, Chipping Norton (1777, 92, 1812, 18) Elephant & Castle, Bloxham (1819) Kings Arms, Deddington (1820) Cartwright Arms, Aynho (1871)

Appendix 3: Administration of Turnpike Trusts - (information from Minutes Books and Parliamentary Papers) (4)

Trust	Clerk	Treasurer	Surveyor	Bondholders	Meetings Venue
12. Gosford	Edward King (1781-84 dec) Wm Elias Taunton of Oxford (1819) John Taunton of Oxford (1835)	Sir Jos Lock (1835)	Richard Dixon (1835)		Talbot, Middleton (1781) Red Lion, Islip (1782) Kings Head, Oxford (1784) Town Hall, Oxford (1785, 90, 1823)
13. Bicester to Aynho & Finmere	Henry Churchill (1790, 92, 1802) Samuel Churchill (1825, 35) Samuel Churchill Field of Deddington (1825-1833 dec) Henry Churchill (1862-) William Hardman Mills of Bicester (1873, 5)	Richard Smith (1825) Tubb & Co (1835)	John Edward Maynard (1825-41) John Harris Jnr (1835, 41-) Charles Cave Snr (-1856 d) Charles Cave Jnr (1856-) George Cave (-1860) Samuel Harris of Bicester (1860-63 sacked) Henry Hawtins of Kirtlington (1863-)	George Cobb, J & R Bathe, Revd Griffiths Lloyd, Mary Catherine Sheperd, William Coleman, George Tubb, Mrs White, H B Churchill, J H Harrison Mrs Rowland	Kings Arms, Bicester (1792-1873)
14. Buckingham, Brackley, Banbury (to Brackley Consolidated Rd)	Robert Weston of Brackley (1835-56)	Edward Bartlett (1835) Edward Parrot (1851)	George Cave (1835-56) Charles Cave 1856-	Earl Brownlow	
15. Bicester, Heyford to Enstone	Samuel Churchill Jnr (1794, 1812, 20, 35)	Tubb & Co (1835)	John Harris (1835)		Kings Arms, Bicester (1812, 20, 73) Hopcrofts Holt (1794)
16. Banbury, Brailes to Barcheston	Samuel Churchill of Woodstock (1802, 20, 35) William Walford of Banbury (1802, 20, 35, 44) John Fortescue of Banbury (1871)	Thomas Wapshot (- 1812) T Cobb & William Gillett (1835)	Richard Gould (1835)		George Inn, Brailes (1802, 20) Red Lion, Banbury (1843, 44) Twistleton Fiennes Arms, Broughton (1844)
Buckingham to Towcester	William Elliot of Towcester (1835)	Bartlett (1835)			
Towcester to Cotton End	Thomas Hughes of Northampton (1835)	Percival & Co (1835)	Thomas March (1835)		

Appendix 4:

An Enquiry into the means of preserving and improving the Publick Roads of this kingdom, with observations on the probable consequences of this present plan
by Henry Homer A.M.
Rector of Birdingbury in Warwickshire and chaplain to the Rt Hon The Lord Leigh
Oxford 1767.

To the Rt Hon The Earl of Aylesford
The Rt Hon The Lord Leigh, high steward of the University of Oxford
The Hon Wriothesley Digby Esq
Sir William Wheeler, bart
Sir Theophilius Biddulph, bart
William Bromley Esq, M.P.
and other acting commissioners upon the two turnpike roads, one leading from Dunchurch in the County of Warwickshire to Stonebridge, the other from Finford, alias Ryton Bridge in the same County to Banbury.

The following enquiry founded chiefly upon the experience which has resulted from his connections with these is with all humility dedicated, as a testimony of his great honour and esteem for them, by their fellow commissioner and most obedient servant, the author.

Chapter 1:   of the Utility of public roads
Chapter 2:   of the ancient institute of roads in this Kingdom, with a sketch of the modern Parliamentary provisions made for the support of this.
Chapter 3:   of the method of constructing roads or bringing them to a proper form
Chapter 4:   of the application of materials to the repair of roads
Chapter 5:   of the causes of the decay of turnpike roads with some remarks upon the defects of the provision made to prevent this
Chapter 6:   of carriages and their operation upon roads with a view of the comparative effects of broad and narrow wheels
Chapter 7:   of inland navigation
Chapter 8:   General reflections

The great objects to be kept in view in management of roads are to support them as a convenient state of use and to effect that with as small expense as is possible, of materials. Neither of these can be effectively obtained without guarding them from unnecessary injury and this must be done either by a Limitation of the weight, the construction of the carriages, or the usage of the roads, or rather by an attention in some degree to every one of these particulars. No breadth of wheels, which is consistent with general use, can for the reasons given in the course of this enquiry, make amends for the effects of excessive weights, nor the improper treatment with even moderate ones. To expect that all parts of the road however circumstanced can be kept in a state fit for travellers upon, or that the use of un-mended paths may be confounded at all seasons without an extraordinary waste of materials, is to expect things to happen contrary to probabilities and experience.

Nothing could have prevented the roads in many parts of England from being entirely destroyed by the increase of weight, but an enlargement of the terms and powers granted to Commissioners, and particularly an increase of their tolls by multiplying gates, which upon examination the author doubts not would be found to have taken place almost universally, at or since the commencement of this scheme over tracts of bad country frequented with heavy draughts. Whether then it can at best be considered in any other light than a temporary expedient, and whether perseverance in a measure, which every bowel of our country must be ransacked to support, be consistent with the duty which we owe to posterity, is a matter which deserves a very serious consideration.

A proper construction of the carriages is certainly the most easy, and of all other perhaps the most efficient means of security to the roads, but then it should not be such a consideration as will enable them to carry heavy, but such as one, as will oblige them to carry light loads. A middling breadth of felly to the wheels, neither so small as to cut deep, nor yet so great as to prevent a little gradual impression, which serves as a guide to keep carriages in regular tracks, is the true method of confining the wearing to a narrow compass, which with judicious management will certainly lessen it, and by lessening that, the road will be kept clean, and will be both more convenient and pleasant for use. A limitation of the number of horses is desirable for no other purpose, but as it tends to lessen the weight, for

Note. This is a brief abstract of the "Enquiry". The pamphlet can be seen in full at the Bodleian Library, Oxford, Oxf. 1767. 8° G Pamph, 1865 1. 24755 e80.

Appendix 5: Routes in Cary's "Roads"

compiled by Jeremy Gibson

My great-great-grandfather Henry Stone (see page 117) was for a short time a Banbury carrier, and a family heirloom from this time is a copy of

Cary's New Intinerary *or an accurate delineation of the Great Roads, both Direct and Cross, throughout England and Wales... 11th edition, 1828.*

The various routes following Turnpike Roads [TP] in the area have been identified and facsimiles of the directions are shown below.

ROADS FROM LONDON

Aylesbury via Stratford to Birmingham.
Cary column 240.
Buckingham to Banbury TP (1794) (p.42).

	M	F	M	F
bpBUCKINGHAM×–P.O. A Corporate Town— 689 *H.* 3465 *I.*—The Assizes are held here alternately with Aylesbury. *On* l. *to Banbury, through Aynhoe,* 18 M.	2	7	57	6
Westbury×	4	7	62	5
bpBRACKLEY. *Northamptonshire* A Corporate Town— 354 *H.* 1851 *I.* *On* r. *to Towcester,* 11¼ M.; *on* l. *to Oxford,* 22.	2	5	65	2
Farthingho×	3	4	68	6
Middleton *Near Banbury, on* r. *to Daventry,* 17¼ M. *Cross the Charwell R. (see p.* 192*), and Oxford Canal (see p.* 154*).*	2	6	71	4
bpBANBURY×—*Church* A Corporate Town— 701 *H.* 3396 *I.* *On* r. *to Daventry,* 15¾ M.; *on* l. *to Chipping Norton,* 12½.	2	1	73	5

Cary column 243. Drayton Lane to Edgehill TP (1753) (p.34); Edgehill via Stratford to Birmingham TP (1726) (p.34).

	M	F	M	F
Through Banbury, on r. *to Southam,* 14 M.; 1 M. *further, on* r. *to Warwick,* 18.				
Drayton—*T. G.*	2	1	75	6
Wroxton×	—	7	76	5

	M	F	M	F
Wroxton× *Within* ¾ M. *of Edge Hill, on* r. *to Warwick,* 14.	—	7	76	5
EdgeHill×-*Rising Sun Warwicksh.* *Over Oxhill and Pillerton Commons to*	5	—	81	5
Pillerton	4	3	86	—
Upper Eatington×— *T. G.*	1	6	87	6
¼ M. *beyond Eatington, on* r. *to Warwick,* 10¼; *on* l. *to Shipston,* 6½. *Near Stratford, on* r. *to Kineton,* 10 M.; *on* l. *to Shipston,* 10½. *Cross the Avon, (see p.* 155*).*				
pSTRATFORD UPON AVON× *(p.* 227*) M.H.* *On* r. *to Warwick,* 8¼ M.; *and Birmingham,* 23. 3 M. *from Stratford cross the Stratford on Avon Canal (see p.* 229*); and about* 4 M. *further cross the Alne (see p.* 227*).*	5	7	93	5

Buckingham via Warwick to Birmingham.
Cary column 257. Through Banbury to Warmington TP (1743); Warmington to Warwick TP (1726-1770) (p.29).

	M	F	M	F
To bpBANBURY, *p.* 252 *Through Banbury, on* r. *to Southam,* 14 M.; 1 M. *further, on* l. *to Kineton,* 11½.	—	—	69	2
Warmington×—*Chur. Warwicksh.*	5	—	74	2
Burton Dasset—*T. G.*	3	3	77	5
Gaydon Inn	1	6	79	3
Harwood House *Near Warwick, on* r. *to Southam,* 9 M.	3	2	82	5
bpWARWICK× *(see p.* 255*)*	5	6	88	3

Bicester via Warwick to Birmingham.

Cary column 252. Bicester to Adderbury TP (1791) (p.43); Weeping Cross to Banbury TP (1744) (pp.42-3).

PBICESTER×	3	2	55	1
486 *H.* 2544 *I.*—Ma. ar. 2-55 Mo.; dep. 11-47 Aft. On r. *to Buckingham,* 11½ M,				
Caversfield×	1	6	56	7
Junction of the Roads×	3	-	59	7
On r. to Brackley, 6 M. On l. to Oxford, 15 M.				
Souldern	2	-	61	7
Aynhoe×	2	-	63	7
On l. to Deddington, 3 M. 1 M. from Aynhoe cross the Oxford Canal (see 154).				
Nell Bridge	1	4	65	3
Cross the Charwell R. (see p. 192).				
Adderbury×, Oxon	1	4	66	7
On l. to Oxford, 19½ M.				
Weeping Cross×	1	4	68	3
bpBANBURY× *(see p. 240)*	1	7	69	2
On r. to Brackley, 9 M.; and Daventry, 16: on l. to Chipping Norton, 12½; Stratford on Avon, 20; Kineton, 12½; and Warwick, 23¼.				

Banbury via Southam to Leamington.

Cary column 252. Banbury to Ryton/ Finford Bridge TP (1755) (p.54).

bpBANBURY× *(see p. 240)*	1	7	69	2
On r. to Brackley, 9 M.; and Daventry, 16: on l. to Chipping Norton, 12½; Stratford on Avon, 20; Kineton, 12½; and Warwick, 23¼.				
Mollington×, Warw.	4	6	74	-
Cross the Oxford Canal twice.				
Ladbroke×	7	6	81	6
PSOUTHAM×—*Griffin*	1	6	83	4
238 *H.* 1161 *I.*—Ma. ar. 6-27 Mo.; dep. 8-10 Aft. *On r. to Daventry, 10 M.; Rugby, 9; and Coventry, 13. At about 1 M. cross Water-gall R.*				
Ufton×	2	4	86	-
Radford×	2	6	88	6
Cross the Warwick and Napton Canal twice.				
LEAMINGTON×	1	6	90	4
Near Warwick, on l. to				

Cross Roads

Chipping Norton via Deddington to Buckingham.

Cary column 732-3, Cross Route 116. Banbury to Burford TP (Aynho [to Swerford] Division) (p.83); Warmington to Buckingham TP (Upper Division) (from Aynho, p.30).

R. 116.—CHIPPING NORTON to Buckingham.				
To Chapel House×	—	—		4
Pomfret Castle×	3	-		3 4
1½ M. further, on l. to Ban-bury, 7½.				
Hempton	5 4		9	-
DEDDINGTON	1 2		10	2
On r. to Oxford, 17 M.; on l. to Banbury, 6,				
Clifton	1 2		11	4
Cross the Charwell R. and Oxford Canal. Near Aynhoe, on l. to Ban-bury, 6 M.				
Aynhoe×, Northamp.	2	-		13 4
Near Aynhoe, on r. to Bi-cester, 8½ M.				
Croughton	1 5		15	1
On l. to Brackley, 2¼ M.; on r. to Oxford, 19¾.				
Barley Mow×	2 2		17	3
Monks House	1 1		18	4
Finmere, Oxon.	2 5		21	1
Tingewick, Bucks.	1 2		22	3
Cross the Ouse R. On l. to Banbury, through Brakley, 16¾ M.				
bpBUCKINGHAM	2 6		25	1

Cirencester; Burford to Cottesbach (Lutterworth).
Cary column 734, Cross Route 118.
Burford, Chipping Norton to Banbury TP (1770) (p.78).
Banbury to Lutterworth TP (p.71).

ᴾBURFORD, *Oxfordsh.*	6 4	17 —	
On r. to *Faringdon,* 10½ M.; *Bampton,* 7; and *Witney,* 7½. *Cross the Windrush R.; and on* l. *to Stow,* 10 M.			
Fulbrook˟	1 —	18 —	
Shipton under Which-wood˟	3 —	21 —	
Cross the Evenlode R.			
ᴾCHIPPING NORTON	7 —	28 —	
On l. to *Stow,* 8 M.; on r. to *Oxford,* 19.			
Chapel House˟	— 4	28 4	
On r. to *Oxford,* 19¼ M.; on l. to *Shipston,* 10.			
Pomfret Castle˟	3 —	31 4	
2 M. *before Sth. Newington, on* r. *to Deddington,* 4½.			
South Newington	3 4	35 —	
Cross the Sarbrook R.			
Bloxham˟	2 —	37 —	
ᵇᵖBANBURY˟	3 4	40 4	
On r. to *Buckingham,* 18 M.; on l. to *Stratford on Avon,* 20; *Kineton,* 12½; *Warwick,* 19¼; and *Coventry,* 27. *Cross the Oxford Canal and Charwell R.; and on* r. *to Brackley,* 8½ M.			
Hulscote, *Northamp.*	1 3	41 7	
Wardington˟, *Oxford.*	3 1	45 —	
Cross the Charwell R.			
Byfield˟, *Northamp.*	5 —	50 —	
Charwelton˟	2 —	52 —	
Badby˟	2 6	54 6	
ᴾDAVENTRY˟	2 4	57 2	
to Dunchurch, *as p.272*	7 6	65 —	
ᴾRUGBY, *as p. 286*	2 6	67 6	
Cross the Avon R. and Oxford Canal.			
Brownsover˟	2 —	69 6	
Near Cottesbatch, on r. *to Northampton,* 21 M.; *on* l. *to Hinckley,* 11.			
Cottesbatch˟, *Leic.*	3 6	73 4	
Entrance of Lutterworth, on r. *to Market Harborough,* 13 M.			

Oxford via Weston to Buckingham (to Cambridge)
Cary columns 882-3. Cross Route 266
Weston-on-the-Green to Towcester TP (1757) (to Barley Mow, p.62).
Warmington to Buckingham Trust (Upper Division) (from Barley Mow, p.30).

R. 266.—OXFORD to *Cambridge* and *Lynn,* by *Buckingham.*	M F	M F
To Gofford Bridge	— —	4 4
Cross the Charwell R. 1½ M. *beyond, on* r. *to High Wycombe,* 27½; *on* l. *to Chipping Norton,* 17. *Near Weston on the Green, on* r. *to Bicester,* 4½ M.		
Weston on the Green˟	4 —	8 4
ᴾMiddleton Stoney˟	2 7	11 3
On r. to *Bicester,* 3 M.; *on* l. *to Chipping Norton,* 14		
Ardeley˟	2 2	13 5
1 M. *beyond, on* r. *to Bicester,* 4; *on* l. *to Banbury,* 9.		
Barley Mow˟, *N. amp.*	4 5	18 2
On l. to *Deddington,* 6¾ M.; *Banbury,* 9½; and *Brackley,* 2¾.		

	M F	M F
Monks House, *Oxf.*	1 1	19 3
Beyond Monks House, on r. *to Bicester,* 7½ M.		
Finmere˟	2 5	22 —
Tingewick, *Bucks*	1 2	23 2
Cross the Ouse R.		
ᵇᵖBUCKINGHAM˟	2 6	26 —
Thence to CAMBRIDGE, *as Route* 265	53 —	79 —
And LYNN, *as p.* 507— 46¾ M.		

Oxford via Deddington, Banbury, Southam to Coventry.

Cary columns 889-890. Cross Route 272.

Oxford to Finford/Ryton Bridge (Southern Division: Kidlington to Adderbury) TP (1755, 1797) (p.58); (Northern Division: Banbury to Ryton Bridge) (1755) (p.52).

	M	F	M	F
Sturgis Castle×	3	5	8	7
On r. *to Woodstock,* 1¾ M.				
Hopcroft's Holt×	3	5	12	4
On r. *to Bicester,* 7 M.; *on* l. *to Chipping Norton,* 9.				
North Aston Inn×	2	2	14	6
At about 1 M. *cross the R. Swere.*				
^{p}DEDDINGTON×	1	7	16	5
On r. *to Buckingham,* 14 M.; *on the* l. *to Chipping Norton,* 9¼.				
Adderbury×	2	6	19	3
On r. *to Buckingham,* 15 M.				
Weeping Cross×	1	4	20	7
^{bp}BANBURY×	1	7	22	6
On r. *to Brackley,* 9 M.; *and Daventry,* 16: *on* l. *to Chipping Norton,* 12½; *Stratford on Avon,* 20; *Kineton,* 12½; *and Warwick,* 23¼.				
Mollington×, *Warw.*	4	6	27	4
Cross the Oxford Canal twice.				
Ladbroke×	7	6	35	2
^{p}SOUTHAM×,—*Craven Arms*	1	6	37	–
On r. *to Daventry,* 10¼ M.; *on* l. *to Warwick,* 9¼.				
Cross the Warwick and Napton Canal.				
Long Itchington	2	2	39	2
Marton×	2	3	41	5
Cross the Leame R.				
Prince Thorpe×	1	2	42	7
Ryton Bridge×	3	4	46	3
On r. *to Daventry,* 14½ M.				
Cross the Avon R.				
^{p}Willenhall×	1	–	47	3
Cross the Sow R.				
Whitley Bridge×	—	6	48	1
^{cbp}COVENTRY—*M. H.*	1	5	49	6
^{cbp}LICHFIELD, *as p.* 303	27	2	77	–
(*Thence to* Holyhead, *as p.* 292—153¼ M.)				

Oxford via Brackley, Towcester to Northampton.

Cary column 895. Cross Route 275.

Weston-on-the-Green to Towcester TP (1757) (p.62); Towcester to Northampton TP (1794) (p.62).

R. 275.—OXFORD to *Peterborough.*

	M	F	M	F
To Barley Mow×, *as p.* 882, *Northamptonsh.*	—	–	18	2
On r. *to Buckingham,* 8 M.; *on* l. *to Deddington,* 6¾.				
Near Brackley, on the l. *to Banbury,* 9¼ M.				
^{bp}BRACKLEY×—*M. H.*	3	2	21	4
On r. *to Buckingham,* 7½ M.				
Silverston×—*George*	7	4	29	–
$_{p}$TOWCESTER×—*Ring of Bells*	3	6	32	6
On r. *to Stony Stratford,* 6¾ M.; *on* l. *to Daventry,* 12½.				
Cross the Grand Junction Canal.				
Blisworth—*Church*	3	6	36	4
Milton	1	6	38	2
Near Northampton, on r. *to Stony Stratford,* 13 M.				
Cross the Nen R.				
^{bp}NORTHAMPTON×—*All Saints Church*	3	4	41	6

Sources

Oxfordshire Studies, Westgate, Oxford	Maps of Oxfordshire *JOJ – Jackson's Oxford Journal* (microfilm) *Victoria History of the County of Oxford (VCH Oxon)* Pigot & Co's *National Commercial Directory* (1830)
Bodleian Library, Oxford	*PP* – Parliamentary Papers *JHC* – Journal of the House of Commons Copies of Ogilby maps and notes Accounts of the Ryton to Banbury Turnpike Trust; 1755-1806: MS Top Oxon d 373 *An enquiry into the means of preserving and improving the Publick Roads of this Kingdom with observations on the probable consequences of the present plan*; Henry Homer; Oxf 1767, 8° G Pamph, 1865 1. 24755 e80
Oxfordshire County Record Office	Minutes of the Bicester to Aynho Trust, 1825-1872: Bicester UDC I/i/1 Accounts of the Gosford Trust, 1847-1872: Mor. II/1

Gloucestershire County Record Office	Minutes of the Banbury to Burford Trust, 1817-1852:
	    D1395 V/1-6
	Accounts of the Chappel on the Heath to Bourton Trust,
	    1731-1767: D621 X4
	Letter of Francis Canning: D2857/2/16

Warwickshire County Record Office	Minutes of the Kineton & Wellesbourne Trust 1770-1872:
	    CR556/860
	Minutes of the Banbury, Brailes & Shipston Trust, 1802-1880:
	    CR580, Box 53
	Minutes of the Drayton to Edgehill Trust, 1753-1871:
	    CR580, Box 57

Northamptonshire County Record Office	Minutes of the Towcester, Brackley & Weston Trust,
	    1820-1874: ML2200 & ML2201
	Minutes of the Banbury, Daventry & Lutterworth Trust, from
	    1765-: D46

Private Collection originally owned by Henry Stone, Banbury carrier or his son Henry Stone, Banbury bookseller	*Cary's New Itinerary: or an Accurate Delineation of the Great Roads, Both Direct and Cross, throughout England and Wales... From an Actual Admeasurement by John Cary... This work shows the Immediate Route from the Metropolis to all parts... from Town to Town...* May, 1828. *Rusher's Banbury List (and Directory)*, 1815-1874 (gaps)

Books and Journals

Bates A. *Directory of Stage Coach Services, 1836*, David & Charles, Newton Abbot (1969).

Beesley, A. *The History of Banbury* (1842)

Cake & Cockhorse (Banbury Historical Society). Articles (by Brooks K.R.S., Gibson J.S.W., and Renold P.), cited in footnotes on pages 7, 35, 52, 91, 100, 107, 117 and 119

Cooper N. *Aynho*, BHS 20, Banbury, and Leopard's Head Press (1984).

Cossons "Warwickshire turnpikes", *Birmingham Archaeological Society, Trans & Proc.*, **LXIV**, 53-100 (1946).

Crossley A. *Banbury, a history*, reprint of a section of *VCH Oxon* (vol. X) Oxfordshire County Library Service (1984).

Defoe D. *A tour through the whole island of Great Britain* (1726), Penguin Classic, London (1971).

Dickins B. "Premonstratension Itineraries from Titchfield Abbey", *Proc. of Leeds Philos. & Lit. Soc*, **4**, 349-361 (1938).

Elliott D. J. *Buckingham - the loyal and ancient borough*, Phillimore, London and Chichester (1975).

Gibson J.S.W. (ed.) *Baptism and Burial Register of Banbury, 1653-1723*, BHS **9** (1968)

Gulland P. *Making the Road from Princes Risborough to Thame,* Buckinghamshire Archaeological Society Occasional Paper No. 5 (2006).

Hedges S. *Bicester wuz a little town*, Bicester Advertiser, Bicester (1968).

Houghton F.T.S. "Saltways", *Trans. Birmingham Archaeological Society*, **54**, 1-17 (1932).

Lawrence K. "Turnpike Roads in Oxfordshire" Oxon Museum Service **5** (1977)

Martin G.H. "Road travel in the middle ages, some journeys of the warden and fellows of Merton College Oxford, 1315-1470", *J. of Transport History*, **3**, (3), 159-178 (1976).

Potts W. *A History of Banbury*, The Banbury Guardian (1958); 2nd edition, E.T. Clark, Gulliver Press, Banbury (1978).

Rule J. *The Vital Century*, Longman, Harlow (1991).

Smedley-Stevenson, G. *Early Victorian Squarson*, BHS 29, Banbury (2007).

Taylor C.C. *Roads and tracks of Britain*, Dent, London (1979).

Toulmin Smith L. *Leland's Itinerary in England and Wales*, Centaur, London (1964).

Wickham Steed V. *Roman roads of the Banbury District* (1967).

Wood V. *The Licensees of the Inns, Taverns and Beerhouses of Banbury...*, Oxfordshire Family History Society (1998)

My thanks are due to the late Christine Kelly for her encouragement to extend this series to cover Banbury and the assistance of staff at Record Offices and Libraries for their assistance and patience.

All enquiries to the author;
Alan Rosevear, <Rosevear1@aol.com>, or http: //www.turnpikes.org.uk

Sources of information for list of Turnpike Trustees from Oxfordshire and the adjoining Upper Thames Valley.

Users should note that the Trustees listed here are the equivalent of modern day company shareholders (except that no dividends were paid), taking no part in running the Turnpike Trust, as described on pages 17 to 26. Only those taking an active part, the equivalent of today's board of directors, are likely to be found named elsewhere in this book.

Symbols used to identify individual trusts. Dates indicate the Acts from which names have been extracted.

Suffix a, n or r - indicates that the individual was mentioned as appointed trustee or referred to in the minutes of the trust.

Suffix d - indicates that, in the minutes of the trust, the individual was recorded as having died

AK -   Adderbury to Kidlington (1818)
AW -   Adderbury to Weston (1755)
BA -   Bicester to Aynho (1790 & 1812)
BBc -   Banbury to Barcheston (1802)
BB -   Burford to Banbury (1770 & 1832)
BC -   Barrington to Campsfield (1834)
BH -   Buckingham to Hanwell (1811 & 1832
BL -   Banbury to Lutterworth (1765, 1807, 1828 & 1840)
BW -   Buckingham to Warmington (1744)
CB -   Chappel on the Heath to Bourton (1731 & 1744)
CC -   Crickley Hill to Campsfield (1751 & 1821)
DE -   Drayton Lane to Edge Hill (1753 & 1822)
F -   Fyfield District (1800)
FB -   Finford (or Ryton) to Banbury (1755, 1802, 1822 & 1859)
GFB -   Faringdon to Burfurd (1812)
G -   Gosford (1821)
HD -   Henley & Dorchester Trust (1734 & 1754)
HS -   Harwell to Streatley (1824)
        Ryton - *see* Finford
SF -   St John's Bridge to Fyfield Trust (1732 & 1738)
SW -   Stokenchurch to Woodstock (1719 & 1739)
TW -   Towcester to Weston (1756)
WR -   Woodstock to Rollright Lane (1730, 1751, 1804, 1825 1846)
WT -   Weston to Towcester (1820)
WW -   Wallingford, Wantage & Faringdon Trust (1752 & 1841)

Turnpike Trustees (exactly as named) extracted from selected Turnpike Acts covering roads in the Upper Thames Valley

Listed alphabetically; trust and date abbreviated according to the guide given on page 162.

Abbey, Thomas BL1765
Abbot, Rev John (clerk)
  HD1754
Abery, John WW1752
Abingdon (Berks.), Mayor &
  principal Burgesses of
  HD1734;
  Mayor of HD1754
Abraham, Henry, aka
  Metcalfe BW1744
Adams, Fitzhebert BL1765
  George (clerk) BB1832
  Humphrey HD1754
  James (clerk) WR1804;
  WR1825
  John BL1765
  Samuel (clerk) BL1765
  Thomas BL1828
  William BL1765
  Rev of Rushton BL1765
  (no forename) BB1832
Addison, John BL1765
  William BL1765
Adkins, John BBC1802
Air, Richard DE1753a
Aires, Charles SW1719
  Robert SW1719
Akerman, John BB1770
Alder, Thomas CC1751
Aldrich, Charles DD HD1734
Aldworth, Richard Nevil
  HD1754
  Robert HD1754
Allen, Allin,
  John HS1824
  Richard HD1754
  Samuel BL1765
  William HS1824;
  WW1841
Alleway, William HD1734
Allibone, Isaac SW1739
Allnatt, Alnut,
  Charles Atherton
  WW1841
  Mathew Snr HD1754
  Mathew Jnr HD1754
  Thomas HS1824
Almond, John HD1754
Alnut see Allnatt
Alt, Justinian (clerk) BA1790

Althorpe see Spencer
Ancell, James (clerk)
  BL1765
Anderson, Matthew HD1754
  Robert HD1754
  Thomas SW1739; HD1754
Andrews, John BL1765;
  BB1770
  John BB1770
  Joseph GFB1812;
  CC1821
  Robert BL1765a
Angell, John HD1734
  William HD1734
Annesley, Arthur AW1755;
  WT1756; BA1790;
  WR1804; WT1820;
  G1821; WR1825
  Arthur Jnr WR1825
  Francis (clerk) BL1765;
  BH1811; BL1828;
  BL1840
  Rev. Dr SW1739
Ansell, Edward BB1770
  John Jordan CC1821;
  BB1832; BC1834
  Parran BB1770
  William BB1770
Appletree, Apletree, John
  AW1755
  Nathaniel BB1770
  Nathaniel Austin BB1770
  William BB1832
Aplin, Benjamin DE1753;
  FB1755; AW1755;
  BL1765; BB1832;
  BL1840; HD1754
  Christopher BA1790
  William (clerk) AW1755
Apperley, Rev Anthony
  WR1751
Applegath, John CC1751
Appletree see Apletree
Arbery ?, John BB1770
Archer, Hon. Andrew
  FB1755
  Henry DE1753
  Thomas FB1755
Arglas, Viscount SF1732

Arnatt, Jonathan CC1821;
  BC1834
Arndell, John WW1752
Arnold, Edward (clerk)
  AW1755
  Edward (clerk) AW1755
  George BL1765; BL1807
  George Henry BL1828;
  BL1840
  Henry BL1840
  James (clerk) BL1828;
  BL1840
  John FB1755; BL1765;
  BL1828
  John Arthur BL1840
  Lumley BL1765a
  Nathaniel FB1802a;
  FB1822
  Richard WT1756
  Robert FB1755
  Thomas WT1820
  (no forename) of
  Blackthorn
  SW1739
Arrowsmith, Rev John
  WR1751
Ash, Joseph FB1755
Ashbrook, William Lord
  Viscount of Shellingford,
  SF1788n
  Lord Viscount SF1806d
Ashby, John BA1790
Ashmead, William CC1751
Ashton, Ellis (clerk) WR1825
Ashurst, Sir Henry SW1719
  Thomas Henry SW1739
  William Henry AK1818;
  DE1822; FB1822
Ashworth, Caleb BL1765
Asslick, James (clerk)
  BL1765
Astley, Sir Edward BL1765
  John Wooley (clerk)
  CC1821
  Solomon BL1765
Aston, Richard SF1732;
  WW1752
  Willoughby SF1732
  Sir Willoughby (bart)
  WW1752, HD1754

Astrey, Rev. Francis
 SW1739
 William SW1739;
  HD1754
Atherton, Joseph HD1754
Atkins, Abraham WW1752
 Edwin Martin SF1803r
 Edwin Martin of Kingston
  Lisle, SF1803n; HS1824
 William FB1755
Aubery, Aubrey, Awberry
 Thomas SW1739
 Sir John SW1739; BA1812
 Thomas Digby BA1812
 Rev Dr SW1719
Austin, John AW1755
 Richard DE1822
Awberry *see* Aubery
Ayre, Robert HD1734;
 SW1739
Ayres, Richard WT1756

Bacon, Rev Isaac G1821
 Nathaniel BW1744
 Rev Phannel DD HD1754
Badcock, Thomas Stanhope
 BH1811
Badger, Samuel WT1756;
 BA1790
Bagnall, John CC1821
 Thomas CC1821; BC1834
Bailey, Richard WW1752
Bailiff(s) etc. *see under*
 Buckingham. Burford,
 Chipping Norton,
 Daventry, Witney
Baker, Edward BB1770
 R Jnr WW1802a
 Robert WW1802a
  HS1824
 Robert WW1752;
  HD1754
 Thomas of Buscott SF1732
 William (clerk) BB1770
 William BB1770
 Wilmot WW1752;
  HD1754
 Dr Archdeacon SW1719
Baldwin, Benjamin SF1788r
 Edmund BBC1802
Ballard, Rev Edward DD
 HD1754
 John (clerk) BB1770;
  FB1822; BB1832;
  BL1840; FB1859

Banbury, Mayor, Recorder,
 Justices, Aldermen &
 Burgesses of AW1755;
 FB1755; BL1765;
 BBC1802;
 Mayor of BW1744;
 DE1753; BH1811;
 JP for DE1753
Banbury, William CB1731;
 FB1822
Bance, John WW1752
Bannister, Edward BBC1802
Banting, John WR1846
Barber, Barbor, Edward
 BW1744; DE1753;
 DE1753a; AW1755;
 FB1755
 John BL1765; BB1770;
 BH1811; DE1822
 (no forename) BA1790
Barker, Daniel BA1790
 Henry HD1734; WW1752;
 HD1754
 John Raymond BC1834
 William SW1739
Barnaby, William SF1791r
Barnard, Robert (clerk)
 CC1821; DE1822;
 FB1822
 William Henry (clerk)
 BH1811
Barnes, James BH1811
 Joseph (clerk) WW1752
 Thomas WW1752
Barnett FB1755
Barrett, John Richard
 HS1824
 William FB1755;
 AW1755; BH1811
Barrington, Haon Daines
 WW1752
 Hon John WW1752
 Lord John SF1732;
 SF1738
 Hon William Keppel
 SF1826a
 Lord William Keppel
 BC1834
 Hon William Wildman
 SF1732
 Lord Viscount HD1754
 see also Wildman
Barter, Charles (clerk)
 WR1825; BB1832;
 WR1846
Bartholomew, H BL1783a
 William SW1719

Bartlett, Edward BH1832
 Isaac Shortland BH1832
 John BH1811
 Philip BH1832
Barton, Rev Phillip LLD
 WW1752
Barton on the Heath
 (Dunsmore, Warw.), Rector
 of CB1744
Baseley, Basley, John
 BL1765
 Richard of Abingdon
 HD1754,
 T FB1755a
Bassett, Francis WR1751;
 AW1755; WT1756
 Thomas WW1752
Bateman, Charles CC1821;
 BC1834
 Henry BC1834
 John BL1765
 John, Lord Viscount
 AW1755; WT1756
 Robert CC1821
 (no forename) Lord
 Viscount HD1754
Bates, Robert (clerk)
 DE1753; AW1755
Bathurst, Benjamin BW1744;
 WT1756
Batson, William BB1770
Batt, Augustine CC1751
 Augustine William
 BC1834
Batten, Battin, John
 WW1752; HD1754
Batteson, Robert Devereux
 CB1731
Baty, William WT1820a
 William (clerk) WT1820a
Bawn, Rev. Dr SW1739
Bayes, William FB1859
Bayley, Arden (clerk)
 BL1828; BL1840
 George SW1739
Bayntum, Stukeley CC1751;
 WR1751; HD1754;
 AW1755; BB1770
Beaford, Richard BL1765
Beardmore, Rev Scope
 SW1739
 Thomas DD BL1765
Beasley, Job FB1755
 Richard of Pusey HD1754
 Thomas FB1755
Beauclerk, John WT1820a
Beauvoir *see* de Beauvoir

Beck, John BBC1802
Becket, William HS1824
Bedford, Thomas CB1731
Bedwell, Richard SW1739;
   HD1754
   Bernard HD1754
Beechey, Walter CC1821
Beeston, Henry SW1719
Belcher, Charles FB1755
   Charles SF1862a
   Joseph WW1752
   Thomas SF1824a;
      BC1834; SF1840a
   William FB1755
Bellamy, John Byrkin
   BBC1802
   William (clerk) BB1770
   William FB1780a
Bellenger, Adam G1821
Benet, Rev Joseph HD1754
Bennett, Daniel of
   Blackheath, SF1863a
   SF1806a
   Edward Leigh (clerk)
      BC1834
   Henry AW1755
   Henry Leigh (clerk)
      WT1820; BA1825;
      BH1832; BB1832
   James WW1841
   John GFB1812; BC1834
   Thomas FB1755;
      GFB1812; BC1834
   William BC1834;
      GFB1812
   William of Blackheath
      SF1819a
   William Lee BB1770
   Wooley Leigh (clerk)
      BH1811; BH1832
Benson, Rev William G1821
Benwell, Joseph HD1734
   William of Bix HD1734
   William of Henley
      HD1734
Berens, Rev Edward of
   Shrivenham SF1806a;
      GFB1812; BC1834
   Archdeacon SF1840a
Berke, Adelphus Meet
   AW1755
Berkeley, Berkley, Hon Henry
   CB1731
   Norborne CC1751
   Thomas DD WR1804
Bernard, Scope BA1790

Berry, Richard, of Clifton
   SW1739
   (no forename), Clifton
      HD1734
Bertie, Hon. Henry SW1719
   Henry HD1734
   Hon. James SW1719
   Rev John (clerk) CC1751
   Norris SW1739; BW1744;
      WR1751; CC1751;
      DE1753; AW1755;
      WW1752
   Peregrine WT1756
   Rev William CC1751
Betteridge, Johnathan
   HS1824
   Richard Hopkins HS1824
Bibbins, Edward FB1755
   Edward Snr FB1755
Bicker, John Jnr FB1755
   John FB1755
Bicknell, Thomas Betrell
   FB1822
Biddulph, Rev Henry
   FB1859
   John (clerk) FB1802a;
      FB1822
   Sir Theophilus FB1755;
      FB1755 1802a; FB1822;
      FB1859
   Theophilus FB1822
   Thomas BA1790
   Walter FB1755
Bigg, Thomas WW1752;
   HD1754
Biggs, Rev Dr Thomas
   WR1730; CB1731;
   SW1739
Bignell, Richard BA1790;
   WT1820
Bigstock, Charles HD1734
Biker, John FB1755/6a
Billingsly, Rev SW1739
Billio, Thomas (clerk)
   BL1765
Bingham, Peregrine (clerk)
   BH1811
Birch, James Snr FB1755
   James Jnr FB1755
   John HD1734
   Rev John SW1739
   Jonathan WR1825
   Rev William DL CB1731
   William HD1734; HD1754
Bird, Charles FB1755
   Henry FB1755
   John FB1755

Bird *contnued*
   John Jnr FB1755
   Robert FB1755
Bishop, Sir Cecil (bart)
   HD1734; HD1754
   Charles BBC1802
   John CC1751; WW1752;
      HD1754
   Richard CB1731
   Thomas WW1752
   William BBC1802
Black, William BL1765
Blackall, George SW1739
   Richard SW1739
   Thomas HD1734;
      HD1754; SW1739
   William of Braziers
      HD1754
   William of Warborow
      HD1754
Blackstone, James DL
   WR1804; WR1825
   James CC1821
   John WR1730; CB1731
   William WW1752;
      HD1754
Blackwell, Joseph HD1754
   Richard HD1734
   ?, Samuel BB1770
Blagrave, John of Watchfield
   SF1732
   John SW1739
   Thomas WW1752
Blake, Daniel SW1719
   John (clerk) AW1755;
      BB1770
Blandford, Marquis of *see*
   Churchill, Godolphin,
   Spencer
Blandy, Adam of Kingston
   Bagpuize SF1806a;
      SF1824a; HS1824
   Adam BC1834
   Charles WW1752
   Francis SW1719; SW1739;
      HD1734
   John of Kingston SF1732;
      WW1752; HD1734;
      HD1754
   John (clerk) WW1752
Blanketters, Master of
   Company of, Witney
   CC1751
Blencowe, George BL1840
   James BL1828
   James Gramer (clerk)
      BL1840

Blencowe *continued*
  John DE1753; AW1755;
    WT1756; BL1765;
    BL1807
  John Jackson BH1811;
    WT1820; BL1828;
    BL1840
  Robert BL1828; BL1840
  Samuel BH1811
  Thomas (clerk) BL1807;
    WT1820; BL1828
  Timothy WT1756
Bletchenden, Rev Dr of
  Kingston SF1732
Blewitt, John WR1730;
    CB1731; WR1751
  Thomas SW1719
Blick, William BL1765
Bliss, John BL1765
Blockley (Worcs.), Vicar of
  CB1744
Blomberg, Edmund Charles
  AW1755; WT1756
Blount, George HD1754
  Richard HD1734
Bloxham, Hopcraft WT1756
  John FB1755; AW1755;
    BL1765; BB1770
Boate, Denton BW1744;
    DE1753
Bobart, Gamaliel Hodgkinson
    WR1804
  Hodgkinson WR1825
  Jacob WR1751
Boddington, Thomas BL1765
Bollard, John (clerk) BL1828
Bolt, William BB1770
Bolton, Henry CC1751
  Richard DD BL1765
  Thomas (clerk) FB1755;
    AW1755
Bond, Richard BL1765
Bonner, Rev Benjamin
    WT1756
Boote, Alexander WW1752
  William HD1754
Booth, Nathaniel WR1730;
    CB1731
  Richard FB1755
Boothby, Sir Samuel BL1765
Boscawen, Hon George
    AW1755
  George BB1770
Bosworth, Joseph BL1765
Bottery, Shreve WT1756
Boucher CC1751
Bouchier, Thomas SF1788r

Bouderie *see* Bouverie,
Boughton, Sir Edward
    BL1765
Boulter, Edward SW1719
Boulton, Christopher
    GFB1812
  Matthew Robinson
    AK1818; BB1832
  Sir Robert BB1832
Bourne, Robert Dr of Physick
    WR1804
Bouverie, Bouderie, Boverie,
  Hon. Bartholomew of
    Coleshill House -
    SF1788n
  Edward (clerk) GFB1812;
    SF1826/40a; -BC1834
  Hon Edward Pleydell
    BC1834
  Rt Hon. EP SF1862a
  Rev HD1754
  Rt Hon Pleydell (Viscount
    Folkstone) HS1824
  Hon William WW1752;
    HD1754
  See also under Folkestone,
    Viscount
Bowater, Edward FB1755
  Richard FB1755
Bowden, John WR1804
Bowen, Thomas (clerk)
    CC1821
Bower, Thomas BB1770
Bowers, John BW1744;
    DE1753
  Thomas BW1744; BL1765
  (no forename) BB1832
Bowler, Francis SW1719
Bowles, Charles WR1751;
    AW1755; WT1756;
    BB1770; BBC1802
  Charles Oldfield FB1822;
    BH1832; BB1832;
    FB1859
  Edward HD1754
  John of Abingdon
    HD1754
  John (clerk) SF1788d
  Oldfield BB1770;
    BA1790; BBC1802;
    WR1804
  Thomas HS1824
  Rev. Thomas, DD
    WT1756
  William HS1824
  William of Abingdon
    HD1754

Bowles *continued*
  William of Hanny
    WW1752; HD1754
  William Thomas WT1756
Box, Edward BW1744
  John BB1770
  Philip BA1812
  Thomas BH1811; BA1812
Boyce, Benjamin (clerk)
    BB1770
Boycott, John (clerk)
    CC1751
Boydell, Thomas FB1755
Boyes, Richard CC1751
Boyle HD1754
Brabon, Stephen of Kingston
    SF1738
Brackley (N'hants.), Mayor &
    Aldermen of WT1756;
  Mayor of BW1744;
    BH1811
Bradcott, Francis AW1755
Bradford, Thomas BW1744;
    DE1753; DE1753a;
    FB1755; AW1755
Bradgate, Richard AW1755
Bradley, John SF1787a;
    SF1794d
  William (clerk) WR1751;
    AW1755
  Rev of Heyford WT1756
Bradshaw, Aholiah FB1822
  Augustus Hill WT1820
  James WT1820
  John CB1731
  Lawrence WT1820
  Robert Haldane WT1820
  William (clerk) WR1751;
    AW1755
  Rev William HD1754
  William Rigby WT1820
  Rev SW1739
Brain, Richard BBC1802
Bray, Col. SW1719
  Reginald CB1731
  Reginald Morgan SW1739
Brayne, Henry BH1832
Brayne, Robert BH1811;
    DE1822; BL1828;
    BH1832; BB1832; BL1840
Brayne, Thomas BH1832;
    BB1832
Bree, Thomas (clerk) FB1755
Breedon, John Symonds DD
    HS1824
  John HD1754
Breerton, Rev Dr SW1719

Brewer, Thomas (clerk)
WW1752
Brewert, George SW1719
Bricknell, Thomas Fox
G1821
William Silcox of Grove
(clerk) WW1841
Brickwell, Charles DE1822;
BH1832; BL1840
Brickwicke BB1832
Brideork, Ralph SW1719
Bridgeman, George FB1755;
BL1765
Henry FB1755
Henry Toy CC1751
Sir Orlando FB1755
Bridger, George BW1744
Bridges, Edmund WW1752;
HD1754
Francis WW1752;
HD1754
Brigham, Thomas SW1719;
SW1739
(no forename) HD1734
Brinkler, John BA1812
Broad, George CC1751
Thomas CC1751
Brockhurst, Benjamin
FB1755
Thomas FB1755
Bromley, John FB1755
Thomas FB1755
William SW1719; FB1755
Brookes, Brooks,
Giles GFB1812
John CC1821
John WW1841
Joseph WR1804
Matthew ? BB1770
Peter BB1770
Thomas (clerk) BB1770
Thomas BB1770
Thomas DD WR1804
William SW1739; BB1770
William of Newland
CC1751
William of Witney
CC1751
Brookland, William
WW1752; HD1754
Brooks *see* Brookes
Broomfield, Henry FB1822
Thomas Ross (clerk)
FB1822
William Williams FB1822
Brotherton, William HD1754
Broughton, Richard BL1765

Brown, Sir Charles WR1730;
WR1751
George WR1730; CB1731;
WR1751
Rev John DD HD1754
Joseph, John Alphonsus
BL1840
Robert FB1755
Stephen HS1824
Thomas CC1751
Thomas WR1804
Rev Thomas WT1756
Walter (clerk) WR1804
William Frederick (clerk)
BA1790
Rev Dr of Lanaton
AW1755
(no forename) of
Bletchingdon WR1751
Browne, John (clerk)
CB1731
John CC1821; BB1832
Mathias WW1752
Richard WW1752
Thomas BB1832
Thomas Trollope AW1755
Walter WR1825
Rev William Frederick DD
G1821; BA1825a
Bruch, Cudworth WW1752;
HD1754
Brunsdon, Thomas BB1770
Bryant, George FB1780/1a
Bryden, William Anderson
FB1859
Buckingham, Bailiff & Chief
Burgess of BW1744,
BH1811
see also Carter, William
Bull, Alban Jnr BL1765
John DD BL1840
William BL1765a
Bullen, Robert CC1821
Bullock, Francis Ferdinando
WW1841
Joseph BA1790
Bumpstead, William
BW1744; DE1753;
AW1755
Bunce, Daniel of Longworth
SF1738
Thomas HD1734
William HD1754
Bunifield, J B FB1802a
Burbery, Thomas FB1755a
Burd, Josiah of Wantage
(clerk) WW1841

Burdett, Wright HD1734
Burford, Bailiffs of CC1751
Burford, Edward DE1753a;
FB1755; AW1755
Edward M.D. BL1765;
BB1770
John BL1765
Richard AW1755;
BL1765; BL1765 78a;
BB1770
Burges, Burgess, Burgis,
Jonas HD1734
James Robert (clerk)
WW1841
Richard WW1752
Burgh, Thomas MD FB1755
Burgis *see* Burges(s)
Burlton, William FB1755
Burnaby, Sir William
HD1754; AW1755;
BB1770
William BB1770
Burnham, Richard FB1822
Burrel, Alexander (clerk)
BW1744
Burroughs, William (clerk)
WW1752; HD1754
Burrows, Burrow, Charles
CC1751
John WT1756
Samuel CC1751
Thomas HD1754
Thomas (clerk) GFB1812
Thomas (clerk) CC1821;
BC1834
Burton, Francis BL1765;
BB1770
James (clerk) BB1770
Rev James G1821
Rev John of Rowsham
WR1730
John BD HD1734;
SW1719
Rev John DD HD1754
Bus ??, John (clerk) BB1770
Busby, Edward DE1753a;
FB1755; AW1755
Bush, Jonathan WW1752;
HD1734; SW1739
Thomas Snr G1821
(no forename) of Childrey
WW1752
Buswell, John of Westcot
Barton AW1755
John of Serswell Barton
AW1755

Buswell *continued*
  Robert (clerk) WR1751;
    AW1755
  Thomas BL1765
Butler, Charles BL1765
  Edward Dr SW1739
  Edward Hunt SF1824a
  George SF1824/40a;
    WW1841; SF1863a
  John WW1752; HD1754;
    FB1755; AW1755;
  John (clerk) DE1753;
    AW1755
  Joseph (clerk) DE1753;
    AW1755
  Robert WW1752; HD1754
  Thomas WW1752;
    HD1754
Butlin, William BL1828
Butterfield, John BW1744;
  DE1753; AW1755
Butterfield, John Jnr WT1756
  Samuel Harding WT1820a
Button, Edward WW1841
  John Viney (clerk)
    WW1841
Byron, Edward HD1754

Ca ?, Crescence BB1770
Cadman, Rev. John BL1765a
  dec 1773
Cadogan, Hon Charles
  SW1719
  Hon Charles Sloane
    HD1754
Calcutt see Callcott
Caldecott, Thomas BL1765
  Thomas BB1832
  William BL1765;
    BL1765a
Callcott, Calcutt, William
  AW1755
  William BL1783a;
    BL1765
Calley, Thomas HD1754
Callman, John (clerk)
  BL1765
Calton, Paul HD1734;
  WW1752
  Paul Jnr HD1734
Campion, Sir George
  WW1752
Cane, Joseph (clerk) HD1734
Canning, Francis Snr
  CB1731
  Francis Jnr CB1731
  Robert BL1840

Capel, Christopher CC1751
Carnall, Robert AW1755
Carnavon, Marquis of, son of
  Duke of Chandos HD1734
Carne, John AW1755;
  HD1754
Carner, Joseph FB1755
Carter, Christopher DE1753;
  AW1755
  Edward SW1719
  Estcourt CC1751
  George Richard SW1739;
    HD1754
  Richard SW1719
  Thomas SW1719
  Thomas BH1811;
    WT1820; FB1822;
    BH1832
  Thomas Richard HD1754
  William, Bailiff of
    Buckingham BW1744
  (no forename) BBC1802
Cartwright, Aubrey BL1840
  Robert BB1832
  Stephen (clerk) BL1840
  Stephen Ralph (clerk)
    BH1832; BB1832
  Thomas SW1719;
    BW1744; FB1755;
    AW1755; WT1756;
    BL1765; BB1770
  Thomas AK1818;
    WT1820; BL1828;
    BB1832
  Sir Thomas BL1840
  William BW1744;
    DE1753a; AW1755;
    FB1755; WT1756;
    BL1765; BB1770
  William Jnr BL1765
  William BA1825a;
    BB1832; BL1840
  William Ralph BA1790;
    BBC1802; BH1811;
    WT1820; FB1822;
    DE1822;BA1825a;
    BH1832; BB1832
Castell, Robert CC1751
Castle, John CC1751
  ?, John (clerk) BB1770
Castleton, Nathaniel BL1765
Caswell, John (clerk)
  BBC1802
Cattle, Hewens DE1753;
  AW1755
Causton, Thomas (clerk)
  WeT1820a

Cautley, Richard (clerk)
  BBC1802
Cave, Charles BL1765
  Sir Thomas FB1755;
    BL1765
  Thomas BL1765
Cawley, Thomas HD1734
  Thomas (clerk) WW1752;
    HD1754
  William HD1734
Chamber, Rev WR1846
Chamberlain, Chamberlaine,
  Chamberlayne
  Edmund Snr CB1731
  Edmund Jnr CB1731;
    CC1751
  Edward BB1770
  Henry Thomas FB1859
  Sir James WR1751
  John BB1770
  Joseph Chamberlayne
    BB1832
  Richard FB1755
  Thomas BL1765
  Thomas Hughes (clerk)
    FB1822
  Thomas Hughes BL1828;
    BL1840
  (no forename), SW1719
Chamberlin, William Hurst
  BH1832
Chambers, William FB1755
Champion, Sir George
  SF1738
Chancellor, Diocese of
  Worcester CB1731
Chandler, George (clerk)
  FB1822
Channey, Wm H BL1771a
  Wm M BL1778a
Chapman, James CC1821
  John CC1821
  Richard BBC1802;
    BH1811
  Thomas FB1755
  William CC1751; BB1770
Charles, John CB1731
Charl(e)wood, Robert
  SF1862a
  William GFB1812
Charlott, Dr SW1719
Charlwood see Charlewood
Charnley, William FB1755
Chauncey, Richard AW1755;
  FB1755; WT1756;
  BW1744; DE1753
  Toby BL1765; WR1730

Chauncey *continued*
  William AW1755;
    FB1755; WT1756;
    BL1765
  William Henry BL1765
Chaunler, John clerk SF1791r
Chaunter ?, John (clerk)
  BB1770
Cheatle, Thomas BC1834
Chefwynd *see* Chetwynd
Cherry, William AW1755
Chester, Thomas CC1751
Chesterman, Thomas
  HD1754
Chetwood, Sir Phillip
  BW1744
Chetwynd, Chefwynd,
    William SW1719
  Lord Viscount BA1834a
Child, Benjamin SW1719
  Robert BL1765
Chipping Norton, Bailiffs of
  WR1730; WR1751
Church, John CB1731
  Rev Ralph SW1739
  Rev Ralph HD1754
  Ralph HD1754
  Richard SF1824a
  William WW1752
  Rev SW1739
Churchill, Alfred Spencer,
    Lord WR1846
  Bartholomew BB1770;
    BBC1802
  Bartholomew Jnr BB1770;
    BBC1802
  Benjamin (clerk)
    BBC1802; CC1821
  Benjamin WR1804;
    WR1825
  Blencow FB1755
  Hon George Spencer
    (Marquis of Blandford)
    AK1818
  Henry BA1790; BBC1802
  John AK1818; BB1832
  John Winston Spencer
    (Marquis of Blandford)
    WR1846
  Samuel BB1770; BA1790;
    BBC1802; BA1812;
    AK1818
Churton, Ralph (clerk)
  WT1820; BL1828
Clark, Clarke, Edward
  BB1770

Clark, Clarke *continued*
  Edward Wiseman
    WW1752
  Francis (clerk) BH1832
  Joseph HD1734
  James GFB1812
  John BL1765
  John GFB1812
  John Alexander (clerk)
    BL1840
  Joseph BL1765 dec 1773
  Richard BL1765
  Richard GFB1812
  Richard BL1828
  Richard Trevor BL1840
  Robert Mayne WW1841
  William BL1765
  William WW1841
  William Nelson HS1824
  William Wiseman HD1754
  William Wiseman HS1824
  William Shaw WW1841
  See also Clerke
Clarson, Henry AW1755
  Samuel FB1755; AW1755
Classon, Abraham FB1755
Clay, Jno BL1765a
Clayton, Kendrick HD1734
  William SW1719
  Sir William HD1734
  William HD1754
Cleaver, Rev John Francis
    vicar of Great Coxwell,
    SF1819/26/40a
Cleeve, William FB1755
Clement, John WW1752
Clerke, Francis (clerk)
    BL1840
  Francis Henry (clerk)
    BL1828
  George SW1719
  John SW1719; SW1739
  see also Clark, Clarke
Clinch, James CC1821;
    BC1834
  John CC1821
  John Williams CC1821;
    BC1834
Clopton, Hugh CB1731
Clough, Alfred Butler
    BL1840
Clowes, Thomas WW1841
Clutterbuck, James (clerk)
    WW1841
Cobb, George DE1822
  Sir George DE1753;
    AW1755

Cobb *continued*
  John DD WR1804;
    WR1825
  Thomas BA1790;
    BBC1802; DE1822
  Thomas Jnr BBC1802;
    BH1811; BH1832;
    BB1832
  Timothy BA1790;
    BBC1802; BH1811;
    DE1822; BB1832
  Timothy Rhodes BH1832;
    BB1832; FB1859
Cockerell, Sir Charles
    BB1832
  Charles BB1832
Cockerton, James WT1820a
Cockman, Rev Dr SW1739
Cocks, Sir Robert WR1730;
    CB1731
  Dr SW1719
Cockshead, Rev Dr SW1739
  Henry (clerk) BW1744
  Thomas William BH1811
  Wenman BL1765
Coker, Charles WT1756
  John BA1790
  John (clerk) BH1832
  Thomas WT1756
  Thomas (clerk) BA1790
  Thomas Lewis BA1825a
Cole, Edward WR1730;
    BW1744; WR1751;
    DE1753; AW1755
  Sir George BW1744
  Harry WR1730; CB1731
  Henry SW1719
  William BA1812
Colebrook, James WW1752
Coleman, Edward BB1770
  ?, Job BB1770
  (no forename) BB1832
Coles, George WR1804
  William AW1755;
    BB1770
Collett, John? BB1770
  Thomas FB1755
Collier, Robert CC1821
  Samuel CC1821
  Thomas WT1820a;
    WT1820
  William BB1770
Collins, Anthony CC1751;
    BB1770
  Charles HD1754
  David AW1755

Collins *continued*
  Ferdinando WW1752;
    HD1754
  Henry HD1754
  John WW1752; HD1754
  John (clerk) HS1824
  John Ferdinando (clerk)
    WW1841
  Paul SW1719
  Thomas BB1770
  William HD1754
Collisson, William WT1820
Collyer, John CC1751
  William CC1751
Colston, Alexander BB1770
  Edward Francis GFB1812
Colton, Barfoot, clerk
    SF1787a; SF1806d
  Caleb (clerk) WW1752
Compere, John CB1744
Compton, Hon Charles
    DE1753; AW1755
  Hon George CB1731;
    DE1753
Congreve, Rev M CB1744
Congreve, Thomas FB1755;
  FB1755/6a
Connant, Dr SW1719
Conway, Hon Henry HD1754
Conybeare, Rev Dr Dean of
  Christchurch SW1739
Coode, Samuel BA1812
Cook, John WT1756
  John DD WR1804
Cooke, Rev John G1821
  John HD1754
  Thomas (clerk) BB1770
Cooper, George MD
    WW1752
  Gislingham HD1734
  John BL1765
  Matthew BL1765
  Thomas SW1739
Cooper, Thomas of
  Faringdon, grocer
    SF1788n; SF1824r
  Thomas of Weston
    HD1754
Cope, Anthony BW1744
  Sir Charles BB1770
  John DE1753; AW1755
  Sir John BA1812; DE1822
  Jonathan BW1744;
    CC1751; DE1753;
    AW1755; HD1754

Cope *continued*
  Sir Jonathan (bart)
    SW1719; WR1730;
    CB1731; BW1744;
    CC1751; WR1751;
    DE1753; AW1755;
    HD1754
  Monoux HD1734;
    SW1739; BW1744
  Sir Monoux DE1753;
    HD1754; AW1755
  Richard BB1770
Corderoy, John HD1734
Corgan, Michael BBC1802;
  WR1804
Cormell, Thomas of Paxford
  CB1744
Cornish, Thomas HD1754
  (clerk) BB1832
Costard, Richard of Abingdon
  HD1754
Cotes, Rev SW1739
Cotgreave, Thomas of
  Faringdon, SF1806a;
  SF1819d
Cotterell *see* Cottrell
Cottingham, John SW1739
Cottrell, Cotterell,
  Charles WR1751;
    AW1755; WT1756
  Charles AK1818
  Sir Clement WR1751
  Stephen BA1790
  see also under Dormer
Councer, George BB1770
  John BB1770
Courtenay, Charles of
  Buckland House SF1819a
Courtney, Francis Reginald
  (clerk) BB1770
Coventry, Mayor & Corp of
  FB1755
Coventry, Hon John Bulkeley
    HD1754; AW1755
  Thomas HD1734
Cowley, John BL1765
  John BL1840
Cowper, William FB1859
  Gilbert WW1752
Cox, Charles HD1754
  Francis (clerk) WW1752
  Francis AW1755; FB1755
  John (clerk) BW1744;
    DE1753; AW1755
  John FB1755
  Joseph WW1752
  Nathaniel FB1755

Cox *continued*
  Peter of Faringdon SF1732
  Richard G1821
  Richard of Ardington
    WW1752; HD1754
  Richard Ferdinand G1821
  Robert Kilby BA1790
  Samuel BBC1802;
    WR1804; BL1828;
    BL1840
  Samuel Fortnom WR1825;
    WR1846
  Thomas SW1719
  Thomas of Borton
    WW1752
Coxe, Charles CB1744
Cozen, Henry BB1770
Crane, Charles (clerk)
  FB1822
Cranke, Rev Edward, rector
  of Hatfield SF1732;
  WW1752
Craven, Henry (clerk)
  WW1752
  John (clerk) SF1788n
  William DE1753; FB1755
Crawley, Thomas SW1739
Crayle ?, Crayle BB1770
Crelwick, Henry BB1770
  Joseph BB1770
Creswell, William BL1765
  see also Wentworth
Creswick, John CB1731
  Joseph CB1731
Crew, Edward HD1754
Cricklow, Samuel FB1755
Cripps, Jeffery HD1754
  John BB1770
  Jo ? BB1770
Crisp, Charles SW1719;
  WR1730
  Sir Charles CB1731
Crofts, Robert BL1765
Croke, Alexander BA1790
  James SW1719
  Richard SW1719
Croley, Edward CC1751
Crook, Alexander BW1744
Croome, John (clerk)
    CC1821; BB1832
  John Jnr BB1832
Crosley, James FB1755
  John HD1734
Crowdy, James GFB1812;
    SF1840a
  Richard Wheeler
    GFB1812; BC1834

Crowdy *continued*
　William GFB1812;
　　BC1834
Crowe, Henry (clerk)
　BH1811; BH1832
Croxall, Edward FB1755
Cullerne, Thomas HD1754
　Thomas Jnr HD1754
Cummins, William, Dr of
　Physick WR1730;
　CB1731; BW1744
Curme, Rev John WR1846
Curteis, Whitfield (clerk)
　BBC1802
　William BBC1802
Curtis, James HD1754
　John HD1754

D'Anvers, Sir Michael
　BL1765
Doyly, D'Oyley, Christopher
　DE1753; AW1755;
　BL1765
　Rev John SW1739;
　HD1754
　Sir John SW1719;
　HD1734
　Robert AW1755
　Thomas SW1739; HD1734
　Sir Thomas (bart) HD1754
　William AW1755
D.. ? John (clerk) BB1770
　John BB1770
Dalby, John HD1734
Dancer, George BW1744
Dandridge, Francis HD1734;
　HD1754
　John Strange (clerk)
　WT1820
Daniel, William FB1755;
　FB1755 81a
　William BL1840
Danvers, Daniel SW1719
Darby, Richard SW1739;
　HD1734
Dashwood, Charles BB1770
　Charles AK1818
　Sir Francis SW1719
　George BA1812; AK1818;
　WR1825
　Sir George BB1832;
　WR1846
　Henry BBC1802
　Sir Henry Watkin BB1770;
　BA1790; BBC1802;
　WR1804; WT1820;
　G1821; WR1825

Dashwood *continued*
　Sir James SW1739;
　BW1744; CC1751;
　WR1751; DE1753;
　AW1755; WT1756;
　BB1770
　Robert SW1719; SW1739;
　WR1751
　Sir Robert SW1719;
　WR1730
Daubeny (clerk) FB1822
Daventry (N'hants.), Bailiff,
　Recorder & Burgesses of
　BL1765
Davies, Henry (clerk)
　WW1752
　James (clerk) CC1821
　John clerk, SF1824r
　Richard FB1755
　Thomas CC1751
Davis, Edward CB1731
　George CC1751; AW1755
　George HD1754
　Harry (clerk) BBC1802;
　BH1811; BB1832;
　BH1832
　John CB1731; AW1755
　John BBC1802; BH1811;
　DE1822; BH1832
　John (clerk) BL1765
　Richard CB1731
　Thomas BA1790
　William HD1734
　William WT1756
　William BB1832
Dawes, Thomas FB1755
Dawkins, Henry BB1770
　Henry WR1804; WR1825;
　BB1832; WR1846
　James WR1730; CB1731;
　CC1751; WR1751
Day, William SW1739
　Rev SW1719
Dayman, Charles (clerk)
　BB1832
Dayrell, Edmund BH1811
　John Langham (clerk)
　BH1811; BH1832
　Richard BW1744
　Richard BH1811; BH1832
　Thomas BW1744
de Beauvoir, Richard Benyon
　HS1824
Deacle, John DE1753;
　FB1755; AW1755
　John (clerk) BA1790

Deacle *continued*
　William DE1753;
　DE1753a;. FB1755;
　AW1755; BL1765a
Deacon, George HD1754
Dean, William HD1754
Deane, Edward BB1770
Dechair, John DD BL1765
Delafield, Rev SW1739
Delanne, Rev Dr SW1719
Denbigh, Earl of BL1773a
Dennet, Richard SW1739
Denton, George BW1744;
　DE1753; AW1755;
　WT1756
Denys, Sir George William
　WT1820
Dew, Henry of Littleworth
　SF1738
　John Jnr SW1719;
　SW1739
　John WW1752
　Tomkins WW1752
　William of Charney
　HD1754
Dewe, John AW1755
　William of Hanny HD1754
Dewee, John CC1751
Dickenson, Rev SW1739
Dickinson, Francis CB1744
　John Marshe WT1756;
　BB1770
　Rt Hon Marshe WT1756
Digby, Hon Wrothesley
　FB1755
Dighton, Richard CB1731
Dilkes, John FB1755
Dillon, Hon Henry August
　WR1804; WR1825
　Viscount WR1846
Dimmock, Henry (clerk)
　BB1770
Diston, James AW1755
　William CB1731;
　AW1755
　(no forename) of
　Shenington DE1753
Dix, Edward BBC1802
Dobree, Nicholas Peter (clerk)
　BBC1802
Dod, John AW1755
Dolben, Sir William BB1770
Dolley, Thomas CC1751
Dolphin, John BB1770
　John (clerk) CC1821
Dormer, Charles Cotterell
　WR1825; WR1846

Dormer *continued*
  Sir Charles Cotterell
    BB1770
  Sir Clement Cottrell
    AW1755; WT1756;
    BA1790; WR1804
  Fleetwood SW1719
  Hon. Gen. James SW1739
  John SW1719
  Robert WR1730
  see also Cottrell, Cotterell
Dottin, Abel HD1754
Doughty, Henry CB1731
Douglas, Sir James SF1788r
Dowdeswell, George
    WR1730; CB1731;
    WR1751
  George Jnr CB1744
  Rev William WR1730;
    CB1731; WR1751
Dowsett, Robert WW1752
Drake, Christopher (clerk)
    CB1731
Draper, William BB1770
  (no forename) AW1755
Drayson, Richard BL1765
Dryden, Sir John WT1756;
    BL1765
Dudley, William AW1755
Duffield, James SW1739
  Thomas HS1824
Dugdale, Dugdale Stratford
    FB1822
Dunce, Samuel BB1770
Dunch, Edmund SW1719
Dundas, Charles HS1824
  George BL1765
Dunkley, Thomas BL1828
Dunscombe, John SW1739
Dunster, Rev Dr SW1719
Durell, David (clerk)
    WW1802a; WW1841
Durham, William CB1731
Dutton, Hon James Henry
    Legge BB1832
  James Lenox BB1770
  Hon James CC1821
  Hon John BB1832
  Sir John CB1731
  Lenox James CC1751
  William BB1770
  William BC1834
Dyer of Hinton HD1754

Eagles, John BL1765
  Woodfield Blake BA1812

Eaglesfield, James HD1734
  John HD1734
Eales, John of Stadham
    SW1719; HD1754
Eariesby, Robert BL1765
Earle, Nicholas (clerk)
    BBC1802; WR1804
Early, Edward CC1821;
    BC1834
  John Jnr CC1821
East, James Buller BB1832
Eaton, John AW1755
  John (clerk) AW1755
  Rev Matthew HD1754
  Richard (clerk) CB1731
  Rev of Steeple Aston
    WT1756
Ebdell, Thomas FB1755
Eddowes, John (clerk)
    BW1744; DE1753;
    AW1755; FB1755
Edgecumbe, Rev Dr SW1739
Edlin, Thomas WW1752;
    HD1754
Edmonds, Henry BB1770
Edmunds, Francis (clerk)
    BW1744
Edoe, Thomas of Faringdon,
    gent SF1788n; SF1824r
Edwards, Anthony CC1751
  Edward D.D. BB1770
  John HD1734
  Thomas SF1732
  Thomas (clerk) FB1755
  William CC1751
Eeles, John HD1754
Egerton, RE of Farthinghoe
    WT1756
  Samuel FB1755; WT1756
Elderfield, William WW1841
Eldridge, John HD1754
  John HS1824
  Simon WW1752; HD1754
  William HD1754
Elers, Paul, CC1751
Elkington, Thomas FB1822
Ellers, Paul AW1755;
    HD1754
Ellins, William CC1751
Elliot, Charles FB1755
  Thomas FB1755
Ellis, Ralph BB1770
  Richard BB1770
  Rev William of Stoke
    WT1756
  William (clerk) BA1790;
    BH1811; BH1832

Ellis *continued*
  William Cornish (clerk)
    BA1790
Elstone, John of Hendred
    WW1752
Elwes, Henry CC1821
  John HD1754
Elweys, John Meggot
    WW1752
Englefield, Sir Henry
    WW1752
Erly, John of Newlands
    BC1834
Esbourne, William FB1755
Euston, Earl of *see* Fitzroy
Evans, Goven (clerk)
    WT1820
  Rev G.S. SF1840a
  Philip BBC1802
  Rev W SF1840a
  Rev SW1739
  (no forename) BB1832
Evelyn, Sir George Augustus
  William Shuckburgh
    BBC1802
Everard, Charles (clerk)
    BL1765
Evetts, Barlow FB1755
  William WR1846
Ewen, Robert HD1754
Eyloe, Richard of Shrivenham
    SF1732
Eyre, Charles Snr HD1754;
    HD1734
  Charles Jnr HD1754
  Francis BL1765
  Joseph (clerk) BA1790
  Richard (clerk) WW1752
  Richard DE1753; AW1755
  William (clerk) BH1811
  William Thomas (clerk)
    BH1832
Eyres, Charles SW1739
Eyston, Charles HS1824
  John HD1754

Fairfax, Samuel FB1755
Falkner, Rev John AK1818
Fane, Charles, Lord Viscount
    WW1752; HD1754
  Francis SW1739
  John BBC1802; DE1822;
    FB1822
Fanshaw, Rev John DD
    HD1754
Faulkner, John (clerk)
    BBC1802

Faulkner *continued*
William CC1821; BC1834
Fawcett, Thomas (clerk)
BH1811; AK1818;
WT1820;WT1820a
DE1822; BA1825a;
BH1832
Fellowes, John BH1811
Felton, Rev Dr SW1739
Fermanagh, Viscount *see*
Verney
Fermor, Henry BA1790
Richard BA1812
Hon. Thomas WT1820
William BA1790;
BA1812; WT1820;
G1821
Fettiplace, Charles WR1751;
BB1770; WR1804
Sir George HD1734
Sir Lorenzo SW1719
Robert CC1751; AW1755;
HD1754; BB1770
Thomas WW1752;
HD1754
Fidell, John SF1840a
Field, John WW1841
John Connor BH1811
Robert FB1859
Samuel Churchill BA1812;
AK1818
Fielding, Rt Hon Basil, Lord
FB1755
Finch, Hon Edward BL1765
Hon Heneage, Lord
Guernsey FB1755
Rt Hon. William BL1765
William SW1739
William DL WR1804
Rev SW1739
Findon, Francis BBC1802
Finmore, SW1719
Firth, William of Letcombe
Bassett (clerk) WW1841
Fisher, Richard SW1739;
HD1734
Thomas FB1755
(no forename) (clerk)
BBC1802
Fitzroy, Augustus Henry, Earl
of Euston WT1756
Hon. Charles WT1820
Flamank, William DD
WR1804
Flesher, Gilbert WT1820a;
WT1820

Flesher *continued*
John Thomas (clerk)
WT1820
Fletcher, Edward CB1744
Richard SW1739;
CB1744; BB1770
William CB1731
William (clerk) BB1770
Flexney, Joseph CC1751
Flight, Thomas HD1734
Fludger, Henry Snr HD1754
Rev John HD1754
John of Abingdon HD1754
William of Longworth
HD1754
William of Wallingford
HD1754
Fludyer, Henry Snr WW1752
Henry Jnr WW1752
William WW1752
Foley, Robert D.D. BB1770
Thomas SW1719
?, Thomas BB1770
Folker, William G1821
Folkestone, Viscount Jacob
Pleydell Bouverie
BC1834
William Lord Viscount
SF1802n
Rt Hon Lord Viscount
SF1840a
See also under Bouverie
Folwell, William BL1765
Ford, Richard Wilbraham
(clerk) CC1821;
BB1832
Thomas BB1770
Forster, William HD1734
Fortnam, Charles BBC1802
Foster, George BA1790
William Snr BA1812
William Jnr BA1812
Fothergill, Thomas BB1770
Fowler, John FB1755;
AW1755
William FB1755
Fox, Charles BW1744;
BL1765; BB1770;
BL1778a; BL1783a
Charles (clerk) BL1765
Daniel SW1739
Foxton, Rev George of Great
Coxwell, SF1791n;
SF1824a
Frampton, John GFB1812
Richard BC1834
France, Thomas BW1744

Francis, Richard BL1765
Franks, Aaron BL1765
Frederick, Gasco??, BB1770
John BB1770
Freeman, Edward FB1755
John SW1719; AW1755;
HD1734; BL1765
Richard CB1731
Robert Berkley BB1770
Sambrooke HD1754
Thomas BL1765;
BBC1802
Thomas Edwards BB1770
William DE1753
Freemantle, Thomas Francis
BH1811
French, Edmund BL1765
Francis BB1770
George BH1832
Thomas WT1820
William BH1832
Friend, William DD
SW1719; HD1754;
CC1751
Frith, William Cokayne
(clerk) WW1841
Frogley, John WW1752
Fulham, John BB1770
Fuller, James HS1824
Fuller, Joseph Humphrey
WW1841
John HS1824
Richard HD1754
Thomas HD1734
Thomas Snr WW1841
Thomas Jnr WW1841
Thomas Humphrey
HS1824
(no forename) of Ginge
WW1752
Furley, Henry CC1751
(no forename) n? Henry
BB1770

Gabel, Henry (clerk)
BW1744; BB1770
Thomas BW1744; DE1753
Gage, Lord Viscount CC1751
Gaisford, Charles (clerk)
CC1821; BC1834
Gales, Bernard AW1755
Gammon, John HD1754
William HD1754
Gardner, John AW1755
Robert FB1755; AW1755
Robert WT1820
Thomas BH1832

Gardner *continued*
  Rev Dr SW1719
  Rev SW1719
Garland, Charles WT1756
  Paul WT1756
Garrard, Charles WW1752
  Thomas WW1752
  Thomas of Wantage
    WW1752
Gas ? Robert BB1770
Gascoyne, Richard FB1755;
    AW1755
Gates, Bernard HD1754
Gayer, Robert HD1734
Geary, John (clerk) WW1752
Geast, Richard FB1755
Gee, Frederick WT1820
Geeves, Anthony CC1751
George, John WT1756
  Jonan BB1770
Gerrard, Nathaniel, (clerk)
    FB1755
Gibbard, Richard BW1744
  Timothy WW1752;
    HD1754
Gibbons, Samuel FB1755
  Rev SW1739
Gibbs, Charles WT1756
  John Snr CB1731
  John CB1731
Gifford, Anthony HD1734
Gilbee, Charles (clerk)
    BL1840
Gilbert, Richard FB1755;
    BB1770
  Thomas BB1770
Gill, Thomas (clerk)
    DE1753a; FB1755;
    AW1755
  T FB1802a
Gillett, William BBC1802
Gilling, Charles WW1752
Gilman, Rev SW1719
Gilpin, James AW1755;
    HD1754
Glass, John CC1751
Glynn, John SW1719
  William SW1719
  Sir William SW1719
Goddard, Samuel FB1755;
    AW1755; BL1765;
    BL1765a
Godfree, John BL1765;
    BL1765a
  William BL1765
Godfrey, George WW1752
  John CC1751

Godfrey *continued*
  William CC1751
  ?? (no forename) BB1770
Godolphin, William (Marquis
    of Blandford) CB1731;
    WR1730
Godson, Richard BBC1802
  Stephen BBC1802
Godwin, Francis BL1765
Goffe, Solomon BB1770
Golby, James BA1790;
    BBC1802; BH1811
  James Wake BBC1802;
    BH1832
Goldicutt, John BB1770
Golightly, Thomas (clerk)
    BL1807; BH1811; FB1822;
    BL1828; BH1832;
    BL1840; FB1859
Gomin, Stephen SW1739
Goodacre, John BL1765
Goode, Francis BH1811
Goodenough, John WW1752;
    HD1754
  John M.D. BB1770
  Samuel (clerk) BB1770
  Samuel James (clerk)
    CC1821; BC1834
  Rev SW1739
Goodlake, Thomas of
    Letcombe Regis,
    SF1806/40a; HS1824
  Thomas WW1752
  Thomas BC1834
  Thomas Leinster ,
    SF1862a
  Thomas Mills HS1824;
    BC1834
Goodman, Joseph BL1840
Goodwin, Augustin (clerk)
    CB1731
Goodwin, Francis AW1755;
    FB1755
  John AW1755; BL1765
  Joseph (clerk) WR1730;
    CB1731; WR1751;
    BB1770
  Joseph CC1751
  Richard (clerk) AW1755
  William DE1753;
    AW1755
Gordon, Pryce Lockhart
    GFB1812; BC1834
  William (clerk) BB1832
Gore, Charles WT1756
  Edward BB1770
Gorges, Richard WR1804

Gough, Drope BW1744;
    DE1753; AW1755;
    WT1756
  Ferdinando SW1739
  George CC1751
  Richard BB1770
  Rev William DD WT1756
Grace, Thomas BL1765;
    BL1773d
Graham, James BBC1802
  John HD1754
  John, surgeon SF1791r
  Robert of Faringdon,
    surgeon SF1788n;
    WW1752
  Thomas BBC1802
Grainger, Rev James
    HD1754
Granby, Marquis of *see*
    Manners
Grant, William WT1820;
    BL1840
  Rev of Stanton Gambold
    SW1739
Gravenor, Abel FB1755
  Edward Jnr FB1755
Gray, Edward Oakley
    BH1811; BA1812
  Robert BH1811; BH1832
  Robert of Faringdon, clerk
    SF1794n; SF1806r
Greathead, Samuel FB1755
Greaves, James BH1832
  Richard (clerk) BB1832
Green, Edward HD1734
  George BA1790
  Hatton GFB1812
  John CC1751
  Thomas FB1755
  Thomas (clerk) BL1828;
    BL1840
  William (clerk) FB1755
Greenall, William BW1744;
    DE1753a FB1755
Greenaway, Charles CC1821;
    BB1832; BC1834
Greenhill, Rev John Russell
    DD HD1754; BH1811
  Robert BH1811
  Samuel SW1739; HD1734
Greenville, Hon. James
    DE1753
Greenway, George FB1822
  Kelynge FB1822
  Randolph WW1752
Greenwood, Charles
    CC1751; HD1754

Greenwood *continued*
  Charles of Castle Street,
    Wallingford WW1841
  Charles of Winterbrook
    WW1841
  John HD1754
  Thomas WR1730; CB1731
  Thomas WW1841
Gregory, Arthur FB1755
Gregory, Henry (clerk)
    BC1834
  Francis SW1719
  John (merchant) WR1730;
    WR1751; AW1755
  John (clerk) WR1804
  Thomas (clerk) BB1770
Grenville, Sir Charles
    FB1822
  Francis FB1755
  George BW1744
  Rt Hon George AW1755;
    WT1756
  Lord George BH1811
  James BW1744
  Hon James AW1755
  Richard BW1744
  Thomas BW1744
Grey, Lord, George Harry
    BL1765
  Henry HD1734
  Rev Richard DD DE1753;
    AW1755; WT1756;
    BB1770
Greyhurst, John CC1751
Griffin, John BB1770;
    BBC1802
  Richard FB1822; DE1822;
    BH1832
  (no forename) (clerk)
    FB1755
Griffiths, Thomas (clerk)
    CC1751; BB1770
Grimes, Abraham BL1765
  Abraham BL1828
  Henry BL1828; BL1840
  William Dixwell BL1765
Grimsdall, William HD1734
Grinsdale, Benjamin (clerk)
    CC1821
Groenal, William AW1755
Grosvenor, John G1821
Grove, Charles (clerk)
    WR1804
  John WW1752
  Richard HD1754
  Robert of Balkin SF1738;
    WW1752

Grove *continued*
  William FB1755
Guernsey, Lord *see* Finch
Gurden, Philip SW1739
  William WT1820
  William (clerk) WT1820
Gutteridge, Benjamin (clerk)
    CC1751
Guy, William HD1734
Gwynne, John BC1834
Gyfford, Anthony (clerk)
    WW1752
Gymingham, Thomason Dyke
    HD1734
Gyse, Sir John CC1751

H...son??, William D.D.
    BB1770
Habcraft, William BL1765
Hacker, Edward Marshall
    BB1832
  Rev John of Glympton
    WR1730
  John (clerk) CB1731
  Nicholas Marshall (clerk)
    WR1825
  Thomas SW1719
  Thomas of Kingham
    WR1730
  Rev SW1719
Hackman, Thomas HD1734
Hackwell, Rev James
    WT1756; BA1790
Hadland, William FB1859
Hakewill, James (clerk)
    BB1770
Hales, James BB1770
  Thomas BB1770
Haley, John BA1790
Halford, Edward BL1765
Hall, Henry HD1734
  Henry of Harden SW1739
  James CC1751; BB1770
  John AK1818; BL1828
  John Jnr BL1828
  Owen HD1754
  Richard BB1770
  Robert HD1754
  Robert John (clerk)
    BB1832
  Thomas HD1754
  Thomas BL1765
  William CB1731
  William G1821
Hallett, William of Faringdon
  House SF1788n; HS1824

Hamilton, Lord Archibald,
  uncle to Duke of Hamilton
    HD1734
Hamington, Richard
    AW1755
Hammerstey, Hugh HD1754
Hammond, George (clerk)
    DE1753
Hampton, George AW1755;
    BL1765
Hanwell, Richard BL1765;
    BL1765a
Harcourt, Hon Simon
    SW1719
Harding, Henry HD1754
Hardinge, Samuel BW1744
Hardway, James FB1755
Harman, Edward HD1754
Harneford, Frances DL
    SF1788rd
Harper, John BL1765
  Thomas SW1739; CC1751
Harrington, Sir James
    BW1744
  Richard SW1739;
    WR1751; HD1754
Harris, Charles SW1739
  ??, Giles BB1770
  Rev Hamlyn BL1773n
  Joseph BBC1802
  Richard CC1751
  Robert HS1824
  Timothy BW1744
  William BB1770
Harrison, Edward SW1719
  George SW1719
  Henry Bagshaw BL1765
  John BH1811; WT1820;
    G1821; BH1832
  Lewis BL1840
  Samuel Wyment BL1828;
    BL1840
  Rev William DD BB1770;
    BA1790
  Rev William FB1859
  Rev , rector of Buscott
    SF1732
Hart, John CB1731
  Percivall WR1730;
    CB1731
Harte, Walter (clerk) BB1770
Hartley, David MD WW1752
Harwood, Kemp HD1734
Hatt, Charles SF1802r
Hatton, John BBC1802
  Richard WW1752
  Robert BBC1802

Hatton *continued*
William WW1752
Haughton, James WR1825
Hawes, Rev SW1739
Hawker, Samuel CC1751
Hawkins, James (clerk)
    CC1821; BC1834
Rev John SF1824a;
    SF1840a
Richard (clerk) AW1755
William SW1719; HD1734
William (clerk) CC1751
Rev William Hawkins of
    Great Faringdon
    SF1802n
William Jnr HD1754
(no forename) of Bagbook
    (clerk) CC1751
Hawtin, Ralph ? BB1770
William BB1770
Hayes, John FB1755
Rev John Lea G1821
Richard (clerk) BB1770
Thomas HD1754
Haynes, Thomas FB1755;
    AW1755
William BBC1802
see also Heynes
Hayton, William WT1756
William WT1756; BB1770
Hayward, Alfred WT1820
Henry WW1841
Thomas (clerk) CC1751
Thomas HD1754
William (clerk) CC1751
William HD1754;
    AW1755; BL1765
William (clerk) WW1841
Hazel, Benjamin WW1841
John WW1841
Hazell, Wm WW1802a
Head, John of Compton
    WW1752
John of Hodcott WW1752;
    HD1754
Sir Thomas WW1752
William BL1828
Heads of Colleges & Halls of
    University of Oxford
    HD1734; AW1755
Hearn, Thomas Snr BH1811
Thomas BA1812
Hearne, John Buckworth
    (clerk) WW1841
Heath, Francis GFB1812
Samuel FB1859
Heather, Matthew BA1790

Hecate, Andrew FB1755
Hedges, Charles WW1841
John Allnatt WW1841
John Kirby WW1841
Hemming, Thomas of Gt
    Barrington CC1751
Thomas of Little
    Barrington
    CC1751
William BBC1802
Henchman, John AW1755
? (no forename) (clerk)
    BB1770
Henderson, Charles Robert
    CC1821; BC1834
Henley, Mayor, Aldermen &
    Burgesses of HD1734;
    Mayor of HD1754
Hensburgh, James Remond
    HD1734
Herbert, James SW1719;
    SW1739
John of Faringdon, surgeon
    SF1788n
John Snr SF1819d
John CC1821
Peregrine SW1739
Philip SW1719
Simon HD1754
Thomas CC1751; BB1770
Thomas CC1821
Thomas Jnr CC1821
Thomas of Faringdon,
    surgeon GFB1812;
    SF1819a
Herbidge, Robert CB1731
Hervey, John HD1754
William GFB1812;
    CC1821; BC1834
Heurtley, Rev Charles Abel,
    DD FB1859
Hewens, Thomas DE1753;
    AW1755
Hewitt, James, Sgt at Law
    FB1755
John FB1755
Joseph FB1755
William FB1755
Heyden, Heydon,
    Elisha BL1765; BL1772
    78a
John BL1807; BH1811
Richard BBC1802;
    BL1807; BH1811;
    DE1822; FB1822;
    BH1832
Thomas BL1828

Heyes, William CB1744
Heynes, Charles BB1770
William BB1770
see also Haynes
Heywood, Francis Snr
    SW1719
Francis Snr HD1734
Francis Jnr HD1734
Nathaniel AW1755
Thead SW1739
Hibert ?, Samuel BB1770
Hickman, Henry BL1773n
William BL1765;
    BL1773d
Hicks, Baptist (clerk)
    CB1731
How CC1751
William (clerk) CC1821
Higginson, John BL1765
Higgons, William GFB1812
Hill, John FB1755
Joseph BL1765
Justly (clerk) BH1832
Robert CC1751
Samuel FB1755
Hilliard, William WW1841
Hillyard, Rev Temple
    FB1859
Hilsborough, Earl of
    DE1753; FB1755
Hinchman, John (clerk)
    AW1755
Hinckley, Richard (clerk)
    BBC1802
Hind, Rev SW1719
Hinde, John (clerk) BL1807
Hindes, John DE1753
Robert FB1755
Samuel FB1755; BL1765
Thomas (clerk) FB1755;
    AW1755
Hinton, Richard CC1751
Hippisley, John WW1752
John (clerk) BB1770
Richard CB1744
Hirons, William BL1765
Hissey, John SF1824a
Richard SF1824r
Hitcham, Thomas DE1753
Hitchcock, James Charles
    (clerk) BL1765
John CB1731
William BH1832
Hitchcox, George DE1822
William BBC1802;
    DE1822
Hitchings, Sir Edward G1821

Hitchman, Simpkins BB1832
Hoard, Thomas CC1751;
  HD1754
Hobbis, John WW1752
Hobbs, Rodolph SW1719
Hodges, Anthony Snr
  HD1754
  Anthony Jnr HD1754
  Henry Danvers BB1770
Hodgkinson, Tilleman (clerk)
  BB1770
Hodgson, Thomas WW1802a
Hodson, John Johnson (clerk)
  BL1840
  Robert BL1765
Holbeach, Henry (clerk)
  BL1807
  William Jnr BL1807
Holbech, Charles (clerk)
  WT1820; FB1822
  Rev Charles William
  FB1859
  Edward FB1822
  George FB1822
  Henry Hugh FB1822
  Hugh BW1744; FB1755;
    AW1755; WT1756;
    BL1765
  William BW1744;
    DE1753; FB1755;
    AW1755; WT1756;
    BL1765; BB1770;
    BH1811
  William Jnr BB1770;
    BH1811; AK1818;
    DE1822; FB1822;
    BH1832
Hole, Dr of Kidlington
  SW1719
Holford, Charles (clerk)
  BW1744
Holland, Dr SW1719
Holled, Knightly (clerk)
  BL1765; BL1765a
  Thomas BL1765
Holliday, Michael of Lt
  Coxwell SF1738
Hollis, John BC1834
Holloway, Benjamin Snr
  BB1770
  Rev Benjamin WR1751;
    WT1756; HD1754
  Benjamin BB1770;
    WR1804; WR1825;
    BB1832
  Edward Vere WR1804;
    WR1825

Holloway *continued*
  John SW1719
  Thomas BB1770
Holmes, Rev Dr SW1739
Holt, Charles SW1719
Holtom, Richard BBC1802
Holton, James CC1751
Homer, Henry FB1755 81a
Hopcraft, Barnet John
  WT1820
  Thomas WT1820
  Thomas Jnr WT1820
  William WT1756
Hopkins, Francis HD1754
  Henry HS1824
  John (clerk) BL1765
  John HS1824; SF1862a
  Richard FB1755
  Robert HS1824
  Robert of Tidmarsh
  HS1824
  Robert Jnr of Tidmarsh
  HS1824
  Robert of Harwell
  HS1824; WW1841
  Thomas HD1754
  William Toovey (clerk)
  WW1841
Horde, Thomas SW1739;
  BB1770
Horncastle, William FB1755
Horne, Edward Jnr SW1739
  Rev Thomas WR1751
  Thomas CC1751; BB1770
  William HD1734
Horner, Henry (clerk)
  FB1755
Horniblow, William
  BBC1802
Hornsby, George (clerk)
  CC1821
Horseman, John (clerk)
  BA1790
Horwood, John WT1820
Hoskins, Charles (clerk)
  BB1770
  James Williams DD
  CC1821; BC1834
Howard, George AW1755
  James SW1739
  John WT1820a
  William HD1734
Howe, Hon. Henry CC1751
  Hon. James CC1751
  Hon. William CC1751
Howell, Henry CC1751;
  HD1754

Howell *continued*
  John of Wolvercote
  SW1739
Howes, Thomas BL1840
Howlett, George BA1790
Howlins, William BL1765
Hubbard, Rev Thomas of
  Sunning HD1754
Hucks, Robert SF1732;
  HD1734
  William SF1732; HD1734
Huddesford, Edmund
  FB1755
Huddesford, Revd Dr of
  Glympton SW1739;
  WR1751
Huddesford, Rev George DD
  AW1755
  John FB1755
  William (clerk) FB1755;
  FB 1755/6a
Hudson, Rev Td SF1840a
Hue, Corbet DD BL1828
Huggins, Rev SW1739
Hughes, David CC1751
  Edward (clerk) DE1753a;
    AW1755; BL1765
  Francis CC1751
  John (clerk) CC1751
  John of Uffington,
    SF1819a
  Robert (clerk) WW1752
  Robert FB1755
  Robert (clerk) DE1822
  Robert Edward (clerk)
    BH1811; BH1832
  Simon (clerk) CC1751
  Thomas DD HS1824
Hulbert, Rev Bertram Brooke
  FB1859
Humfres, Edward BL1765
Humfrey, Joseph HD1754
  Thomas HS1824
  Thomas Jnr HS1824
Humphrey, Nathaniel DL
  BW1744; DE1753
  Nathaniel Pargiter
  AW1755; BL1765
Humphris, Rd BL1771a
Hunt, George CB1731
  Henry CB1731
  John Higgs (clerk)
    BL1828; BL1840
  Joseph (clerk) BL1840
  Peter WW1752
  Thomas CC1751;
    HD1734; BB1770

Hunt *continued*
  Rev Thomas DD HD1754
  Rev SW1739
  (no forename) of Bix
    HD1734
Hunter, Richard WW1752
  Rev SW1739
Huntley, Joseph BBC1802
  Robert SF1824a
  Thomas BB1770
  Thomas CC1821
  Wadham (clerk) CC1821
Hurd, John (clerk) CC1821
Hutton, John ? (clerk)
  BB1770
Hyde, Charles FB1755;
  AW1755; BB1770
  John (clerk) CC1821;
    WR1825; BC1834
  John Derby BC1834
Hyett, Benjamin CC1751
  Nicholas CC1751

Iliff, William (clerk) BL1765
Inge, William FB1755
Ingles, James (clerk) CB1744
Ingram, Hastings CB1731
  Rev John WR1730;
    CB1731; WR1751
  Samuel CC1751; HD1754;
    BB1770
  Thomas BB1770
Innes, George (clerk) FB1822
Ireland, Rev John DD G1821
  John G1821
Iremonger, Joshua CC1751;
  WR1751
Ireson, Thomas BL1765
Ironmonger, Jonathan
  HD1754
Isham, Sir Edmund BW1744;
  WT1756
Ives, Cornelius WT1820
  Cornelius (clerk) WT1820
  William CC1751;
    WR1751; AW1755;
    HD1754

Jackson, Edward DD FB1755
  Gilbert SW1719
James, John WW1752
  Rees (clerk) BB1770
Jarvis, Richard BB1770
Jeaffreson, Christopher (clerk)
  BB1832
Jefferys, Thomas (clerk)
  HD1734

Jenkins, John Clarke (clerk)
  BL1828; BL1840
  Nathaniel BL1840
Jenkinson, Edward (clerk)
  BA1790; BBC1802
  Sir Robert SW1719;
    WR1751
  Sir Robert Banks
    WR1730; CB1731;
    CC1751
  William SW1719
  William WR1730; CB1731
Jennens, William HD1754
Jenner, Rev Thomas DD
  CB1744; WT1756
Jennings, Henry HD1734
  James SW1719; HD1734
  James Richard DE1753;
    AW1755
  Moses HD1754
  Richard SW1719;
    AW1755; WT1756;
    BL1765
  William HD1734;
    WW1752
Jephcott, Thomas BL1765
Jerram, Charles (clerk)
  BC1834
Jervoise, George Purefoy
  BH1811; BH1832
Jeston, Rev Robert Green
  FB1822; FB1859
Jodrell, Paul SW1739
  Paul Jnr SW1739
Johnson, James (clerk)
  GFB1812
  Joseph (clerk) GFB1812
  Thomas GFB1812
Jones, Anselm (clerk)
  WT1820; WT1820a
  Arthur WR1804
  Charles Wake BW1744
  Sir Charles Wake DE1753;
    AW1755
  Henry Whitmore BB1832
  James HD1754
  John CB1731; WR1730
  John (clerk) BB1770
  John WR1804
  Richard FB1755
  Robert (clerk) WT1820
  Rev Samuel WR1751
  Rev of Cassington
    SW1739
  (no forename) DD
    BBC1802

Jones *continued*
  (no forename) (clerk)
    FB1755
Jopson, James FB1755
Jordan, John CC1751
  William CC1751
Joyce, Richard CB1744
Judd, William BH1811;
  DE1822
Justice, Francis HD1734
  Francis HS1824
  James HD1754
  John Thomas HS1824
  Richard HD1754
  Thomas HD1734
  Thomas of Sutton HD1754
  Thomas of Abingdon
    HD1754
Juxon, Sir William WR1730;
  CB1731

Keats, Richard (clerk)
  BB1770
Keck, Anthony SW1719;
  CB1731; SW1739;
  BW1744; WR1751;
  DE1753; DE1753a;
  HD1754; AW1755
  Francis SW1719
Kemble, Thomas CB1744
Kempster, Christopher
  BB1770
Kempthorne (clerk) CC1821
Kendrick, Ezekiel FB1755
Kening, Richard FB1755
Kenn, John CC1821
Kennicot, Rev Benjamin
  HD1754
Kenrick, Scawen DD
  HD1734
Kent, John BA1790
Kerie, Rev George WR1730
Kessing, Rev of Besselsleigh
  HD1754
Key, John FB1755
Kime, Augustus BH1832
Kinch, William Thomas
  SF1862a
King, Edward CC1751;
  FB1755
  Francis AW1755
  James BBC1802; BL1807;
    BH1811
  John SW1739; HD1754
  John BA1790; BA1812
  John BH1832; WW1841
  Isaac WW1841

King *continued*
   Rev, of Kingston HD1754
Kingdon, John WR1804;
   BB1832
Kingston, John WT1756
Kingston, Robert WT1756
Kirby, Burrows Matthias
   BH1832
   John WW1752
   John BA1790
   John WW1841
   John Jnr BA1812
   John Malsbury WT1820
   Richard Jnr BA1812
Kirkman, John FB1755
Kitson, Robert SW1739
Knapp, Henry WW1752
   Henry Jnr HS1824
Knibb, Rev George DD
   HD1754
Knight, Dormer WR1751
   Hon. Henry DE1753
   Henry AW1755
Knightley, Charles BL1765;
   BL1807
   D BL1778a
   Henry BL1807
   James BL1765
   John Snr FB1755
   John Jnr FB1755
   John (clerk) BL1765
   John FB1822
   Lucy BL1765
   Rainald BL1840
   Richard (clerk) BL1765
   Thomas FB1780/1a
   Valentine (clerk) BL1765
   Valentine BL1807
   Valentine (clerk) BL1840
Knipe, Revd John BA1825a
Knollis, Francis WR1730;
   SW1739
   Hon Francis (clerk)
   CC1821
Knollys, Rev of Blackborton
   SW1739
Knott, Rev James Monkhouse
   FB1859
Kyte, Sir William CB1731

La Roque, Peter (clerk)
   BL1765
Lacy, Rowland SW1719;
   WR1730; CB1731
Ladbroke, Sir Robert FB1755
Ladbrooke, Felix FB1822

Lamb, George (clerk)
   BA1790
   James AW1755; BB1770
   John (clerk) DD BA1790;
   BBC1802; BH1811;
   DE1822; BL1828
   Joseph BBC1802
   Matthew (clerk) BL1765;
   BL1772 1778a
   Richard Howson BL1828;
   BL1840
Lamball, John WW1752;
   HD1754
Lambern, Richard SW1719
Lambert, William FB1755;
   AW1755
Lamborne, Ovey SW1739
Lampet, Anthony BBC1802
   Daniel BB1770
   Lionel (clerk) BB1770
   Lionel BBC1802
Lampriere, Rev George, vicar
   of Buckland SF1738;
   HD1754
Lancaster, Thomas William
   (clerk) DE1822; FB1822;
   BB1832; FB1859
Lancelot, Langston WR1825
Lander, SW1739
Lane, Rev Charles SW1739
   Dr HD1734
Lang, William (clerk)
   BL1765
Langley, John (clerk)
   WW1841
   (no forename) (clerk)
   WW1752
Langston, James Haughton
   BB1832; WR1846
Langton, John WR1804
   William Gore WR1804
Large, Joseph CC1751
   Joseph CC1821
Lassar, James WW1752
Latimer, Edward G1821
Law, William BH1832
Lawley, Francis DE1822;
   FB1822
Lawrence, Broderick DD
   BW1744
   Isaac Newton CC1821
   John of Childrey WW1752
   Richard of Coleshill, clerk
   SF1788n
   Robert CC1751
   Walter Lawrence CC1821
   William CC1751

Lawrence *continued*
   William WW1752
Le Marchant, Rev James
   HD1754
Lea, David CC1751
   Rev James of Cromarsh
   HD1754
   Rev Thomas FB1822;
   FB1859
Leader, Rev Charles
   SW1739; WR1751
Leake, Charles CC1821;
   BC1834
   James BC1834
   Thomas CC1751
Lechmere, John WR1846
Ledwill, William SW1739
Lee, Charles (clerk) WR1825
   Hon Fitzroy Henry
   CB1731
   Hon. Fitzroy Lee WR1730
   Rev Sir George BH1811;
   BA1812
   George Henry, Viscount
   Quarendon SW1739
   Richard BW1744
   Hon. Robert CB1731;
   SW1739; CC1751;
   WR1751; HD1754;
   AW1755; WT1756;
   BB1770
   Thomas (clerk) AW1755
   Rev William Blackstone
   WR1846
   Rev of Wooton WR1730;
   WR1751
   Rev SW1739
   (no forename) (clerk)
   BL1765
   (no forename) BL1765
Legge, Hon. Heneage
   DE1822; FB1822
Leigh, Charles CB1731
   Egerton BB1832
   Egerton Jnr BB1832
   James CB1744; AW1755;
   BB1770
   James Henry FB1822
   Theophilus DD Master of
   Balliol WR1730;
   CB1731; WR1751
   Rev Thomas, Fellow of All
   Souls WR1730; CB1731
   Thomas HD1734
   Thomas (clerk) WR1751;
   BB1770

Leigh *continued*
Rev Thomas of Barding
HD1754
William CB1731
Rev Dr, Vice Chancellor of
Oxford SW1739
Lenten, Herritage SW1719;
SW1739
Lenten, John SW1719
Lenthal, John CC1821
Lenthall, John SW1719;
WR1730; WR1751;
CC1751; AW1755;
HD1754
John Jnr HD1754;
AW1755; BB1770
William WR1730;
WR1751; CC1751;
AW1755; HD1754;
BB1770
William Jnr BB1770
Lenton, Heritage HD1754
Leonard, Francis Mapletoft
(clerk) BB1832
Richard Weston (clerk)
WT1820a; BH1832;
BB1832
Leverett, James CC1751
Lewen, George HD1734
Lewes, Thomas (clerk)
CC1821; BB1832
Lewingdon, John HD1754
Lewis, David FB1755
Rev SW1739
Leyborne, Robert, DD
CC1751
Leyborne William BB1770
Leyson, Rev Morgan, rector
of Longworth SF1732
Lickorish, Rev Richard
FB1859
Liddiard, Charles WW1841
Lightboun, Thomas FB1755
Lindow, Henry Londow
BB1832
Litchfield, Francis (clerk)
BH1832
Littlepage, Robert SW1719
Lloyd, Griffiths (clerk)
BA1812
Henry William (clerk)
WW1841
Humphry (clerk) CB1731
Leonard BW1744
William DE1822
(no forename) (clerk)
BL1765

Lockey, Richard BB1770
Lockman, John (clerk)
BB1770
Loder, Charles CC1751;
BB1770; HD1754;
SF1787a; SF1803r
Loder, Charles GFB1812;
SF1824a; CC1821;
BC1834
John WW1752
Rev John HD1754
Rev Seymour, rector of
Hinton SF1732
Loe, Francis SW1739
John SW1739
William SW1739
Loggin, Edmund DE1753;
AW1755
Francis CB1731
John (clerk) BL1765
William CB1731
William BBC1802
William (clerk) BBC1802
London, Recorder of City of
WT1756
Long, Sir Robert WT1756
William AW1755;
FB1755; BL1765
William CC1821
Longe, William BB1770
Lord, John BA1812;
GFB1812
Lawrence SW1719;
SW1739
Loudell, George FB1822
Lousley, Job HS1824
Joseph HS1824
Love, Cater FB1755
Loveday, Arthur BL1840
John BL1783a
John Jnr BL1807; FB1822;
BL1828; BL1840;
FB1859
Thomas SW1739
Thomas (clerk) BL1840
William BW1744
Rev William FB1859
William Taylor BL1840
William Thomas (clerk)
WT1820
Lovegrove, Robert HD1754
Lovell, John WT1820
Lovenden, Edward of Buscott
SF1738
Edward Lovenden
SF1787a; WR1804
Capt John SF1732

Lovenden *continued*
Joseph BB1832
Lovett, William BL1765;
BL1765a
Lowe, Rev John AK1818
Lowke, John FB1755
Lowndes, Joseph BW1744
Richard BW1744;
DE1753; AW1755;
WT1756
William of Winslow
WT1756
William of Whaddon Hall
BH1811
William Selby BH1832
Lucas, John CC1751;
FB1755
William BL1765
Lucy, George DE1753
Ludford, John FB1755
Lush, James BH1811
John WW1752
Robert WW1752
Luxborough, Earl of DE1753
Lybb, Anthony SW1719
Richard SW1719
Lydall, John SW1739;
HD1754
Lyford, John HD1754
Lygon, Hon Edward CC1821
Lyndon, Richard FB1755
Lyon, Robert CC1751

Macey, William CC1821
Mackarness, John CB1731
Maddock, Robert CC1751
Maggot, John of Marcham
SF1738
Malins, George Wallington
WT1820
Malkin, Samuel FB1755
Mallaber, George BL1828;
BL1840
Mallam, Richard SF1824a
Man, Francis SW1719;
WR1730
Mander, Daniel FB1755
John FB1755
Thomas CB1731
Manners, John, Marquis of
Granby BL1765
Mansell, Henry CB1731
Henry Longueville (clerk)
WT1820
Thomas (clerk) CB1731
Thomas WR1730

Mantell, George of Faringdon,
  surgeon SF1819/24/40a;
  WW1841
Mapletoft, Francis (clerk)
  BL1765
  Nicholas (clerk) BL1765
  (no forename) (clerk)
  BA1790
Marfell, Thomas BL1828;
  BL1840
Marnott, George, barrister
  BL1828
  Robert (clerk) BL1828
Marriett, Marriot, Marriott,
  Francis BB1770
  John BB1770
  Hugh BL1765
  ?, Humphrey BB1770
  Richard CB1731
  Robert BL1765
  Robert (clerk) BL1840
  Thomas BB1770
  see also Merriot
Marsh, William (Dr of
  Physick) FB1802
Marshall, Christopher
  BB1770
  Edward (clerk) BBC1802;
  WR1804; WT1820;
  WR1825
  John WW1841
  Nicholas WR1751;
  BB1770
  Nicholas (clerk) WR1804
Marsham, Charles (clerk)
  BA1812
  Hon Rev Jacob BA1790
Marten, John, Dr of Physic
  SW1739
Martin, James (clerk)
  BB1770
  John WR1730
  Richard CC1751
  Robert BB1770
  Thomas WR1730;
  CC1751; WR1751
  Sir Thomas Byam (bart)
  WW1841
  William BL1765
  Rev SW1739
  ? (no forename) (clerk)
  BB1770
Martyn, Francis CB1731
  George CB1731
  James (clerk) CB1744
  John CB1731
  Thomas CB1731

Mashborne, Robert BW1744
Masket ??, BB1770
Mason, Francis SW1719;
  HD1734
  John, Recorder of
  Buckingham BW1744
  John HD1734; SW1719;
  SW1739
Massey, John (clerk)
  BBC1802
Master of Company of
  Blanketters, Witney
  CC1751
Masters, Streynsham
  SW1719; WR1751
Mather, Challis FB1755
  Rev Dr SW1739
Matthews, Mathews, Daniel
  SF1824a
  Peter HS1824
  William WW1752;
  HD1754
Matthes, William AW1755
Mattingley, Thomas, of
  Faringdon, common brewer
  SF1791n; SF1824r
Mavor, William (clerk) DL
  WR1804; CC1821;
  WR1825
  William LLD BC1834
Maxey, John WW1752
Mayd, William (clerk)
  CB1744
Maynard, Rev Robert
  ·FB1859
Mayne, Robert WW1752
  William WW1802a
Mayor of (etc) *see under*
  Abingdon, Banbury,
  Brackley, Coventry,
  Henley, Oxford,
  Wallingford,
  Woodstock (New)
Mayow, Joseph GFB1812
Mayward, Sir Thomas
  SF1806r
Meadowcourt, Rev SW1739
Meads, Jehoiada BBC1802
  Richard CC1751
Meddoms, John DE1753;
  FB1755; AW1755
Medley, Charles WW1841
Medleycott, Edmund
  HD1734
Meller, (clerk) BB1770
Merriot, John CC1751
  see also Marriot

Merthwaite, George (clerk)
  BA1790
Metcalfe, Edward DE1753;
  FB1755; AW1755;
  BL1765
  Henry WR1804
  (no forename) BW1744
Methuen, Sir Paul BW1744
Michener, Jonathan
  FB1755/6a
Micklem, Edward G1821
Middleton, Henry FB1755
  Thomas (clerk) BB1770
Mill, Richard SW1739
Miller, Charles of Frittwell
  AW1755
  Edward (clerk) DE1822
  Fiennes Sanderson
  BH1811; DE1822;
  BH1832
  James BL1765
  John DE1753a; AW1755;
  FB1755
  John HD1754
  Robert BA1812
  Sanderson BW1744;
  DE1753a; DE1753;
  HD1754; AW1755;
  BL1765; BB1770
Mills, Edward CC1751
  John (clerk) DE1753
  Samuel BL1773n
  William (clerk) BC1834;
  GFB1812; SF1826/40a
  William Yarnton of Wadley
  GFB1812; SF1803n;
  SF1824r
  William Yarnton (clerk)
  BC1834
Millward, John BW1744;
  WT1756
Minchin, William BB1770
Minckin, Thomas CC1821
Mister, Samuel Wright (clerk)
  WR1825
  William BBC1802
Mitchel, Rev SW1719
Mitchenor, John (clerk)
  FB1755
Montague, George WT1756;
  BB1770
  Hon George WT1756
Montgomery, Francis
  BL1765; BL1765a
Moor, Sir John WW1752

Moore, James BA1790
 Rev John of Abingdon
  HD1754
 William BW1744;
  HD1754
Mordaunt, Sir Charles
  DE1753; FB1755;
  AW1755
 John HD1734
Mordaunt, Sir John BBC1802
Moreton, John SW1719
 John Jnr SW1739;
  WR1751; FB1755;
  AW1755
 Sir William WT1756
Morewood, Charles Rowland
  Palmer FB1859
 Charles Turville SF1824r
 William Frederick Palmer
  FB1859
 George BH1811; WT1820
  BH1832
 Gregory WT1820a
 James WW1752
 John of Brightwell (clerk)
  HD1734; WW1752
 John of Wallingford (clerk)
  WW1752
 Rev John HD1754
Morice, William (clerk)
  WR1825
Morland, Benjamin HS1824
 Benjamin Jnr HS1824
 Francis Bernard BA1812
 Thomas Thornhill HS1824
 William HS1824
 William Jnr HS1824
 William Bernard BA1812
Morrell, Baker WW1841
 Charles Snr WW1841;
  WW1802a
 Charles Jnr WW1841
 James G1821; WW1841
 Jeremiah WW1752;
  HD1754
 Mark G1821; WW1841
 Robert WW1841
Morrice, James (clerk)
  BL1807
Morris, Harry BL1765
 William CC1821
Morton, John WR1730;
  CC1751; HD1754
 ?? (no forename) BB1770
Mostyn, Charles WR1804
 Charles Browne WR1804;
  WR1825

Mostyn *continued*
 George WR1825
 Sir Thomas WT1820
Moulden, Joseph Snr
  WW1752
 Joseph Jnr WW1752;
  HD1754
 Joseph WW1841
Moye, Edward (clerk)
  FB1755
Munday, Thomas AW1755;
  HD1754
Murcott, Henry FB1755
 William FB1755
Myers, Thomas GFB1812;
  BC1834

Nailer Dr, Dean of Winton
  CB1731
Naish, John of Abingdon
  HD1754
Nappier, Thomas SW1719
Nares, George HD1754
Nash, Edward SF1824r
 Francis HD1734
 Francis (clerk) HD1734
 Rev Russel HD1754
 Treadway (clerk) HD1754;
  AW1755
 Rev of Chalgrove DD
  HD1754
Neal , Zachary HD1734
Neale, John FB1755
 Thomas Snr FB1755
 Thomas Jnr FB1755
 William FB1755
Neate, Arthur (clerk) BC1834
 Thomas (clerk) GFB1812;
  BC1834
Needham, Robert WW1752;
  HD1754; CC1751;
  AW1755
Nelson, George BH1811;
  BA1812; WT1820a;
  BH1832
New Woodstock *see*
  Woodstock
Newcomb, Henry (clerk)
  HD1734
 Thomas BL1765
Newcome, Joseph HD1734
Newdigate, Sir Roger (bart)
  HD1754; AW1755;
  FB1755
Newe, Alexander HD1754
 Nathaniel SW1739

Newell, John SW1719;
  SW1739
Newell, Thomas HD1734
 Thomas Blackman (clerk)
  CC1821
 William SW1719
 Rev William SW1739
Newman, George BH1811
 Henry SF1824r
 John Snr DE1753a;
  AW1755; FB1755
 John Jnr BH1811;
  FB1755; BL1765
 John BH1811; BA1812
 John Dorset AW1755;
  BL1765
 William SF1824a
Newmarch, Charles CC1821
Newsam, Clement (clerk)
  FB1822
Newsham, James DE1753;
  AW1755
Newton, Rev James SW1739;
  HD1754
 Richard WW1841
 Robert Aldworth WW1841
 Thomas Snr WW1841
 Thomas Jnr WW1841
Niblet, Rev Drq SW1739
Niblett, Rev Stephen DD
  WW1752
Nichol, John DD BA1790
Nicholls, Richard (clerk)
  BB1770; BL1783a
Nichols, John AW1755
Nicholson, Jeremiah (clerk)
  CC1751
Nicoll, John BL1807;
  BH1811
 Rev Richard BH1811
Nobbs, John CC1751
Noble, William (clerk)
  WW1752
Noel, Rev Augustus
  Wriothesly FB1859
 John (clerk) BB1770
Norman, Samuel HD1754
 William HD1734
 (no forename) of Henley
  SW1739
Norris, James SW1719
North, Hon. Rev Brownlow
  BL1765; BB1770
 Dudley BBC1802;
  BH1811
 Hon Francis BBC1802

North *continued*
Rt Hon Lord Frederick
DE1753; AW1755;
FB1755; WT1756;
BL1765; BB1770
Hon Frederick BBC1802;
BH1811
George Augustus, Lord
BA1790
Henry John WR1804;
WR1825
Norton, Cornelius HD1734
John BW1744
Norwood, William CC1751
Nott, Theatiplace FB1755
Nourse, Charles HD1754
Francis SW1719; WR1730
John SW1739; WR1751;
AW1755; WT1756;
HD1754
Nucella, Rev Thomas
WR1846
Nugent, Edward BA1812
Nutt, Joseph SF1824r

O'Brian, Sir Edward WR1730
Offley, Rev SW1719
Oldham, Thomas Snr
FB1755
Thomas Jnr FB1755
Thomas William FB1859
Onely, John Snr BL1765
John Jnr BL1765
John (clerk) BL1765
Oram, Josiah FB1755
Ormond, William WW1841
Osbaldeston, Sir William
SW1719; WR1730;
CB1731
Osgood, Lawrence Head
WW1752; HD1754
Osmond, George BA1790
Overbury, Thomas WR1730;
CB1731
Overton, John AW1755;
FB1755
William AW1755; FB1755
Ovey, Thomas HD1754
Owen, Thomas WW1841
Oxford, City of, Mayor,
Recorder & Aldermen,
AW1755 ; HD1734;
Mayor of HD1754
Oxford, University of, Heads
of Colleges & Halls of
HD1734; AW1755;

Oxford University *continued*
Vice Chancellor of
HD1734; AW1755
Queen's College, Provost
of *see* Smith
Oxenden, Sir George
HD1734; WW1752;
HD1754; CC1751
George CC1751
Henry CC1751; WW1752;
HD1754

P.., Samuel BB1770
Packer, Henry SF1732
Robert SF1732
Winchcombe Howard
SF1732
Packwood, Gery FB1755
Page, Francis WR1751;
AW1755; FB1755;
BA1790; BBC1802
Francis Bourne DE1753
Paget, John BB1770
???., Francis BB1770
Pagett, Thomas Bradley
WR1804
Pain, John AW1755; FB1755
John BH1811; DE1822;
BH1832; BL1828
Joseph BH1811; DE1822;
BH1832
Palmer, Benjamin FB1755
Benjamin Wyment Snr
BL1828; BL1840
Benjamin Wyment Jnr
BL1840
Charles FB1755
Charles (clerk) FB1802a;
FB1822; FB1859
Peregrine HD1754;
AW1755; WT1756
V. FB1755/6a
William FB1755
William FB1822
William Jocelyn (clerk)
WT1820; WT1820a;
BA1825a; BH1832
Pardoe, Rev Thomas DD
HD1754
Pares, Thomas BL1807
Parker, Charles FB1755
Hon George Lane HD1754
Sir Henry John CB1731
James (clerk) BB1770
John (clerk) BL1765
Richard CC1821
Hon Thomas SW1719

Parker *continued*
Thomas, Lord HD1754;
AW1755; WT1756
Hon Thomas CC1821;
BC1834
Lord Thomas Augustus
Wolstenholm WR1846
Parkhurst, Capt. Fleetwood
BL1765
John BL1765
Parnell, Thomas HD1734
Parrat, Edward of Northleigh
SW1719
Parrott, Parrot, Francis
FB1822
George BH1811; BH1832
Henry SW1719
Richard FB1755
Thomas SW1719
Thomas DL CB1731
Parry, Francis HD1754
William (clerk) CB1731
Parsons, Rev Anthony
HD1754
George Lodowick (clerk)
WW1841
Herbert G1821
James (clerk) BB1770
Robert (clerk) CB1731
Thomas of Sandford
SW1739
Passand, Rev Henry John
WR1846
Patey, Thomas HD1734
Patrick, Samuel CC1751
William CC1751; BB1770
Patten, John CC1751
Pattin, John BB1770
Ro... BB1770
Pawlett, Hon. Armand
Charles WR1751
Paxford, John BB1770
Payne, Francis (clerk)
AW1755
John CB1731; WT1756
(no forenam) (clerk)
BB1770
Paynton, Thomas AW1755
Pearce, Rev Joseph Francis of
Hatford, SF1819a;
SF1824r
(no forename) (clerk)
FB1822
Pearse, William (clerk)
DE1822; BH1832
Pearson, George FB1755
Thomas (clerk) HS1824

Peck, William SF1824r
Peers, Charles HD1754:
    AW1755
    Rev Richard vicar of
    Faringdon SF1732
    Rev of Stanford HD1754
Pegge, Sir Christopher Dr of
    Physick WR1804
Pennington, John (clerk)
    BB1770
Penniston, Rev John Kerry
    SW1719
Penstone, Joseph SF1824a
Penyston, Fairmedow
        CB1731; WR1751;
        BB1770
    Francis WR1804; WR1825
    Francis Jnr WR1825
    Rev John WR1730
Perbrick ??, James BB1770
Perkins, James BW1744
    John BW1744
    Thomas BL1765
    William Banbury FB1859
Pern, Robert WT1756
Perratt, Richard of Faringdon,
    currier SF1791n;
    SF1824/40a
Perret, Edward John
    WR1751
Perrot, Thomas CB1731
Perrott, Henry WR1730;
    SF1732
    John CC1751
    Richard BC1834
    Thomas DL WR1730
    Thomas LLD of Fyfield
        SF1732
    Thomas BB1832
Perry, Weeden SW1719
    William HD1734
Peters, Rev John William
    SF1824a
Pettatt, Thomas (clerk)
    CC1821
Pettipher, Michael BBC1802
Peyton, Sir Henry WT1820;
    BH1832
    Henry WR1846
Phelps, John Snr SW1719
Philips, John WW1752;
    HD1754
    Mathew WW1752
    Thomas WW1752
    ..? (no forename) (clerk)
        BB1770

Phillimore, Robert (clerk)
    CC1821; BB1832; BC1834
Phillips, John HS1824
    William Jnr BA1812
    (no forename) HD1734
Philpot, William (clerk)
    BL1828
    William Doveton BL1828
Phipps, George SW1719
Pickering, John FB1755
    Leonard BC1834
    Richard (clerk) CC1821
Pierrepoint, Hon. Philip
    Sydney WT1820;
    WT1820a; BH1832
Piggott, James Noel (clerk)
    BA1812
    John WW1752; HD1754
Pigott, William BA1812
Pilkington, Rev Charles
    FB1859
Pinfold, Giles Jnr CC1751
Pinnell John (clerk) CC1751;
    HD1754; AW1755
    John CC1821; BC1834
    Richard SF1824a
    Thomas BC1834
Pitt, Benjamin HD1734;
    SW1739
    Cornelius (clerk) CC1821
    Edward, (Dr of Physick)
        CC1751
    Henry HD1734
    ?, James (clerk) BB1770
    see also Pytt
Pittman, Charles HS1824;
    WW1841
Pixell, Thomas (clerk)
    BB1770
Planpin, Thomas BL1765
Plantwright, W WT1820a
Platt, Head WW1752;
    HD1754
Pleydell Champneys
        SW1739; HD1754
    Sir Mark Stuart (bart)
        SF1732; WW1752;
        HD1754
    see also under Bouverie,
    Folkestone
Pocock, Henry HD1734
    John Blagrove HS1824
    William HD1734
Pole, Charles BB1832;
    BC1834
    Charles Jnr BC1834
    Charles Richard BB1832

Watson Buller (clerk)
    BB1832
Pollard, John BW1744;
    WR1751; WT1756
    John Carter BB1770
Poole, John CC1821
    Robert FB1822; FB1859
Popham, Alexander
    WW1752
    Edward CB1731;
    WW1752; HD1754
Potenger, Richard HD1734
Potter, Fitzherbert (clerk)
    BB1770
    Rev John SW1739
    Thomas BB1770; BA1790
    William BA1790
Pottinger, John SW1739
    Head (clerk) HS1824
Pottle, John CC1751
Potts, Charles BL1765
Poulett, John BH1811;
    BH1832
    see also Powlett
Poulter, EH SF1840a
Powell, Thomas Snr
    SW1739; HD1754
    Thomas Jnr HD1754
Powlett, Hon Lord Harry
    SW1719
    see also Poulett
Powney, Penyston HD1734;
    WW1752; CC1751
Powys, Philip HD1734;
    SW1739
Praed, Humphrey Mackworth
    CC1751
Pratt, William BA1790
Preedy, Benjamin BBC1802
    James (clerk) WT1820
    John BBC1802
    William BBC1802
Preest, William Shuttleworth
    FB1755
Prentice, John BH1811
Presbury, William FB1755
Prewett, William BB1770
Price, Barrington of Beckett,
    SF1794n
Price, Bartholomew WW1752
Price, Benjamin BH1811;
    WT1820; BH1832
    Campbell BW1744
    Charles Snr HD1734
    Charles Jnr HD1734
    David (clerk) CC1751;
    WR1751

Price *continued*
  Howell (clerk) CC1751;
    HD1754
  James Scarlet BC1834
  John SW1719
  John of the Ham WW1752
  Ralph (clerk) WW1752
  Thomas (clerk) BW1744;
    WT1756
  William BW1744
  William (clerk) CC1821
  William (clerk) HS1824
  see also Pryse
Prince, Jasper SF1824a;
  BC1834
  Rev John, Vicar of
    Uffington SF1738
  Thomas HD1754
  William SW1739; HD1734
Princep, Rev of Bicester
  WT1756
Prinn, William CC1751
Prinsop, John (clerk)
  AW1755
Prior, John CC1751;
  BB1770; WR1804
  Thomas WR1804;
    WR1825
  see also Pryor
Pritchard, John HD1734
Prowse, James WW1841
  Richard HD1754
  Thomas WT1756
Pryor, Thomas WT1756
  see also Prior
Pryse, Lewis SW1739;
  WR1751
  Pryse WR1804; WR1825;
    BC1834; WR1846
  Walter SW1739
  see also Price
Pujolas, James CC1751
Pumfrey, Robert WW1841
Purdo, Rev Dr SW1739
Pusey, John Allen WW1752
  Hon. Philip of Pusey
    SF1788n; GFB1812
Pye, Benjamin (clerk)
  WW1752; HD1754
  Benjamin Dr at Law
    SF1791r
  Charles SF1787a
  Henry Snr SF1732;
    CC1751
  Henry Jnr SF1732;
    WW1752; HD1754
  Henry James SF1787a

Pye *continued*
  Robert DL SF1788rd
  Thomas of Faringdon
    SF1738
  Sir William SF1788d
  (no forename) MD
    CB1731
Pytt, James (clerk) CC1751
  Robert Henry CC1821;
    BC1834
  see also Pitt
Pytts, Jonathan BB1770

Quarendon, Viscount *see* Lee
Quinney, William FB1755

Radcliffe, Rev Dr SW1739
Rain, John HD1734
Raine, Richard BC1834
Ramsey, James Francis
  BH1832
Rash, Sir John HD1754
Rathbone, John DD
  GFB1812
Rattray, Charles Dr of
  Physick BL1828
Rattray, David MD BL1765
Rawlins, Rev Michael
  HD1754
Rawlinson, Abram Lindow
  BB1832
  Abram Tysac BB1832
  Thomas HD1754
  William SW1719
Raymond, Sir Jammet,
  WW1752
  Richard WT1756
  (no forename) WW1752
Read, Thomas of Ipsden
  SW1739
Read, Colonel George
  SW1719; CB1731;
    HD1754; AW1755
  George WR1730; CC1751;
    WR1751
  John CC1751
  Sir John (bart) HD1754;
    AW1755; WT1756
  John of Ipsden HD1754
  Sir Thomas SW1719;
    WR1730; CB1731;
    CC1751; WR1751
Reade, Hon. John BB1770
  Sir John CC1821; BC1834
  Sir John Chandos BB1832
Reading, Edward FB1822
  Thomas BA1790

Ready, Alexander SW1739;
  CC1751
  Chaunter BB1770
  Robert (clerk) BB1770
  Robert SF1787a
Recorder (etc.) *see* London,
  Woodstoock (New)
Redhall, Ambrose BB1770
Remington, John (clerk)
  FB1755
Reynell, Carew (clerk)
  SW1739; WW1752
  WT1756
Reynolds, Bryan of
  Faringdon, mercer
    SF1791n; SF1819d
  Charles GFB1812;
    SF1824a
  James SF1738
  James GFB1812; SF1824a
  Richard GFB1812
  Thomas Reynolds
    SF1824a
Ricardo, Mortimer WR1846
Rice, Hon. Edward DD
  CC1821; BB1832
  Edward Gilbert CC1751
  Hon. George CC1821
  Lionel of Faringdon
    SF1732
  Rev. Richard SF1862a
  Richard Jnr GFB1812
  Sir Robert SW1719
Rich, Daniel of Goosey
  WW1752; HD1754
Richards, George (clerk)
  GFB1812
  George DD CC1821;
    BC1834
Richardson, Thomas
  BBC1802
Richmond, Symour WW1752
  Toby WW1752
Rider, Hon. Rev. Henry
  BL1807
Riggins, Thomas HD1754
Riley, Jas BL1765
Risley, John Snr (clerk)
  BH1811; BA1812
  John Jnr (clerk) BH1811;
    BH1832
  Risley BW1744
  William Cotton (clerk)
    BH1832; BB1832
Roberts, Edward HD1734
  Henry FB1802
  John (clerk) WR1804

Robertson, David WW1841
Robins, Francis CB1744
    John WW1752; HD1754
    Robert of Aston CB1744
Robinson, Rev. Francis
    WR1846
    George North AK1818;
        BB1832
    John BL1765
    Robert SW1739
    Thomas WR1825; BC1834
Roche, Michael BBC1802
Rock, Samuel HD1754
Rockall, Christopher HD1734
Rocke, Richard (clerk)
    BL1828
Rodd, Rev. John CB1744;
    WT1756
Rogers, Richard CC1751
    William (clerk) CB1731
    William CC1751
Role, Richard BB1770
Roles, Henry WT1756
Rolles, Thomas SW1719
Rollinson, Lock BB1770
    Thomas CB1731;
        WR1751; BB1770
    William CB1731; WR1751
Rolls, Henry BA1790
    Thomas BA1790
    William BA1790
Rooke, Archdale SW1739;
    AW1755
    Thomas CB1731
    Thomas Archdale BB1770
Rosbarts, Nathaniel HD1754
Rose, Charles (clerk)
    BL1840; BL1828
    George BL1840
    Henry (clerk) BL1828;
        BL1840
    John CC1751
    John (clerk) BL1840;
        BL1828
    Richard HD1754
    William BL1765a
    William Rose BL1840
Rosse, Rev. SW1739
Rothwell, Richard (clerk)
    FB1755
Rowney, Edward (clerk)
    CB1731
    Thomas SW1719;
        WR1730; CB1731;
        HD1734; CC1751;
        WR1751; AW1755;
        WT1756

Rowney continued
    Thomas Jnr SW1719
Rudge, Rev Benjamin
    HD1754
    Edward SW1739; HD1754
    Edward WW1841
Rush, George WT1820
    Sir John WW1752
Rushout, Sir John CB1731
Rushworth, John BL1765
Russell, John (clerk)
    CC1751; AW1755
    Rev John of Souldern
        WT1756
    John FB1822
    John (clerk) BH1832
    Joseph FB1822
    Robert Greenhill WT1820
    William SW1739
    William FB1822
    (no forename) (clerk)
        BB1770
Rutter, Daniel CC1821;
    BC1834
Ruxton, John (clerk) CC1821
Rye, Dr. DD SW1719;
    WR1730
Rymill, John BL1765
    Robert BL1765; BL 1771a
Ryves, Edward SW1739;
    WR1751; FB1755;
    AW1755; HD1754

Sabin, Charles Heath
    WT1820
    John FB1859
Sadler, Joseph Snr SW1739;
    HD1754
    Joseph Jnr HD1754
Sale, John BL1765
Salmon, George FB1755
    John DE1822; FB1822
Samman, David BBC1802
Samwell, John (clerk)
    BB1770
    Sir Thomas WT1756
    Thomas WT1756
Sanders, Thomas WW1752
    Thomas BL1828; BL1840
    Thomas (clerk) BL1828
Sandford, William, DD
    CC1751
    William BB1770
Sandys, J FB1802
    Samuel CB1731
Sansbury, Nathanial
    DE1753a

Sansbury continued
    Samuel BW1744; DE1753;
        AW1755; FB1755
Sappin, Richard WW1752
Sarncy, Peter HD1754
Sarney, Daniel HD1734
Satchwell BL1765
Saunders, John of Woolston
    SF1732
    Samuel BC1834
    Thomas BA1790
Savage, John CB1731
Sawyer, Anthony of Clifton
    SW1739; HD1734
Saxton, Edward HD1754
Sayer, James BB1770
    Jonathan HD1734
Scheler, Rev SW1719
Schutz, Augustus HD1754
    George HD1754; AW1755
Scoggs, William WW1752
Scot, Rev. SW1719
Scott, James clerk SF1788r
    Thomas (clerk) BH1832
Scriven, John Sgt at Law
    BL1828
Scrope, John SW1719
Scudamore, Charles SF1824a
Scull, John BB1770
Scundritt, William AW1755
Seagrave, Samuel (clerk)
    DE1753a
    Samuel AW1755
    Rev Samuel Young
        WR1846
    (no forename) (clerk)
        DE1822
Secker, George FB1755
    John CC1821
Sedgley, John HD1754
Seeley, George BH1811
Sellman, Joseph Snr CC1751
Sellwood, Richard WW1752;
    HD1754
    Robert HD1754
Selwood, Robert (clerk)
    HD1734
Senhouse, William BL1840
Severne, John Michael
    BL1828; BL1840
    Samuel Amy BL1828;
        BH1832; BL1840
    (no forename) BB1832
Sexton, Edward WW1752
    John WW1752
Seymour, Edward WW1752
    John WW1752

Shakespear, William FB1755
Sharp, ? BB1770
Sharrant ? BL1765
Shaw, Edward, (clerk)
    HS1824
    John BL1765
    Robert of Lutterworth
        BL1773n
Shayler, James BC1834
Sheldon, Edward WR1730;
    CB1731
    Edward BBC1802
    Ralph BBC1802
    William CB1731; WR1751
    William BBC1802
Shenton, Peter WW1752
Shepherd, Sir Thomas Cotton
    BH1832
Sheppard, John CC1751
    Sir Thomas BH1811
    Thomas Cotton BH1811
    William SW1719;
        WR1730; CB1731
Sherrard (clerk) FB1755
Sherrock, Joseph WT1756
Sherwood, Charles HD1754
Shewell, John of Didcot
    WW1752
Shilfox, Daniel AW1755
Shippen, Rev. Dr SW1739
Shipton, John FB1755
Shirley, Hon. George
    DE1753; AW1755
    Hon. Sewallis BW1744
Shorter, John BBC1802
Shortland, John Vincent
    G1821
Shuckborough, Charles
    CB1731
Shuckburgh, Sir Charles
    BL1765; BL1773d
    Sir Francis FB1822;
        FB1859
    John FB1822
    Richard FB1755
    Sir Stukeley FB1755
Shuffrey, Samuel BC1834;
    CC1821
Shute, Christopher (clerk)
    CB1731
Shuttleworth, James BL1765
Sibley (clerk) BB1832
Sills, Joseph HD1734
    Samuel HD1734
Silver BB1832
Silvester, John gent; SF1787a
    SF1791r

Simcock, John BA1790
Simeon, Sir Edward HD1734
Simes, Richard HD1754
Simmes, Elias HD1734
Simon, William CC1751
Simonds, John Blackall
    HS1824
Simons, Thomas BB1770
Skeeler, Rev. Thomas
    WR1730; CB1731;
    WR1751
Skelton, Henry CC1821
Skillicorn M (clerk) BB1832
    (no forename) BB1832
Skinner, Matthew Sergeant at
    Law HD1734
    Thomas CC1821
Skipwith, Sir Francis
    FB1755; BL1765
    Francis BL1765
    Thomas BL1765
Slade, John HS1824
    Richard (clerk) CC1751
    Thomas (clerk) BB1770
Slater, Thomas BH1832
Slatter, Thomas (clerk)
    WR1825
Slaughter, Charles CB1731
Smallbone, Francis HD1754
Smart, William CC1751
Smith, Benjamin gent
    SF1791a
    Daniel HD1734
    George Gainsford (clerk)
        WT1820
    Henry HD1734
    Henry SW1739
    Henry (clerk) BL1828
    Henry Lilley FB1822
    Holled BL1765
    John FB1755; BL1765;
        BB1770
    John MD AW1755;
        BL1765
    John Thomas Henry (clerk)
        BL1840
    Joseph WT1756
    Lilley FB1755
    Richard SW1739 Smith,
    Richard BA1790
    Samuel FB1755
    Samuel (clerk) BL1807;
        BL1828
    Samuel DD BL1828
    Sir Sebastian SW1719
    Sebastian SW1739
    Stephen FB1755

Smith *continued*
    Thomas of Cassington
        SW1739
    Thomas HD1754
    Thomas of Ascot HD1754
    Thomas FB1755; BL1765
    Thomas (clerk) BL1807;
        BL1828; BL1840
    Thomas Lander FB1755
    Ward CC1751
    Rev. William WR1751;
        HD1754
    William Henry Ashton
        CC1821; BC1834
    Rev of Cotsford WT1756
    (no forename) Provost of
        Queen's College
        AW1755
Smyth, John CB1744
    John LD AW1755
    Dr John DE1753; BL1765
Smythe, Joseph BL1765;
    BB1770
Snell, Powell CB1744;
    BB1770; CC1751
    Thomas (clerk) CC1751
Snelling, John of Faringdon,
    cheesefactor SF1788n
Snow, Birn George FB1780/1
    &1802a
    Joseph BBC1802
    Thomas BBC1802
    William FB1802
Snowshill, Isaac BB1770
Somerscale, Rev. Joseph
    CB1744
    William CB1731; BB1770
Somerville, Ralph FB1755
Sotham, Thomas WR1804
    William WR1804;
        WR1825
Sothern, James WT1820
Southam, Edmund BH1832
    George BW1744
    John BW1744; BH1811
    Richard AW1755; FB1755
Southby, Edward SF1732;
    HD1754; WW1752;
    SF1794d
    Henry of Coxwell, esq.
        SF1794n
    Nathaniel SF1738
    Richard SF1732; HD1754
    Robert HD1734; HD1754
    Robert BB1770
    Robert HS1824

Southby *continued*
   Thomas Hayward
      SF1824a; SF1840a
Southcote, Philip WW1752;
   HD1754
Southwell, Edward BB1770
Sparrow, Robert BL1765
   Samuel BL1765; BL1772a
Speidell, John (clerk CC1821
Speke, Rev SW1739
Spence, John (clerk) BL1840
Spencer, Hon. Augustus
   Almeric WR1825
   Lord Charles BB1770;
      WR1804
   Charles (Viscount
      Althorpe) FB1822
   Lord Francis Almeric
      BBC1802; WR1804
   Hon. Francis WR1825
   Hon Francis George
      BB1832
   George (Marquis of
      Blandford) WR1804;
      G1821; WR1825
   Hon. George WR1825
   Hon. John WR1730;
      CB1731; HD1754;
      FB1755; AW1755
   John WT1756
   John (clerk) BL1765
   John WR1804
   Hon John Charles
      (Viscount Althorpe)
      WT1820
   Joseph BBC1802
   Lord Robert BB1770
   (no forename) Rev
      WT1756
Spenlove, John Francis
   HS1824
   John Francis Jnr HS1824
Spense, John (clerk) BL1828
Spicer, James BBC1802
Spindler, John HD1734
   Samuel SW1739; HD1734
   Thomas SW1739; HD1734
   Rev, vicar of Eaton
      Hastings SF1738
Spires, John DD BL1765
Spokes, John WW1841
Spraggett, Richard FB1859
Spry, John (clerk) WW1752
   Rev of Hendred HD1754
Spurrett, Bernard AW1755;
      BL1765
   William BB1832; BH1832

Stafford, Edward (clerk)
   BL1807; BL1828; BL1840
Staley, Thomas FB1859
Stamp, Berenberg WW1752;
   HD1754
Stanhope, Sir William
   WT1756
Stanley, William WW1752
   ?, Henry BB1770
Stanyan, Temple HD1734
Stapleton, Sir Thomas
   WW1752; HD1754
   Sir William WR1730;
      CB1731; HD1734
   Rev HD1754
Staverton, Thomas HD1734;
   SW1739
Stead, Benjamin of Wadley
   SF1788n; SF1806r
Stearne, Richard FB1755
Stephens, Charles Loder
   CC1821
   Henry BB1770
   John BB1770
   William CC1751; BB1770
   William HS1824
Stevens, Henry HD1734
   Henry Stuart HD1734
   John (clerk) HD1734
   John of Long Wittenham
      HD1754
   John BA1790
   Robert (clerk) BB1770
      SF1788d
   Thomas HD1754
   William , surgeon HD1754
   ? (no forename) BB1770
Stevenson, John of Faringdon,
      maltster SF1791n
   Joseph DE1753
Stewart, Daniel FB1822
Stilgo, Nathaniel FB1859
Stirling, William WW1752;
   HD1754
Stockwood, Rev William
   SW1739; HD1754
Stokes, Peter SW1739
   Thomas BW1744
Stone, Edward (clerk)
   DE1753; BB1770
   Edward AW1755
   James HD1754
   John SW1719
   Richard HD1754
   Thomas HD1754
   William WW1752;
      HS1824; WW1802a

Stone *continued*
   William Jnr HS1824
   William of Charlton
      WW1841
Stonehouse, Sir John (bart)
   SF1732; HD1734;
      CC1751; WW1752
   Richard WW1752;
      HD1754
   William WR1751
Stonhouse, Rev James
   HD1754
Stonor, Thomas HD1734
Stopes, Rev James HD1754
   (no forename) (clerk)
      BL1765
Stowe, George BB1770
Stratford, Francis FB1755
   John CC1751
Stratton, George WR1804
   George Frederick
      BBC1802; WR1804
   John BBC1802; BA1812
Street, Charles CC1821
   Rev. SW1739
Strickland, Edward Rowland
   BC1834
   Walter CC1821; BC1834
   Walter Jnr CC1821;
      BC1834; WR1846
Strivens, Henry Stuart
   SW1719
Stroud, Joseph WW1752
Stuart, Daniel BB1832;
   DE1822
   Hon. Rev. Henry Windsor
      Villiers FB1859
Sturgess, Rev. Nathaniel
   WR1730; WR1751;
      CB1731
Style, Francis HD1734
Sudlow, John WT1820
Summerfield, William
   BB1770
Sutton, John WR1730;
      CB1731; SW1739
   Rev SW1739
Swainson, Charles Litchfield
   (clerk) BL1840
   James (clerk) BL1840
Swinborne, William HD1754
Sylvester, Paul BB1770
   Thomas BB1770
Symonds, John Loder
   BC1834; SF1824/40a
   Robert (clerk) BC1834;
      GFB1812; SF1826a

Symonds *continued*
    Thomas (clerk) BC1834;
      CC1821

Tait, Rev. Thomas Henry
    FB1859
    Talbot, George BB1832
    John Chetwynd BB1770
    William DE1753a
    William (clerk) DE1753;
      AW1755
Tanner, Joseph HS1824
Tape, Robert WT1756
Tate, Robert BL1765
Tatham, Edward DD
    WR1804
Tattom, Robert (clerk)
    BL1765
Tatton, Richard BL1765
Taunton, Daniel G1821
    Thomas Henry G1821
    William Elias CC1821;
      G1821
    Sir William Elias G1821;
      BC1834
Tawney, Charles DE1822;
    FB1822
    Henry BB1832
    Richard DE1822; FB1822
Tayler, Richard HD1734
    Thomas Snr HD1734
    Thomas Jnr HD1734
    William BL1765; HD1734
Taylor, Charles WW1841
    Henry (clerk) WW1841
    James SW1739
    James WR1804; WR1825
    Rev. John DD CB1731;
      AW1755
    John of Didcott WW1752
    John of Wantage WW1752
    Joseph WR1730; WR1751
    Joseph of Sandford
      SW1739; AW1755
    Thomas (clerk) CB1731
    William CB1731; DE1753;
      AW1755; FB1755;
      BB1770; HD1754
    William WR1804
    William WW1841
    William Addington (clerk)
      BL1840
    Rev of Whitfield SW1739
    Rev SW1739
Temple, Earl, Rt Hon Richard
    Nugent Chandos BH1811
Tenant, Miles BBC1802

Tench, John (clerk) WR1825
    (no forename) BB1832
Theobalds, Francis CB1731
Thomas, Robert GFB1812
    Vaughan (clerk) WR1825
    Walter (clerk) BB1770
    William BB1770
Thompson, Edward BL1840
    Marmaduke (clerk)
      WW1841
Thornborough, Rev SW1739;
    WW1752
Thornbury, Rev. SW1739
Thornhill, Edward SF1787a;
    SF1819d
    Thomas WR1846
Thornton, Edward BL1840
    Henry WT1756
    John Jnr BL1807
    Philip (clerk) BL1828;
      BL1840
    Thomas WT1756; BL1765
    Thomas Cook BL1807;
      BL1840
    Thomas Cook (clerk)
      BL1828
    Thomas Lee WT1756;
      BL1765
    Thomas Reeve BL1840
    William Snr BL1828
    William Jnr BL1828
    William (clerk) BL1840
Thorold, James (clerk)
    CC1821; BC1834
Thorp, Edward BL1765
    John Wise G1821
    Samuel BL1765
    Rev William AK1818
Thrale, Henry HD1754
    Ralph HD1754
Throckmorten, R.G. SF1840a
Throckmorton, Sir Charles
    BC1834
    Sir John bart SF1819d
    Sir Robert (bart)
      WW1752; HD1754;
      SF1794d
    Robert George BC1834
Thuroy, G H FB1755/6a
Thursby, John Harvey
    FB1755; WT1756
Tilley, Rev Dr SW1719
Tillings, James BB1770
Tilson, Christopher WR1751
    John AW1755; HD1754
Tipping, Bartholomew
    SF1732; WW1752

Tipping *continued*
    Sir Thomas SW1719
    William SW1719
Tombs, John K SF1862a
Tomes, Edward FB1822;
    FB1802a
    John FB1822
    Richard FB1822
Tomkins, Benjamin HD1734;
    HD1754
    Charles MD HS1824
    Edmund FB1822
    George AW1755
    Joseph HD1734; HD1754
    William BW1744
    William DE1753;
      AW1755
    William HD1754
    William HS1824
Tonson, Richard WW1752
Toovey, Caleb HD1734
    John of Wallingford
      HD1734; WW1752;
      HD1754
    John of Henley HD1754
    Richard of Wallingford
      HD1734; WW1752;
      HD1754
    Samuel SW1719;
      SW1739; HD1754
    Thomas SW1719; HD1734
    Thomas Jnr of Sherborne
      SW1739
    Rev Thomas HD1754
    William Jnr HD1734;
      WW1752; HD1754
    William of Wallingford
      HD1754; WW1752
    William Snr WW1802a;
      WW1841
    William Jnr WW1841
    Rev SW1739
Topham, Rev Edward Charles
    FB1859
Tordiff, Thomas (clerk)
    CC1821
Tourville, William BB1770
Tower, Thomas HD1734;
    WW1752
Towl, Richard GFB1812
Townesend, Gore BBC1802
Towney, Richard AW1755
Townsend, Edward DE1753
    George CB1731
    John CC1751
    John of Langford, clerk,
      SF1791d

Townsend *continued*
  John GFB1812
  Thomas BL1765
  William Snr CC1751
  William CC1821
Townshend, Anthony
  B1770
  Rt Hon Charles BL1765
  James DE1753; AW1755
  John WW1752
  Joseph WW1752
  (no forename), of Alkerton
  DE1753
  (no forename), of Kingham
  AW1755
Towsey, Edward WW1752;
  HD1754
  William WW1752;
  HD1754
Tracey, Thomas CC1751
  Lord Viscount CC1751
Tracher, Thomas HD1754
Tracy, John CB1731
  John Jnr CB1731
  Robert CB1731
  Thomas BB1770
Travel, Ferdinand Tracy
  (clerk) BB1770
  Francis BB1770
  John Snr SW1719;
  WR1730; CB1731
  John Jnr WR1730;
  CB1731; SW1739
  John BW1744; WR1751;
  DE1753; AW1755;
  HD1754
  (no forename) (clerk)
  WR1804
Treacher, John AW1755
Treadwell, Thomas AW1755
Tredwell, Richard FB1755
Trevor, Hon George Rice
  BB1832
Trinder, William WW1841
Trollope, Thomas SW1739;
  HD1754
Trotman, Fiennes BW1744;
  WR1751; DE1753;
  AW1755; WT1756
  Fiennes BA1790;
  BBC1802
  Henry BA1790
  Samuel SW1719;
  WR1730; WR1751;
  DE1753a; AW1755;
  WT1756

Trotman *continued*
  Samuel (clerk) DE1753;
  AW1755
Troughton, Bryan Snr
  FB1755
  Bryan Jnr FB1755
Tubb, Thomas BA1812
Tuckwell, Henry BB1770
  Humphrey CC1821;
  BB1832; BC1834
  John HD1734; WW1752
  John CC1821
  Joseph WW1752
Tuke, John (clerk) SF1802r
Tull, Edward HS1824
  Edward Jnr HS1824;
  WW1841
  Richard WW1841
Turner, Abraham BL1765
  Cholmondly SW1719
  Sir Edward SW1739;
  WR1751; AW1755;
  WT1756
  Edward (clerk) BA1790
  George (clerk) WR1804
  Sir Gregory Page BA1790
  Sir Gregory Osborn Page
  BA1812
  J.. BB1770
  James FB1822
  Richard AW1755; FB1755
  Vincent John WR1846
  William WR1804; G1821;
  H1832
  William Beckett WW1841
Turrell, John HD1734
Turton, William HD1734;
  HD1754; WW1752
Twistleton, Fienes SW1719
  Fiennes BB1832
  Francis BL1765; BB1770
  John DE1753; AW1755
  Thomas BL1765; BB1770
  Captain BW1744
Tyler, Henry GFB1812
  John BL1765
  Joseph CC1821; BC1834
Tyrell, Avery of Stanford
  WW1752; HD1754;
  SF1732; SF1788d
  James Snr SW1719
  James Jnr SW1719
  John of Hatford SF1732
  Joseph of Kidlington
  SW1739
  Walter of Stanford
  SF1732; SF1788d

Tyrril, Joseph HD1754;
  AW1755
Tyrrill, William CC1751;
  HD1754
Tyrer, John CB1731
  Thomas CB1731

Underhill, Samuel CB1731
Underwood, George (clerk)
  CC1751; BB1770
  Robert HD1734
Upston, John BB1770
  William CC1751; BB1770
Upton, James BBC1802

Valencia, Viscount WR1846
Valpy, Anthony Blagrave
  HS1824
Vansittart, George HS1824
  Robert L.L.D. BB1770
Vaughan, William (clerk)
  AW1755
  Rev of Fritwell WT1756
Vavasour, Richard (clerk)
  BB1832
Venables, Charles William
  CB1744
Venour, John (clerk) FB1822
Vere, Hon. Poulett BH1811
Verney, Hon Ralph (Viscount
  Fermanagh) BW1744
  Ralph, Earl WT1756;
  BA1790
Vernon, Henry AW1755
  Robert WW1841
  Thomas CC1751; FB1755
  William (clerk) BB1770
Vesey, Rev SW1719
Veysie, Daniel (clerk)
  BL1840
  George Buffy, Lord
  WT1756
  Hon. John Charles
  WT1820
  Rev SW1739
Vincent, William BBC1802
Vinor, John (clerk) FB1755
Vizard, William BC1834
Vyner, Robert FB1822
  Thomas FB1755/6a

Wade of Faringdon HD1754
Wain, Thomas CC1751
Wainwright, John (clerk)
  BL1765
  William HD1754
  Rev SW1719

Wakefield, George AW1755
Walford, Edward Gibbs
   (clerk) BBC1802;
   DE1822
  Thomas DE1753;
   AW1755; BB1770;
   BA1790
  William BBC1802;
   BH1811; DE1822;
   FB1822; BL1828;
   BH1832; BB1832
  William (clerk) BL1840
Walker, John HD1734
  John BA1790
  Joseph BB1770
  Thomas HD1754;
   AW1755; BB1770
  Thomas Richards
   WR1804; G1821;
   WR1825
  William (clerk) AW1755
  William gent SF1787a
  William Joseph (clerk)
   CC1821; BC1834
  Rev Master HD1734;
   WW1752; WR1751
Wall, Martin Dr of Physick
  WR1804
Waller, Edmund CC1751
  Edmund Jnr CC1751
  Harry (clerk) CC1821
  Harry Edmund (clerk)
   CC1821
  Harry Edmund BB1832
  Robert BB1832
  William BC1834
Walles of Signet CC1751
Wallingford (Berks.), Mayor
  & Aldermen of HD1734
Wallis, John SW1719;
  HD1734
Walls, Richard BW1744
Walter, Sir John SW1719
  John CC1751; WR1751
  Sir Robert WR1730;
   CB1731
  Rolle BB1770
Wanley, William CB1731
  William Jnr CB1731;
   CC1751
Wansell, Thomas CB1731
Wapshare, Charles (clerk)
  HS1824; WW1841
Ward, Christopher William
  GFB1812
  Henry SF1819d
  Henry William GFB1812

Ward *continued*
  John FB1755
  Poyntz (clerk) FB1822
  Robert BL1765
  William Jnr of Faringdon
   SF1791n
Wardle, John (clerk)
  DE1753a; AW1755;
  FB1755
Waring, Elijah CC1751
  W BB1770
  (no forename) FB1755
Warington, Samuel BB1770
Warmington, John BBC1802
Warneford, Samuel Wilson
  DD BB1832
Warner, Henry SW1739
  James of Hagborn
   WW1752; HD1754
  Nathaniel HD1734;
   SW1739
  Richard WR1751; BL1765
  Rev of Milton HD1754
Warnford, Francis WW1752;
  SF1791a
Warren, Sir John Borlase
  BA1790
  Rev Master of Heath
   AW1755
Warriner, George BB1832
Warwick, Daniel SW1719
Wasey, George (clerk)
  FB1822
Wastie, Francis HD1754
  Thomas of Cowley
   SW1739
Watkin, John (clerk) BL1765
Watkins, Charles BL1765;
  BL1765a
  Fleetwood CB1731
  John BW1744
  William BL1828; BL1840
Watson, John of Barford
  SW1739
  Thomas BL1765; BL1765a
Watts, Conoway WT1756
  George (clerk) WW1752
  George (clerk) SF1787a
  John BW1744; FB1755;
   WT1756; HD1754
Wayne, Edward BB1770
Webb, Daniel Coggs
  WR1825
  John (clerk) CC1751
  Richard SW1739
  Sir Thomas BL1765

Webber, Rev. of St Clement's
  SW1739
Webster, Richard (clerk)
  BL1807; BL1828
Weckes, Richard SF1819r
Welchman, John WT1756
  Rev Richard BL1773n
  Robert Frederick FB1859
  Jnr BB1770
Wells, Edward WW1752;
  WW1802a
  Edward of Slade End
   WW1802a; WW1841
  George HD1734
  Hicks BH1811; DE1822
  Richard BB1770
  Richard SF1824r
  ?, Thomas BB1770
  Thomas WW1841
  Rev. of Coggs SW1739
Weller, William BB1770
Wenman, Viscount Philip
  SW1739; HD1754;
  CC1751; AW1755;
  WT1756; BB1770
  Richard HD1754
  Hon Richard BB1770
  Hon Thomas Francis
   BB1770
Wentworth, William alias
  Creswell BL1765
West, James AW1755
  John DE1753
  John BH1811; DE1822;
   BL1828; BL1840
  Temple DE1753; AW1755
  Rev. Thomas DD WT1756
  Thomas HS1824
Westcar, Samuel BA1790
  Thomas BB1770
  William BA1790
Westell, Daniel BC1834
Western, Charles (clerk)
  WR1804; WR1825
  Maxamillian of Longworth,
   SF1794n
  (no forename) BB1832
Weston, Anthony HD1754;
  AW1755
  John BH1811; WT1820
  Robert WT1756; BA1790
  Robert BBC1802;
   BH1811; WT1820
  William BL1765
Weyland, Richard WR1846
Whalley, Robert MD
  HD1754

Whalley *continued*
  William (clerk) BB1832
  (no forename) (clerk)
    BB1832
Wheat, Sir George WR1751
Wheate, George SW1719;
    WR1730; CB1731
  Thomas SW1719
  Sir Thomas SW1719;
    WR1730; CB1731
Wheatland, Rev SW1739
Wheatley, John BL1765;
    BA1790; BBC1802;
    BH1811
  Samuel BBC1802
  Thomas AW1755; BL1765
Wheeler, Charles (clerk)
    FB1755; FB1780/1a
  Charles John FB1802
  Devereux (clerk) WW1752
  Francis FB1755
  Henry WW1752
  John Charles FB1822
  William FB1755/6a
  Sir William FB1755;
    BL1765
Whichloe, Thomas WW1752
Whippy, Benjamin BC1834
  Benjamin John WR1846
Whistler, John SW1719
  Ralph HD1734
Whitaker, Edward (clerk)
    CC1821
  Frederick GFB1812;
    CC1821; BC1834
White, Francis of Fyfield
    SF1732
  James GFB1812
  John (clerk) WW1752
  William SW1739
  Zachary SW1739
  Rev SW1739
  (no forename) of
    Blechingdon AW1755
Whiteing, Thomas SW1739
Whitfield, Rev Henry
    SW1739
Whithorne, John CC1751
Whitley, Rev Richard Vernon
    SF1862a
Whitmell, John BL1765
Whitmore, John (clerk)
    WR1730; CB1731
  Rev Thomas WR1751
  William CC1751
  Hon Lieut Gen William
    BB1770

Who... Groves BB1770
Whorwood, Rev Edmund
    WR1730
  Simon, a Dean SW1739
  Thomas SW1719;
    WR1730; SW1739;
    WR1751; HD1754
Whyle, Francis AW1755
  Humphry (clerk) DE1753
Wiblin, Daniel HD1754
Wickham, William SW1739;
    AW1755
  Rev William HD1754
  (no forename) of Swacliffe
    AW1755
Wicks, Edward HD1754
  John (clerk) CC1751
  Robert HD1754
Wicksted, Rev Stephen
    SF1738
Widdows, Charles WW1752;
    HD1754
Wieldon, George BL1840
  George Jnr BL1840
Wiggons, William SF1824a
Wigley, James FB1755
Wilcox, Richard DE1753;
    AW1755
Wildegose, John BL1828
  Robert BL1828
Wilder, John HS1824
Wildman, Rt Hon William
    (Viscount Barrington)
    WW1752; SF1794d
  see also Barrington
Wilkes, John BBC1802
  Sebastian BBC1802
  William BBC1802
Wilkins, John BB1770
  John Jnr BB1770
  John North CC1821
  Thomas BW1744;
    WT1756
Wilks, Richard of Blockley
    CB1744
Willes, Charles (clerk)
    BB1770
  Edward DE1753;
    AW1755; WT1756
  Edward Sgt at Law
    FB1755
  Edward FB1822
  John BW1744; DE1753a;
    AW1755; FB1755;
    WT1756; BL1765;
    BB1770
  Sir John WT1756

Willes *continued*
  John WT1820
  John Freke BA1790
  Robert BL1765
  William BH1832; BB1832
  Rev. William Shippen
    BH1811; AK1818;
    WT1820; DE1822
Williams, Charles (clerk)
    BL1828; BL1840
  Christopher SF1824a
  David (clerk) BL1807
  Edward (clerk) BB1770
  ?., James (clerk) BB1770
  Joseph BBC1802
  Thomas (clerk) FB1755
  Thomas of Ladbroke
    FB1755 81a
  Thomas BB1770
  Dr of Physick WR1804
  (no forename) (clerk)
    BB1832
Williamson, Richard BL1765
  (no forename) (clerk)
    BB1770
Willinsle, Sir Edward
    BL1765
Willis, Browne BW1744
  Cornelius AW1755
Willoughby, Henry WW1752
Willson, Corbett (clerk)
    FB1822
  Richard (clerk) BL1765
Wilmot, Samuel SW1739;
    HD1754; AW1755
Wilson, Daniel (clerk)
    BB1832
  John (clerk) CB1731
  Joseph AK1818; BB1832
  Rev William Worcester
    HD1754
  William (clerk) BB1832
Winchester, William of
    Faringdon SF1738
Wingrave, Richard SW1739
Winkley, William FB1822
Winkworth, John WW1752
Winnington, Edward CB1731
  Francis CB1731
  Francis Jnr CB1731
Winter, Thomas (clerk)
    BB1832
Winterton, William FB1755
Wintle, Robert, Dr of Physic
    SW1739
  Robert (clerk) WW1841
  Thomas WW1802a

Wintle *continued*
Thomas (clerk) WW1841
William Wheeler SF1862a
Wisdom, Simon CC1751;
BB1770
Wise, Edward SW1739
Edward of Drayton
HD1754
Francis (clerk) AW1755
Henry (clerk) FB1822
John SW1739
John of Fifield WW1752;
HD1754
John (clerk) FB1822
Matthew FB1822
Richard HD1734
Robert of Stadham
HD1734; SW1739
Thomas HD1734;
HD1754; SW1739;
AW1755
Rev of Greys HD1754
Rev SW1739
Witherington, George
FB1859
Withers, Benjamin Price
WT1756
Witney, Bailiffs of CC1751
Witney, Master of Company
of Blanketters, CC1751
Wittenham, Samuel (clerk)
WW1841
Witts, Edward CC1751;
BB1770
Francis Edward (clerk)
CC1821; BB1832
Francis Edward BB1832
Thomas CC1751
Wodhull, John DE1753
Michael WT1756;
BL1765; BB1770;
BH1811
Wodnoth, Charles BW1744
Wolstenholme, Henry
SW1719
Wood, James BB1770
? , Philip Snr BB1770
Thomas of Stanton
Harcourt SW1739
Thomas FB1822
William (clerk) BL1807
Woodcroft (clerk) BB1770

Woodfield, Richard
AW1755; FB1755
Woodman, Haines CB1731
Philip CB1731
Thomas Bartholomew
(clerk) WT1820
Woodroofe, James WW1752
Thomas (clerk) DE1822
Woodruff, (clerk) BB1770
Woods, Harding AW1755
Thomas (clerk) HD1734
Thomas HD1754
Woodstock (New), Mayor &
Aldermen of AW1755;
WR1804;
Mayor of WR1730;
WR1751
Woodstock, Recorder &
Mayor of CB1731;
Recorder & Assistants of
AW1755
Woodward, George (clerk)
WW1752
Thomas B WT1820a
Woolley, John CC1751
Woolly, Rev of St Peter's
SW1739
Wooton, Richard G1821
Worcester, Chancellor of the
Diocese of CB1731
Wright, Atkyns SF1824r
Christopher Snr FB1755
Christopher Jnr FB1755
Henry WT1756
John HD1734; HD1754
John SW1739
John BC1834
Oliver BL1765; BL1773d
Rev Robert AK1818
Thomas CC1821
William SW1719;
SW1739
Wrottesley, Henry WT1820
Wroughton, Bartholomew
HS1824
Francis SW1719
Philip HS1824
Seymour HD1734
Wyat, Thomas of Cropredy
SW1739
Wyatt, Charles AW1755;
FB1755; BL1771/2a

Wyatt *continued*
Charles BBC1802;
BH1811; BL1828;
BL1840
Charles (clerk) BH1832
Charles Francis (clerk)
DE1822; BB1832;
FB1859
Thomas BH1811; FB1822;
BH1832
Thomas (clerk) DE1822
William AW1755;
FB1755; BL1765
Wybrow, Rev Henry FB1859
Wyckham, Richard BW1744
William SW1719
Wykes, William SW1719
Wykham, Richard BL1765
William Humphrey
BL1765; BB1770
(no forename) SW1719
Wymondesold, Charles
WW1752
Francis WW1752
Mathew WW1752
Wynniatt, Reginald (clerk)
CC1821; BB1832
Reginald Jnr BB1832

Yarborough, Francis (clerk)
BW1744; DE1753;
WT1756
Yardley, Thomas FB1755
Yate, William (clerk)
CB1731
Yateman, Francis HD1754
Robert BB1770
Yates, Edward WT1756
Rev John WT1756
John WT1820a
York, Humphrey WW1752
John HD1754
Thomas WW1752;
HD1754
Youick, Thomas BL1765;
WT1756
Young, Edward Snr BB1770
Edward Jnr BB1770
John (clerk) BB1770
Richard WT1756
Thomas SW1739
William BB1770

Index of Personal and Corporate Names

Only one place and occupation or office can be shown here against each name, though individuals often may in fact have several. 'Clerk' indicates the clerk to a trust, usually an attorney. 'Collr.' = (toll) collector. Dates are the earliest (only) for the name.

Turnpike trustees appearing in the text are asterisked (*); see also the list of *all* trustees, pages 163-193, mostly not also occurring in the text.

Above all, names are (usually) as taken from printed Acts and newspaper advertisements, with all the opportunities for contemporary mis-readings and misprints these offer.

The Index of individual Place Names is arranged by English Counties and Wales. **Toll-gates** are shown in **bold**, inns in *italics*. This is followed on page 213 by one covering Roads, Rivers, the Coventry to Oxford Canal, and Railways. It concludes with a list of Turnpike Roads.

Roads, Rivers, Canals, Railways

Turnpike Trusts and Roads

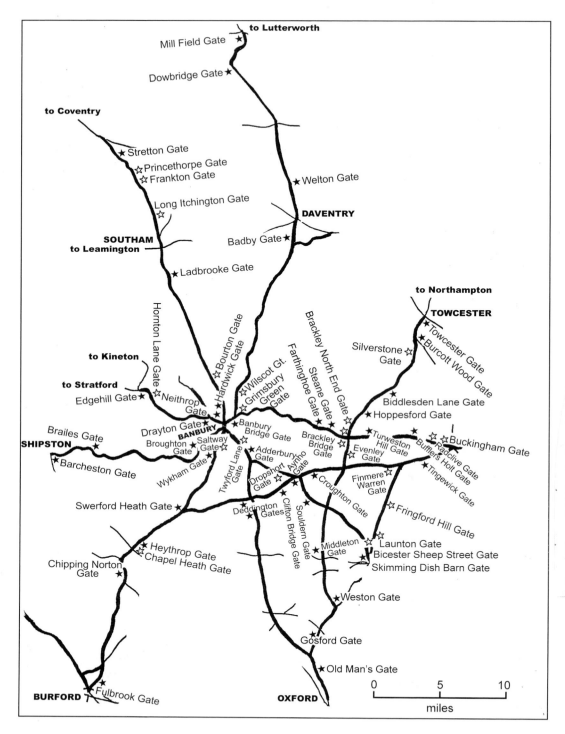

Location of toll-houses in the area around Banbury and Brackley
(*black stars = permanent location; white stars = location used for a few years only*).